Promise
and
Challenge

Catholic Women Reflect on Feminism, Complementarity, and the Church

EDITED BY MARY RICE HASSON

With a Foreword by Mary Ann Glendon, Former U.S. Ambassador to the Vatican

Our Sunday Visitor Publishing Division
Our Sunday Visitor, Inc.
Huntington, Indiana 46750

ISBN: 978-1-61278-868-5 (Inventory No. T1664)
eISBN: 978-1-61278-869-2
LCCN: 2015933887

Cover design: Lindsey Reisen
Cover art: Shutterstock
Interior design: Maggie Urgo

PRINTED IN THE UNITED STATES OF AMERICA

CONTENTS

PART THREE
PRACTICAL CONSIDERATIONS
TOWARD A "MORE INCISIVE FEMALE PRESENCE IN THE CHURCH"

Toward a Deeper Appreciation of Complementarity

By Mary Ann Glendon, JD

This timely book is the fruit of a venture launched by Helen Alvaré and Mary Hasson—two remarkable women whom I've long admired for their exemplary dedication to marriage, motherhood, professional life, and service to the Church. As attorneys active in the Church as well as in the public sphere, they were quick to respond to Pope Francis's call for Catholic women to think deeply with him about the ways that women can further the work of the Church in today's world.

Inspired by the Holy Father's call, they organized a symposium on women whose inaugural session in April 2014 brought together a distinguished group of scholars to think with the Church about women, complementarity, and the challenges currently facing the Church in her evangelizing mission.

Why Complementarity?

One of the signal achievements of this book is to illuminate a concept that is too little known and all too often misunderstood. A dictionary will tell you that complementarity refers to situations where one of two things adds to, completes, or fulfills a lack in the other. But complementarity is much more than that. Indeed, as Pope Francis has pointed out: "To reflect upon 'complementarity' is nothing less than to ponder the dynamic harmonies at the heart of all creation.… All complementarities were made by our creator, so the author of harmony achieves this harmony."

To understand complementarity is to enter into the spirit of 1 Corinthians 12, where Saint Paul tells us that the Spirit has endowed each of us with different gifts so that—just as the human body's members work together for the good of the whole—everyone's gifts can work together for the benefit of each, and for the good of all.

Complementarity thus invites us to think more deeply about a broad range of relationships, including those between men and women, and those between clergy and laity. Where relations between men and women are concerned, Pope Francis draws an important distinction between a simplistic idea of complementarity, which sees "all the roles and relations of the two sexes [as] fixed in a single, static pattern," and the recognition that "complementarity will take many forms, as each man and woman brings his or her distinctive contributions…his or her personal richness, personal charisma."

The Holy Father's observations lead to some important questions: What can reflection on complementarity teach women and men about themselves and their relationships? How does it suggest we should think about various forms of feminism? And what does complementarity mean for the Church, her institutional presence, and her evangelizing mission?

Pope Francis has invited women to explore these questions alongside him. Like his predecessors Pope Saint John Paul II and Pope Emeritus Benedict XVI, Pope Francis clearly values the "distinctive contributions" of men and women in the Church. And he has expressed his desire to expand the opportunities within the Church for greater collaboration between men and women, and between clergy and laity, all toward the end of creating a more "dynamic harmony" and reflecting more authentically the image of God.

As we travel along the path toward fulfilling those aspirations, there will be various practical and theological challenges. And that is just what makes the essays in this collection so timely and welcome.

The authors of these chapters—some of the Church's most thoughtful and eloquent writers—have opened new vistas, offered fair critiques, and identified areas ripe for further study, reflection, and discussion. Perhaps most importantly, these writers give testimony, in word and deed, of the key roles that women have played and continue to play in the life of the Church, and in the Church's mission to evangelize the world.

In his November 2014 remarks at a Vatican conference, Pope Francis felt moved to comment humorously on the fact that complementarity is a rather obscure word "that does not roll lightly off the tongue." With the present book, however, one may hope that not only the word, but also the concept, will find its well-deserved place in the vocabulary of the New Evangelization.

Mary Ann Glendon is the Learned Hand Professor of Law at Harvard University and a former U.S. ambassador to the Holy See. In 2013, she was appointed by Pope Francis to a commission to study and make recommendations concerning the Vatican Bank, and she currently serves as a member of the Board of Superintendence of the Vatican Bank. She has also served the Holy See as president of its Pontifical Academy of Social Sciences, from 2004 to 2014, and as its representative at various UN conferences, including the 1995 women's conference in Beijing, where she headed the Vatican delegation. A member of the U.S. government's Commission on International Religious Freedom, she writes and teaches in the fields of human rights, religious liberty, comparative law, and political theory.

An Invitation...
and a Response

By Mary Rice Hasson, JD

I believe that we have much more to do in making explicit this role and charism of women...

—Pope Francis, July 28, 2013, Press Conference[1]

Since early in his papacy, Pope Francis has spoken, and continues to speak, "with his customary frankness and spontaneity"[2] about the role of women in the Catholic Church. He expresses his desire for the Church to address women's "deep questions"[3] about the meaning of womanhood and to "develop a profound theology of womanhood."[4] He acknowledges the need to make "greater room" for a "more capillary and incisive female presence in the Church,"[5] including the "presence of women...

---

1   "Press Conference of Pope Francis during the Return Flight" (apostolic journey to Rio de Janeiro on the occasion of the XXVIII World Youth Day), July 28, 2013, *http://w2.vatican.va/content/francesco/en/speeches/2013/july/documents/papa-francesco_20130728_gmg-conferenza-stampa.html.*

2   GianPaolo Savini, SJ, "Climbing Higher," *L'Osservatore Romano*, April 2, 2014, *http://www.osservatoreromano.va/en/news/climbing-higher.*

3   Antonio Spadaro, SJ, "A Big Heart Open to God" (interview with Pope Francis), *America*, September 30, 2013, *http://americamagazine.org/pope-interview.*

4   "Press Conference of Pope Francis," July 28, 2013.

5   VIS, "Pope Francis Receives the Italian Women's Centre: Broaden the Space for Women in the Church," Official Vatican Network, January 25, 2014, *http://www.news.va/en/news/pope-francis-receives-the-italian-womens-centre-br.* The official Vatican translation differs slightly from the news translation: "I

where important decisions are made, both in the Church and in social structures."[6]

Given the richness of the Church's existing teachings[7] on women, what might a more "profound theology of woman" cover? And where, and in what new ways, might women serve the Church, so as to become a more widespread and influential presence?

The pope doesn't exactly say.

Like his predecessors, however, Pope Francis reiterates the Church's definitive teaching[8] that the path forward does *not* include ordaining women to the priesthood. "Women in the Church must be valued, not 'clericalized,'"[9] he says. While women and men possess equal dignity, the Church teaches, "reservation of the priesthood to males, as a sign of Christ the Spouse who gives himself in the Eucharist, is not a ques-

---

have expressed my hope that greater room can be made for a more capillary and incisive female presence in the Church."

6   Pope Francis, apostolic exhortation *Evangelii Gaudium* (On the Proclamation of the Gospel in Today's World) (2013), 103, *http://w2.vatican.va/content/francesco/en/apost_exhortations/documents/papa-francesco_esortazione-ap_20131124_evangelii-gaudium.html.*

7   See, for example, Pope Paul VI's statement in the Messages of the Council at the Closing of the Second Vatican Council (1965), Pope John Paul II's apostolic letter *Mulieris Dignitatem* (1988), Pope John Paul II's post-synodal apostolic exhortation *Christifideles Laici* (1988), Pope John Paul II's *Letter to Women* (1995), and the document by the Congregation for the Doctrine of the Faith, *Letter to the Bishops of the Catholic Church on the Collaboration of Men and Women in the Church and in the World* (2004).

8   In his apostolic letter *Ordinatio Sacerdotalis* (On Reserving Priestly Ordination to Men Alone), Pope John Paul II wrote: "Wherefore in order that all doubt may be removed regarding a matter of great importance, a matter which pertains to the Church's divine constitution itself, in virtue of my ministry of confirming the brethren (cf. Lk 22:32) I declare that the Church has no authority whatsoever to confer priestly ordination on women and that this judgment is to be definitively held by all the Church's faithful." See *http://www.vatican.va/holy_father/john_paul_ii/apost_letters/1994/documents/hf_jp-ii_apl_19940522_ordinatio-sacerdotalis_en.html.*

9   Madeleine Teahan, "I Won't Create Female Cardinals, Says Pope Francis," *Catholic Herald UK*, December 16, 2013, *http://www.catholicherald.co.uk/news/2013/12/16/i-wont-create-female-cardinals-says-pope-francis/.*

tion open to discussion."[10] In the sacramental economy, Pope Francis emphasizes, the ordination of men should not be identified with power or "superiority" but with service, oriented toward the "holiness of Christ's members."[11] Men and women, then, as Pope Saint John Paul II wrote, are called to "collaboration," with "mutual respect for their difference."[12]

Indeed, women are more visible than ever within the Church, collaborating with men in a variety of ways.[13] In his encyclical letter *The Joy of the Gospel*, Pope Francis praises

10 Pope Francis, *Evangelii Gaudium*, 104. Perhaps not surprisingly, some media outlets seized upon Pope Francis's remarks as an opportunity to highlight disaffected Catholic women still agitating for women priests. For example, Erin Saiz Hanna, the executive director of the Women's Ordination Conference, said that "women are weeping and yearning for justice in the church," and yet Pope Francis is "just another enforcer of the stained glass ceiling." Erin Saiz Hanna, "Why Would Pope Francis Keep Women Out of the Priesthood?" *The New York Times*, November 27, 2013, *http://www.nytimes.com/roomfordebate/2013/11/27/the-new-popes-new-direction/why-would-pope-francis-keep-women-out-of-the-priesthood*.

11 Pope Francis, *Evangelii Gaudium*, 104. Similarly, Saint Pope John Paul II reminds both men and women, "The greatest in the Kingdom of Heaven are not the ministers but the saints." Pope John Paul II, *Ordinatio Sacerdotalis*, 3.

12 Congregation for the Doctrine of the Faith, Letter to the Bishops of the Catholic Church on the Collaboration of Men and Women in the Church and in the World (2004), 12, *http://www.vatican.va/roman_curia/congregations/cfaith/documents/rc_con_cfaith_doc_20040731_collaboration_en.html*.

13 In *Christifideles Laici*, Pope Saint John Paul II wrote of the Church's desire, especially since Vatican II, to have women participate more fully in decision-making in the Church: "An example comes to mind in the participation of women on diocesan and parochial Pastoral Councils as well as Diocesan Synods and particular Councils. In this regard the Synod Fathers have written: 'Without discrimination women should be participants in the life of the Church, and also in consultation and the process of coming to decisions.' And again: 'Women, who already hold places of great importance in transmitting the faith and offering every kind of service in the life of the Church, ought to be associated in the preparation of pastoral and missionary documents and ought to be recognized as cooperators in the mission of the church in the family, in professional life and in the civil community'" (footnotes omitted). Pope John Paul II, *Christifideles Laici* (On the Vocation and the Mission of the Lay Faithful in the Church and in the World) (1988), 51. Of course, religious sisters have long held positions of leadership and responsibility in Church-run educational, health, and service ministries. See *http://www.vatican.va/holy_father/john_paul_ii/apost_exhortations/documents/hf_jp-ii_exh_30121988_christifideles-laici_en.html*.

the "many women [who] share pastoral responsibilities with priests, helping to guide people, families and groups and offering new contributions to theological reflection."[14] Women increasingly outnumber men on Church marriage tribunals, serving as auditors, notaries, and defenders of the bond.[15] In recent years, the Vatican also has appointed women not only to serve on pontifical councils, but also to hold leadership positions on those bodies.[16] Similarly, women now shoulder significant responsibility on Vatican commissions and boards,[17] at pontifical universities,[18] and in Vatican administrative and managerial positions.[19]

And Pope Francis seems intent on breaking new ground, according to his own style and timing. In September 2014, he appointed five female scholars to the influential International Theological Commission,[20] which examines doctrinal questions for the pope and the Congregation for the Doctrine of the Faith. Two "renowned [female] theologians,"[21] including

---

14   Pope Francis, *Evangelii Gaudium*, 103.

15   Agnese Camilli, "Pride and Responsibility," *L'Osservatore Romano*, April 2, 2014, *http://www.osservatoreromano.va/en/news/pride-and-responsibility*.

16   Cindy Wooden, "Pope Names Woman Undersecretary of Justice and Peace Council," Catholic News Service, January 21, 2010, *http://www.catholicnews. com/data/stories/cns/1000271.htm*. Women also have held positions within the Pontifical Council for the Laity.

17   Josephine McKenna, "Pope Francis' Promised Reforms Start to Take Shape with New Leaders for Vatican Bank," Religious News Service, July 9, 2014, *http://www.religionnews.com/2014/07/09/pope-francis-promised-reforms-start-take-shape-new-leaders-vatican-bank/*.

18   Zenit.org News Agency, "First Woman Ever Appointed Rector of a Pontifical University: Says Church Doesn't Need Gender Quotas to Grow, but Collaboration," Pontifical Council for the Laity, July 4, 2014, *http://www.laici.va/ content/laici/en/media/notizie/mary_melone.html*.

19   Savini, SJ, "Climbing Higher."

20   "Pope Francis Appoints Five Women to Theological Panel," *Catholic Herald UK*, September 23, 2014, *http://www.catholicherald.co.uk/news/2014/09/23/ pope-names-five-new-female-members-of-international-theological-commission/*.

21   "Pope Francis Names New Members to the International Theological Commission," *Vatican Radio*, September 23, 2014, *http://en.radiovaticana.va/*

one contributor to this book, Sister Sara Butler, MSBT, served the ITC in two previous terms. Sister Prudence Allen, RSM, a new appointee, is an expert on the theology of women, and several contributors to this book build upon her work as a foundation for further insights. According to the Vatican press release, the ITC appointments affirm the "growing female involvement in theological research."[22]

Still, critics chafe at the general slowness of measurable progress for women in the Church. Journalist John L. Allen Jr., who applauds Pope Francis as "the real deal," nonetheless questions why, when Pope Francis has "had a chance to chip away at the Vatican's glass ceiling for women" by appointing more women to high-level positions, "quite often he's whiffed."[23] Allen interprets Pope Francis's selections of five new women for the International Theological Commission as a tilt toward "fairly conservative" theology more than as a sign that women's influence is on the rise.[24]

Other progressives betray an unfortunate tendency to discount the value of *certain women's* increased participation in the Church. Women who show no "evidence of progressive views or

---

news/2014/09/23/pope_francis_names_new_members_to_the_itc/1107111.

22   Ibid.

23   John L. Allen Jr., "Hard Questions We're Not Asking Pope Francis," *Crux*, September 2, 2014, *http://www.cruxnow.com/church/2014/09/02/hard-questions-were-not-asking-pope-francis/*.

24   Allen notes the "fairly conservative" positions taken by several male and female appointees to the International Theological Commission and highlights the work of several female appointees in opposing the positions of female "progressive" Catholics. For example, he points out that ITC-appointee Sister Prudence Allen criticized "progressive Catholic sisters who broke with the bishops" over health care and abortion funding, and that another appointee, Tracey Rowland of Australia, writes for "conservative" publications and defends "traditional Catholic doctrine." He also reminds readers that another male appointee, Father Thomas Weinandy, supported "the Vatican's investigation of the Leadership Conference of Women Religious, the more liberal grouping of American nuns." John L. Allen Jr., "Maybe Francis Isn't after a Lurch to the Left, but a New Balance," *Crux*, September 23, 2014, *http://www.cruxnow.com/church/2014/09/23/pope-francis-international-theological-commission-new-balance/?s_campaign=crux:email:daily.*

an inclination to challenge authority"[25] within Church structures represent little progress, according to some critics, if those women hail from "the most conservative edges of theology or philosophy," oppose women's ordination, or "find arguments to support church teachings on any of the neuralgic social issues of the day, from the nature of homosexual relations to birth control."[26]

Many of us—the contributors to this book and other like-minded Catholics—would argue, however, that measuring "success" mostly by the numbers, counting female heads of this and that, and insisting on soft gender quotas not only misses the point but also narrows the discussion over the range of possible ways women might—or already do—serve and influence the Church and society.

Pope Francis himself stresses that more work remains to be done in order to better understand and integrate women's gifts within the Church and society. In sharing his "wish" for the Church to deepen her understanding of women's "presence" and vocation, Francis notes that these concerns are "close to my heart."[27] He also suggests that Catholic women themselves have a vital role to play in determining the theologi-

---

25 Mollie Wilson O'Reilly, "Confirmed: There Are Five Whole Women on the CDF's New Advisory Board," *Commonweal Magazine*, September 23, 2014, *https://www.commonwealmagazine.org/blog/confirmed-there-are-five-whole-women-cdfs-new-advisory-board.*

26 Ibid. Phyllis Zagano, "Getting the Message," *National Catholic Reporter*, September 24, 2014, *http://ncronline.org/blogs/just-catholic/getting-message*. See also Patricia Miller, "3 Ways Pope Francis Has Let Women Down," *Huffington Post*, June 27, 2014, updated August 27, 2014, *http://www.huffingtonpost.com/patricia-miller/three-ways-pope-francis-h_b_5535022.html*. Miller, who views the Church's teaching against contraception and abortion as "damaging to women," argues that "feminist theologians…who take a very different view" have no "say in formulating church doctrine." Because they cannot become priests, bishops, or cardinals, progressive women are thus locked out of the opportunity to "make the rules" of the Church.

27 Pope Francis, "Address of Pope Francis to Participants in a Seminar Organized by the Pontifical Council for the Laity on the Occasion of the 25th Anniversary of 'Mulieris Dignitatem,'" October 12, 2013, *http://w2.vatican.va/content/francesco/en/speeches/2013/october/documents/papa-francesco_20131012_seminario-xxv-mulieris-dignitatem.html.*

cal and practical contours of a more fruitful collaboration. He invites women to "consider" the issue, to "go deeper into this," saying: "Let us carry [this undertaking] forward together."[28]

The pope's warmth and openness sparked, and continues to spark, wide-ranging conversations[29] among Catholic women over whether and what kind of new directions might be desirable for women and the Church.

This book grew out of one such conversation.

In April 2014, the Ethics and Public Policy Center[30] and the Catholic Information Center,[31] both of Washington, D.C., co-sponsored a symposium on women,[32] which brought together a cross-disciplinary group of thirty-eight outstanding female Catholic scholars, thinkers, and ministry leaders to engage Pope Francis's observations in a serious way. The symposium aimed to move the conversation about women and the Church forward by probing the teachings on complementarity and envisioning ways to bring "a more incisive female presence" into the culture and the Church. It was an outstanding event, rich in scholarship and challenging discussions—a vivid testament to the "presence" of talented Catholic women serving the Church.

---

28 Pope Francis, *Mulieris Dignitatem* seminar.

29 Some women hope the pope's openness means the Church will "catch up" on various agenda items, from "finding feminine ways to describe the divine to church support for paid maternity leave." See Elizabeth Tenety, "What Catholic Women Want," *The Washington Post*, August 22, 2013, *http://www.washingtonpost.com/local/what-catholic-women-want/2013/08/22/bb2df208-0b59-11e3-9941-6711ed662e71_story.html.*

30 The Ethics and Public Policy Center of Washington, D.C., under the leadership of President Edward Whelan, is Washington, D.C.'s premier institute dedicated to applying the Judeo-Christian moral tradition to critical issues of public policy. Notable senior fellows include George Weigel and Mary Eberstadt. See *http://eppc.org/.*

31 The Catholic Information Center, led by Father Arne Panula, offers a variety of spiritual, intellectual, and professional programs for Catholics working in the Washington, D.C., area. See *http://www.cicdc.org/.*

32 The full title of the symposium on women was "Women and the Church: Present Considerations and Future Directions."

The symposium presentations, enriched by the fruits of in-depth discussions among the participants, form the substance of this book. As such, this book represents one effort by particular Catholic women to respond, in a spirit of service and fidelity, to the pope's invitation.

This book also affirms that, despite the media's fairly common portrayal[33] of Catholic women as a disaffected lot, the Church has a wide reservoir of intellectually and spiritually well-formed women with hearts on fire for the Lord *and* the Church *and* her authoritative teachings. As one symposium attendee put it, "we're here," and the wider world needs to know that. In particular, the members of the "JP II Generation" have embraced the faith in all its beauty—doctrines, sacramental life, and evangelistic mission. Whether young, middle-aged, or mature, single, married, or religious, countless Catholic women are already at work serving the Church, their families, and society with great love—an "incisive and capillary presence," if you will.

Our hope is that this book, written by "daughters of the Church,"[34] will prompt further conversations among women (and men), as well as additional research and exploration of these ideas. We hope that the book will prompt action as well. The book's final chapter, "Promise and Challenge," includes

---

33   Tom Roberts, "The 'Had-It' Catholics," *National Catholic Reporter*, October 11, 2010, citing a Pew survey that shows 39 percent of former Catholics who are now religiously unaffiliated cite their unhappiness with "how the Church treated women" as a reason for abandoning Catholicism. See *http://ncronline.org/news/faith-parish/had-it-catholics*. See also Cathleen Kaveny, "The Big Chill: '*Humanae Vitae*' Dissenters Need to Find Voice," *Commonweal*, October 10, 2013, *https://www.commonwealmagazine.org/big-chill*; Tina Beattie, "Pope Francis Has Done Little to Improve Women's Lives," *The Guardian*, August 27, 2014, *http://www.theguardian.com/global-development/poverty-matters/2014/aug/27/pope-francis-womens-lives-catholic-church*.

34   During his in-flight press conference returning from Rio de Janeiro in 2013, Pope Francis was asked what position he takes on homosexuality. He replied: "The position of the Church. I am a son of the Church." "Press Conference of Pope Francis," July 28, 2013. Similarly, the chapter authors of this book are united in their fidelity to the Church's teachings.

some additional points raised in the symposium discussions—theological and practical considerations that warrant future exploration.

This book's expert contributors—female theologians, philosophers, attorneys, and an economist—are a diverse group. They offer intriguing insights and analyses pertinent to the theological and practical aspects of expanding women's roles within the Church and society. Some of them present original scholarship, others synthesize new ideas with established teachings, and several analyze the practical challenges inherent in possible changes. All bring their personal experience and spiritual depth, as well as their professional expertise, to the task.

Although unequivocal in their support for the Church and her teachings, these writers do not shy away from tough questions. Several contributors address frankly the clericalism, insularity, and disengagement of some Church leaders, on various levels, which hinder the fruitful collaboration of men and women within the Church. Others observe that previous promising calls for "the promotion of women" have fallen short on the practical level. As a result, women's potential contributions to "the moral dimension of culture" and the Church's "mission of evangelization" have been underdeveloped.[35] But the writers also praise warmly the Church's long history, long before feminism, of affirming women's dignity, leadership, and service, and they acknowledge the beauty of Church teachings proclaiming the dignity and vocation of women.[36] Indeed, these teachings form the cornerstone of the ideas shared in this book.

And that leads me to an important point. This book does *not* advocate for changes in Church teachings on ordination or sexuality; our premise is that the Church's teachings represent a sure guide for women (and men) along the path to human flourishing and eternal salvation. Nor does this book attempt to represent all the many perspectives found among Catholic

---

35   Pope John Paul II, *Christifideles Laici*, 51.

36   See note 8, supra.

laywomen and women religious concerning the role of women in the Church. We do expect that much of what is written here, however, will resonate intellectually and experientially with many Catholics—men and women, cleric and lay. Purposely, this book offers a collection of ideas—not a consensus from the symposium—that we hope will be a catalyst, spurring others in the Church to engage these ideas or propose their own.

Overview

The book itself is divided into three parts.

Part One, "The Context for Change," identifies threshold issues and provides important context as the Church looks to expand the role of women.

In Chapter One, "Even Our Feminism Must Be Service," Professor Helen M. Alvaré, JD, one of the Church's leading voices in America and a driving force behind the symposium on women, establishes the basis for evaluating "every single work in and of the Church"—it must have "as its rightful end, the giving of our gifts to God and to one another." Within this framework of service, Professor Alvaré, a family law professor at George Mason University School of Law and an adviser to the Pontifical Council for the Laity, describes the implications of women's "presence" and "service." Professor Alvaré argues that the Church's successful integration of women into "the Catholic project in the world" will not only "make God more visible in the world," but also "offer a revolutionary model for the world to follow." She makes the case that "the time is now" for the Church to expand the presence of women "at the front lines" and to manifest "a more developed Marian [pastoral] face" to the world.

In Chapter Two, Sister Sara Butler, MSBT, STL, PhD, professor emerita of Dogmatic Theology at the University of Saint Mary of the Lake (Mundelein Seminary) and past member of the International Theological Commission, offers "Some Thoughts on the Theology of Woman in the Church."

Sister Sara, whose previous works[37] provide an authoritative defense of the Church's teaching on the priesthood, draws upon her wealth of experience to address several overarching theological issues relevant to the development of a deeper theology of women. She stresses the importance of building on recent papal teaching on women, the wisdom of promoting a "theology of man along with a theology of woman," the need to recognize the effects of sin on the history of male-female relationships, the perils of confusing the notions of equality and vocation, and the crucial need to define "full participation" in light of the baptismal call to holiness. Sister Sara highlights as well the importance of enlisting "the collaboration of women themselves in this project."

Professor Elizabeth Schiltz, JD, the Thomas J. Abood Research Scholar and co-director of the Terrence J. Murphy Institute for Catholic Thought, Law, and Public Policy at the University of Saint Thomas Law School, rounds out Part One with Chapter Three, "The Promise and the Threat of the 'Three' in Integral Complementarity." In this chapter, Professor Schiltz summarizes Sister Prudence Allen's idea of integral complementarity,[38] where the collaboration of women and men, each whole and complete in themselves, yields an "amplified" result, the creation of something new and greater. Professor Schiltz argues that "women's voices" and "the creative dynamism of men and women working together" are often absent within Church structures and the Church's work, and

---

37 Sister Sara's recent writings include, among others, *The Catholic Priesthood and Women: A Guide to the Teaching of the Church* (Chicago: Hillenbrand Books, 2007); "Redeeming Relationships," *L'Osservatore Romano,* May 9, 2014 (countering feminist arguments against complementarity); and her chapter, "Catholic Women and Equality: Women in the Code of Canon Law," in *Feminism, Law, and Religion,* ed. Marie A. Failinger, et al. (Burlington, VT: Ashgate Publishing, 2013).

38 For a short summary, see Sister Prudence Allen, RSM, "Man-Woman Complementarity: The Catholic Inspiration," *Logos* 9:3 (Summer 2006), *http://www.laici.va/content/dam/laici/documenti/donna/filosofia/english/man-woman-complementary-the-catholic-inspiration.pdf.*

why that must change for the Church to confront today's challenges effectively. Professor Schiltz highlights barriers—such as fear and distrust—within the Church, and within men and women themselves, which must be overcome for the desired "creative dynamism" to emerge. Encouraging the Church to move forward, she closes with the words of Pope Saint John Paul II: "Do not be afraid!"

Part Two, "Theological Considerations: Toward a Richer Understanding of Complementarity," takes a fresh look at complementarity, highlighting several important aspects that, several authors suggest, require further development theologically.

Chapter Four, "Two Women and the Lord: The Prophetic Voice of Women in the Church and in the World," by Sister Mary Madeline Todd, OP, STL, opens the book's theological section with a reflection on the feminine genius, as illuminated by two women of "exceptional influence," Saint Catherine of Siena and Mary of Magdala. Sister Mary Madeline highlights each woman's "receptivity, openness to persons, and compassion in adversity." This feminine genius opens them to healing encounters with the Lord, which in turn allows each woman to receive, and respond to, a call of "exceptional prophetic character." Mary of Magdala's "fulfillment of her prophetic vocation…awakens hope in the apostles," while Catherine's prophetic mission calls Pope Gregory XI to courage and leadership. Drawing parallels from these two women to Catholic women of today, Sister Mary Madeline demonstrates that women will have an impact on the Church and the world only if they "first encounter Christ in prayer," in a spirit of service and humility, because true reform must be "motivated by love and rooted in truth."

In Chapter Five, "The Feminine Genius and Women's Contributions in Society and in the Church," Professor Margaret Harper McCarthy, PhD, of the John Paul II Institute for Studies on Marriage and the Family, Washington, D.C., argues that society must move beyond "modern egalitarian functionalism" to value and privilege the work specific to women; in a similar way, the Church must value and privilege its Marian dimension. Dr. McCarthy emphasizes the value of women's presence at the "decision-making level," *provided* women contribute from the point of view of their "feminine genius"—an "aptness" for motherhood, physical and spiritual, which is iconic of something deeper, the gift of self. As such, the presence of women, in society and the Church, corrects temptations to power and moderates tendencies that marginalize the most vulnerable.

In Chapter Six, "The Genius of Man," Professor Deborah Savage, PhD, maintains that the "genius of women cannot be understood apart from that equally significant reality...the genius of man," particularly now, when "relationships between men and women are characterized by confusion and disorder." She revisits Genesis 1 and 2 to sketch the masculine genius in light of man's natural relationship to the created order. A man's "place," writes Dr. Savage, "is in the midst of created order... and his task is to care for it." Man "creates things outside himself" to contribute to human flourishing, particularly the good of the family. "Properly understood, the particular genius of man has proven throughout history to be an essential gift in sustaining families and creating social order...it has been the key to the very building up of civilizations." Dr. Savage closes by calling on the Church to explore "the masculine genius" in order to understand complementarity in all its fullness.

Chapter Seven, "The Dignity and Vocation of Men: Why Masculinity and Fatherhood Matter to Women," follows naturally from the previous chapter's discussion of the "genius of man" and argues that fatherhood is similarly related to a fuller understanding of complementarity. In this chapter, Theresa Farnan, PhD, a consultant to the United States Conference of Catholic Bishops' Committee on Laity, Marriage, Family Life, and Youth and an adjunct professor at Franciscan University of Steubenville, highlights the importance—to women, the

Church, and society—"of illuminating fatherhood and its relationship to the dignity of women and motherhood." Drawing on the "fundamental anthropological principles in *Mulieris Dignitatem*" and "the rich vision of masculine virtue and faithful fatherhood found in *Redemptoris Custos*" (Pope Saint John Paul II's apostolic exhortation on Saint Joseph), Dr. Farnan examines "motherhood and fatherhood as inseparable, complementary, and irreplaceable for human flourishing." She argues that a "more profound theology of women must be supported by an equally profound theology of men and placed in the context of Christian anthropology's rich vision of the person" in order to bring hope and healing to a world "wounded by sin."

Part Three, "Practical Considerations: Toward a 'More Incisive Female Presence in the Church,'" considers several practical issues related to the "place" of women in the Church and proposes ways that women's heightened presence will help spread the Gospel message, amplify the Church's good works, and provide an essential contribution to the Church's evangelizing mission.

In Chapter Eight, "With Motherly Care: Addressing the Crisis of Human Flourishing in Our Time," Professor Catherine Ruth Pakaluk, PhD, of Ave Maria University, insists that women have an "important role…[to] play in implementing Catholic social teaching" and that "the Church's teaching on family and education is just as much a part of its social doctrine as are the economic encyclicals." Because, in today's culture, "the social crisis" is often a crisis of education and family stability, women must play a "pivotal role" in "revitalizing families, communities, and the mission of the Church." Dr. Pakaluk proposes that the Church expand women's influence and strengthen male-female collaboration in three areas: "the social sciences, education, and care-oriented work." She argues, first, that social scientists who are women "are especially suited to play the needed integrative role" between "Catholic social doctrine" and "social science research." Second, she maintains that women "have a special role in restoring a correct understanding of education," including the value of Catholic education and the need to educate children for their vocations. Third, because women have a "special vocation to nurturing and healing," Dr. Pakaluk believes women can help the Church assume a much-needed "feminine posture" in providing care and "social relief."

In Chapter Nine, "Engaging Women: Finding a New Translation for Catholic Sexual Teaching," legal scholar Erika Bachiochi, JD, makes the case that the Church needs new language to express its teachings on sexuality and reproduction, in order to reach "the world's sojourner," a woman deeply formed by "the secular feminist worldview, whether or not she knows it." Catholic women must play a significant role in effecting that translation. Referencing Pope Francis's language in *The Joy of the Gospel*, Bachiochi calls us to "go out into the streets of feminist discourse, unafraid to get dirty, but without getting lost." We must listen, understand, and discover "shared concerns" before "translating" important teachings; areas of dialogue include the body, concern for the poor and vulnerable, the gift and obligations of sexual asymmetry, and tensions between work and caretaking roles. Bachiochi urges us to "accompany" all women, but particularly the poor and vulnerable. "Straying from Church teaching on contraception, abortion, sex, and marriage has harmed all women, but it has harmed poor women the most." The "kinship" between the Church's social teachings and sexual teachings "must be better articulated" at all levels in the Church, she writes, because when the Church "advocates her sexual teachings, she is advocating for the poor and vulnerable above all."

Chapter Ten, "Can Catholic Women *Lean In*? Working Women in the Church," offers the experienced perspective of attorney Mary Hallan FioRito, JD, for twelve years the executive assistant to Francis Cardinal George, OMI, now the archbishop emeritus of Chicago. FioRito, who has served the

Church for nearly thirty years in different capacities, believes that implementing a truly Catholic vision of women, family, and work could "change the conversation" about women's work, inside and outside the home. "The Church can help to create workplaces where gender differences are not only respected but also celebrated, where those with different vocations are accommodated, where marriage and family life…are supported, and where work—for both women and men—is a path to holiness." But practice has not caught up to belief, FioRito argues. "The secular world, not the Church, has been more innovative in offering those benefits that provide women with [the support] they need…to serve both the Church and their children." She suggests concrete changes that the Church, in its role as employer, might consider in order to facilitate women's "presence" in the Church—because "it is simply the right thing to do."

Chapter Eleven, "Offense, Defense, and the Catholic Woman Thing," features author Mary Eberstadt's often witty and always insightful take on women's ability to shape the culture for the better. A senior fellow at the Ethics and Public Policy Center, and the author of *How the West Really Lost God: A New Theory of Secularization*, Eberstadt describes "the duty of the public Catholic woman…to take what men have made and to perform social and moral alchemy on it, the better to attract those who have shut their heads to logic and, in some cases, have shut their ears to *any* arguments made by the sons of the Church." Pope Francis's call for women to help heal the Church, then, is a "mandate to do what women do organically in our families and communities." Eberstadt makes the convincing case that women today are called to do "nothing less than…change reality itself by replaying it through the higher keys of a feminine heart and mind, and in so doing lend lightness and…clarity to the larger symphony of our times."

The book closes with a look at the "Promise and Challenge" of the future. In this chapter, I share additional observations and practical points that arose from the symposium discussions. These noteworthy insights merit fuller discussion and deeper analysis, in ways not possible here. They also symbolize the great promise of future collaboration between clergy and laypersons, and among laypersons (men and women) themselves.

As Pope Francis reminds us, women have "a particular sensitivity for the 'things of God,' above all in helping us to understand the mercy, tenderness, and love that God has for us." So essential are women to the Church, says Pope Francis, "the Church cannot be understood without women."[39] And so, women not only have a place in the Church, we are *irreplaceable* in the heart of the Church. Our challenge is to find that place for women and, in so doing, to realize the great promise of our mutual collaboration. This book represents a modest step toward that goal.

A final word...I want to express deep thanks to the benefactors who saw promise in this initiative and supported the inaugural symposium on women. We—the symposium speakers and attendees as well as the Ethics and Public Policy Center and the Catholic Information Center—are incredibly grateful to the Our Sunday Visitor Institute, the Chiaroscuro Foundation, and the Knights of Columbus, as well as several generous individuals, including Betsy McCormack, Gregory S. Folley, Charles P. Rice, Anne and William Burleigh, and Carol and Roger Naill. Their generosity made the symposium a tremendous success and led to the publication of this book. We express thanks also to our excellent (and patient) editor, Cindy Cavnar, as well as to our publisher, Our Sunday Visitor, for bringing these important ideas and insights to a wider audience. And last but not least, a special thanks to Helen M. Alvaré for her tireless service to the Church and her valuable guidance on this project.

---

39 "Press Conference of Pope Francis," July 28, 2013.

Mary Rice Hasson, JD, is a fellow in the Catholic Studies Program at the Ethics and Public Policy Center in Washington D.C., where she writes on Catholicism, sexual morality, women's issues, and family life. She co-authored, with Michele Hill, the groundbreaking report What Catholic Women Think about Faith, Conscience, and Contraception *(2012) and is completing a book that explores Catholic women's views on faith, sexual morality, and reproduction. An attorney, Hasson writes commentary for a variety of websites and publications and has been interviewed by media outlets such as CNN, MSNBC, EWTN, the BBC, and the AP, as well numerous Catholic radio programs and print publications. The mother of seven children, she also has served the Catholic Church for twenty years in apostolates focused on women, marriage, family, and education.*

Part One

The Context for Change

CHAPTER ONE

Even Our Feminism Must Be Service

Helen M. Alvaré, JD

The secular feminism of the latter half of the twentieth century made more than a few just demands, especially in light of the global, historical record concerning women's dignity. But still it could not be reconciled with a wholly Catholic project for women, including the project of conceiving the work of women in the Church. Even stripped of a few of its most objectionable elements—an intrinsically combative approach to men, the derogation of childbearing, and the championing of abortion—something has always been clearly missing from the secular feminist project.

What is it? Nothing other than the framework, the foundation of any program or philosophy concerning human dignity or anthropology within the Church: a true account of the meaning of life, which is neatly expressed in *Evangelium Vitae* as being a "gift which is fully realized in the giving of self,"[1] the giving of self to God, our author, and to our every "neighbor," our sisters and brothers in the Lord who are also "authored" by God. This is the framework, the condition, for every single work in and of the Church, whether by its sons or by its daughters. Even the rightful striving to surmount what Pope Francis has called the "servitude" to which some women in and outside the Church have sometimes been relegated

---

1 Pope John Paul II, *Evangelium Vitae* (On the Value and Inviolability of Human Life) (1995), 49, *http://www.vatican.va/holy_father/john_paul_ii/encyclicals/documents/hf_jp-ii_enc_25031995_evangelium-vitae_en.html.*

must have as its rightful end the giving of our gifts, to God and to one another.

Even if we begin on this foundation, however, more specific conclusions about how to make women's presence in the Church more "capillary" and "incisive"—in Pope Francis's words—remain elusive. Even after the last fifty years of secular feminism, most reasonable people have no trouble understanding how vital are women's contributions in the familial and domestic milieu. In fact, if anything—in the currently fluid, expensive, insecure, and hyper-paced world—women's willingness to have children and to care for them is a kind of miracle, and many observers are more grateful to women for this than they were in the past. And not only to bear children but also to breast-feed them, to perform the lion's share of child-rearing in the aggregate, especially if you consider that *worldwide* more than 90 percent of single-parent households are headed by women. Then there is the care for the sick, the elderly, the disabled...all disproportionately undertaken by women.

A great deal has been and will continue to be said on this subject. But as a woman who has worked in the Church for about thirty years (if you count my three years representing the Archdiocese of Philadelphia as outside legal counsel starting when I was twenty-three), I would like to speak about women's service specifically as Catholics representing the Catholic Church, either as part of some Catholic institution or by speaking publicly in their capacity as Catholics.

Implications of Women's "Presence" and "Service"

What to say about women's presence there? I will offer six observations.

First, the Church's burgeoning material in this arena includes both the language of women's "rights"[2] and wom-

---

2   Pope John Paul II, *Letter of Pope John Paul II to Women* (1995), 4, 6, *http://www.vatican.va/holy_father/john_paul_ii/letters/documents/hf_jp-ii_*

en's "dignity," "gifts," "vocation," and "genius," all within the framework of that "service"—which (as the *Letter of Pope John Paul II to Women* says) "when it is carried out with freedom, reciprocity and love, expresses the truly 'royal' nature of mankind."[3] To this set of concepts, Pope Francis adds the line dividing "service" from "servitude." In other words, reasoned notions of women's dignity and rights are not independent of the project of women in the Church, even while they must be enacted within the framework of service.

Second, given the service framework, immediately we can see that Catholic women have to eschew standard secular feminist notions such as quotas or identical outcomes for women as for men. In the secular system, these outcomes pose as *ends,* not just means; but the Church, of course, has different and higher ends.

Third, we have a lot of great theory to work with, especially from the last fifty years' treasury of teaching documents, and also from female and male theologians and philosophers and other scholars—lawyers, economists, sociologists, and so forth. While the theoretical track is always important, we are right now facing the question of how to realize this theory in *practice.* I was delighted to see the same observation recently on the front page of the Pontifical Council for the Laity website. I can't explain exactly why, but I have been feeling this same impulse for the last few years. Pope Francis is really giving it voice.

Fourth, and broadly speaking, in the visible, practical world, giving flesh to the image of God as male *and* female means integrating women into the Catholic project in the world, regularly in partnership with Catholic men, and also regularly as an individual voice, depending upon the work at hand. It is (again in the words of the PCL Women's Sec-

---

let_29061995_women_en.html.

3   Ibid., 11.

tion[4] website, April 2014) the "great anthropological theme of our times," this theme of the *meaning* of two-sexed humanity, created in God's image. It is becoming increasingly obscured by everything from the recent Australian invention of a "third sex" to the recently discovered sociological status of LAT (couples "living alone together"), to the sociological classification of some sexual intercourse as "non-relationship" sex, to the notion that there could be such a thing as same-sex marriage.

Women never achieved in the worlds of work, politics, media, entertainment, and business the sort of humanizing, person-centered influence that some secular feminists claimed women would achieve. But should the Church start down this path of integrating women into more fields of action, it will not only—according to its own theology—make God more visible in the world, but offer a revolutionary model for the world to follow. I won't go into the details here, of course, but it is easy to imagine that such a commitment will require the Church—women and men together—to figure out how many women can answer their vocational calls to serve the Church while doing what women have continued to desire even over the last fifty years of feminism: assure themselves first that justice is being done at home, to their husbands and children. The amount of coming and going in and out of the workforce, flexible hours, job-sharing, benefits-negotiating, and other strategies this may involve could be considerable. This is why it hasn't been done well in many places. (But may I say—not exactly modestly—on behalf of women, that anyone who has watched forty mothers set up and break down "international food day" at a Catholic high school in less than two hours flat, feeding 500 boys, caring for each other's toddlers, serving up food from twenty-five countries, and leaving the school hall spotless in time for first lunch period, simply has

---

4   See, generally, The Pontifical Council for the Laity, Women's Section, website at *http://www.laici.va/content/laici/en/sezioni/donna.html.*

no doubt that women will be of tremendous aid to the Church in figuring out how to get this whole "home and work" thing sorted out.)

An essential contribution, a great innovation that the Church brought to feminism, is the insistence that men and women are naturally oriented toward each other, in a collaborative, mutually gifting way. But Pope Benedict XVI was also wont to say that this regular rubbing together of elbows and shoulders is not only bound to generate friction, but even be touched by original sin. As Catholicism innovated feminism *theoretically,* it is a natural next step that it should innovate collaboration *practically* speaking as well.

Fifth, it is quite possible that we will see in the Church what we have seen in the world in the matter of the intersection of women's desires and the needs of others: Women may well cluster in certain vocational areas and be less represented in others. I mused to the *Washington Post* a few years ago that my experience heading a commission investigating clerical abuse in a large archdiocese led me to believe that having women, particularly mothers, in the complaint-intake office at a diocese would have made a historical difference to the Church. That was simply my sense after one year of sorting through the abuse complaints and the diocese's responses. In the past few weeks, Pope Francis has appointed an international commission to handle this issue, and for the first time in this arena, women constitute nearly half the commission. On the banking commission on the other hand, there is one woman among five. This will have to play out according to women's gifts and the Church's needs over time. That is the way of true vocations. Other obvious areas probably include medicine, administration, education, immigration, and I think law, based upon what I'm seeing of women in law over the last fifteen years of teaching.

Sixth, Pope Francis is confirming that one of the practical realizations of women's work in the world precisely as Catholics will involve the Church moving toward women, not just women moving into specific roles within the Church. By this I mean the following: Pope Francis is saying that *what women are doing already*—their loving, merciful, person-centered ways of working and living—are what the Church wants to be, as an institution with both a Petrine and a Marian face. In other words (and to paraphrase John Allen) women are where the action is, as Pope Francis understands the action. And again, Allen offers something similar when he says that Pope Francis grasps that "if the Catholic Church is a 'field hospital'... women are its primary medical staff."[5] This has similarly been verbalized by Cardinal Walter Kasper, who rightly concludes that one way of reading what Pope Francis is thinking is that he is suggesting, "Women are already *ahead* and *out there* in a Church like Francis's that is '*going out*'"[6] (emphasis added).

This doesn't mean only that the Church will more vocally affirm this work and pronounce that it is indeed an important face of the Church. It appears from Pope Francis's words that he also means that every Catholic, male and female, lay and clergy, needs to incorporate the Marian face of the Church into his or her outreach. The pope's own words and actions suggest this. Archbishop Vincenzo Paglia of the Pontifical Council for the Family observes that Pope Francis displays a spirit of "familiarity"—that is, family closeness. He pays attention to individuals; he touches and hugs and jokes with people depending on their particular needs and situations. He sacrifices comforts while affirming the rights of the vulnerable to more. He demonstrates and begs for mercy for

---

5   John L. Allen Jr., "Women; the Old Guard; Pope v. Pope; Graffiti; and All Things Catholic," *National Catholic Reporter*, January 31, 2014, *http://ncronline. org/blogs/all-things-catholic/women-old-guard-pope-v-pope-graffiti-and-all-things-catholic.*

6   Andrea Tornielli, "Kasper Proposes Appointing Women as Heads of Pontifical Councils," *Vatican Insider*, March 1, 2014, *http://vaticaninsider.lastampa .it/en/inquiries-and-interviews/detail/articolo/curia-curia-curia-donne-women-mujeres-32413/.*

wayward children. And he instructs his pastors to go forth similarly. He exhorts them to be "close to the people," to "smell like their sheep" versus operating like "managers." He calls for their attention to the uniqueness of their particular churches. He wants "mercy," which goes hand in hand with reaching out to those on the "periphery." He evocatively calls the Church a "field hospital" for the sinner and asks pastors to find "the courage to spend their lives for the flock," especially for "those whom the world would throw away." All of these qualities and actions have recognizably maternal and Marian aspects, on behalf of a Church that Francis regularly refers to as female.

Now Is the Time: From Theory to Practice

I want to conclude by suggesting that there are two signs of the times that I believe indicate that now is precisely the time to put our marvelous theory into practice regarding the rights, the dignity, the gifts of women on behalf of our faith.

The first sign is Pope Francis himself. The public's nearly frenzied reaction to him indicates that the world senses its need for a Church manifesting the kind of "capacity for the other" that Francis, and so many women, have been gifted with. For example, Pope Francis reminds the world of every person's equality in dignity. And in a world of increasingly divided life experiences—not just at the level of money, but respecting education, work, even marriage—in a world where Mr. and Mrs. Gates can hang out with eighty influential politicians on five minutes' notice, but governments have no persistent agenda for the poor or the displaced or the immigrant or the disabled—people want bold reminders of our radical equality in dignity before God and one another. They want a pope (and a Church) who wait in line for coffee with the other participants at a meeting.

In a world of automated penalties and full prisons, people want more mercy and less legalistic "justice."

In a world where more people are saying "maybe" or "for a while" to marriage, in a world where fewer and fewer children will know and be loved by both of their parents, people want a pope and a Church always ready to talk to you as Mother and Father…so they respond to a pope who makes monthly calls to a widow who has lost her only son.

In a world of hoarders, credit card debt, and technological one-upmanship, they want a pope who wears out his dress shoes and rides in an old car.

I submit that women have a particular gift for manifesting this particular attention to particular persons with particular needs and for demonstrating the priority of people over things. In "Catholic-speak," part of discerning a vocation is to identify *needs lacking adequate responses.* The world's response to Pope Francis indicates the need for the kind of virtues I have just described, the kind women often manifest, the kind a Church with a more developed Marian face might manifest overall.

A second sign that now is the time to put theory into practice is the following dynamic: among the most pressing and momentous questions of our time are the meanings of sexual difference, human sexual relations, marriage, and parenthood. And a great deal of the contested territory concerns women—the meaning of women's freedom and the place of sexual expression, sexual license therein, the line between service and servitude, the handling of both work and mothering, and so on. And a great deal of the fallout—not all, but a great deal of the fallout of experimentation within these areas—is borne by women and by the children they more often care for or have responsibility over. The Catholic Church happens to be among the leading intellectual, historical, and social forces on all these matters. But *despite* this, and *despite* the fact that society is losing ground rapidly, with the result that *huge* numbers of vulnerable people are suffering, the Church is regularly deemed *persona non grata* in this arena. Women, as well as male/female couples together, are needed at the front lines in order to discuss all the hotly contested matters they are well-suited to address, such as the meaning of freedom and justice for women, the goods of marriage, and the case for a preferential option for children.

In other words, I don't think it is any accident that Pope Saint John Paul II and Pope Benedict XVI advanced the anthropological questions involving men and women so brilliantly precisely at this sexually confused moment in history. I don't think it's any accident that Pope Francis has called for a Synod on the Family, a more incisive presence of women in the Church, and a heightened Marian pastoral sense, now and all at the same time.

So these are some of my initial observations at this moment in time. It is the understatement of my adult life to say that I am looking forward to where this is going, praying fervently for the guidance of the Holy Spirit, and simultaneously praying for and cheerleading the Holy Father.

Helen M. Alvaré, JD, MA (theology), is a professor of law at George Mason University School of Law, Arlington, Virginia. She is a consultor to the Pontifical Council for the Laity at the Vatican and cooperates with the Permanent Observer Mission of the Holy See to the United Nations, serving as a delegate to United Nations conferences concerning women and the family. She writes regularly for the Jesuit monthly, America, *and the Witherspoon Institute's publication,* thepublicdiscourse.com. *Her articles have appeared in prominent news outlets including* The New York Times, *the* Washington Post, *the* Huffington Post, *and the* Weekly Standard. *Chairwoman of the Task Force on Conscience Protection at the Witherspoon Institute, Professor Alvaré is also president of the Chiaroscuro Institute and an adviser to the U.S. Conference of Catholic Bishops. She and her husband have three children.*

CHAPTER TWO

Some Thoughts on the Theology of Woman in the Church

Sister Sara Butler, MSBT, STL, PhD

Many Catholic women are happy to learn that Pope Francis wants to "create still broader opportunities" for their participation in the Church's life—for example, by involving them in "settings where important decisions are made."[1] They are glad that he intends to include them more fully in roles that do not require priestly ordination. When the pope calls for the development of a more profound "theology of woman," however, as he did on the return flight from World Youth Day in Rio de Janeiro[2] and in his exclusive interview with Father Antonio Spadaro, SJ,[3] many Catholic women are puzzled and less than enthusiastic.[4] Pope Francis has mentioned this repeatedly since then—for example, in addressing one hundred Catholic women gathered for a seminar on *Mulieris Dignita-*

---

1 Pope Francis, apostolic exhortation *Evangelii Gaudium* (On the Proclamation of the Gospel in Today's World) (2013), 103.

2 "Press Conference of Pope Francis during the Return Flight" (apostolic journey to Rio de Janeiro on the occasion of the XXVIII World Youth Day), July 28, 2013, *http://w2.vatican.va/content/francesco/en/speeches/2013/july/documents/papa-francesco_20130728_gmg-conferenza-stampa.html.*

3 Antonio Spadaro, SJ, "A Big Heart Open to God: The Exclusive Interview with Pope Francis," *America*, September 30, 2013, *http://americamagazine.org/pope-interview.*

4 See, for example, Pat Gohn, "A Theology of Women? What Does Pope Francis Mean?" Patheos.com, August 15, 2013, *http://www.patheos.com//Catholic/Theology-Women-Pat-Gohn-08-16-2013.html.*

tem (On the Dignity and Vocation of Women),[5] in his apostolic exhortation *Evangelii Gaudium* ("The Joy of the Gospel") (103-104), and in an address at the Italian Women's Center.[6] Catholic feminists, both "old" and "new,"[7] have some misgivings about what a deeper "theology of woman" might look like and who might be enlisted to develop it. What advice would we like to offer? I have come up with five points.

Build Carefully on Recent Papal Teaching

Given the magisterium's concern for consistency, this advice might not seem necessary. Still, it is worth mentioning, because papal teaching of the past fifty years has brought forward and developed the Catholic tradition on the equality, dignity, and vocation of women in important ways, and it provides a common point of reference for an ongoing dialogue. Popes Paul VI and John Paul II both addressed questions raised by feminists on the occasions of the UN International Women's Years (1975 and 1995).[8] In the apostolic exhortation *Mulieris Dignitatem* (1988), Pope Saint John Paul II expresses and advances the Church's teaching in a meditation that responds to critical questions posed by feminist theologians. In his *Letter to Women* (1995), he summarizes a vision of woman's equality and dignity that is clearly in dialogue with the feminist critique.

---

5   Megan Fincher and Colleen Dunne, "Women Resistant to Pope Francis' Call for New Theology," *National Catholic Reporter*, November 4, 2013, *http://ncronline.org/news/women-resist-call-new-theology*.

6   Pope Francis, "Pope Francis Receives the Italian Women's Centre: Broaden the Space for Women in the Church," Official Vatican Network, January 25, 2014, *http://www.news.va/en/news/pope-francis-receives-the-italian-womens-centre-br*.

7   See Pope John Paul II, *Evangelium Vitae*, 99, for reference to the "new feminism."

8   See Pope John Paul II's *Letter to Women* (1995), *http://www.vatican.va/holy_father/john_paul_ii/letters/documents/hf_jp-ii_let_29061995_women_en.html*, and *Pope John Paul II on the Genius of Women* (Washington, DC: USCCB Publishing, 1997).

Some Catholic women have read and received this teaching with gratitude. They follow and promote it and support the theologians and philosophers who attempt to interpret it. Others, on the basis of different analyses and methodologies, and influenced, perhaps, by secular feminist critics and the popular culture, continue to object to the theology of sexual complementarity set out by the Holy See.[9] While Catholic women do not speak with one voice, they express their views in dialogue with the papal teaching. This dialogue needs time to mature.

In recent years, the debate among Catholic women is often carried on in light of this teaching. "New" feminist Michele M. Schumacher, for example, analyzes the different assumptions about human nature and freedom found in the competing views.[10] Tina Beattie,[11] in response to Schumacher and Nancy Dallavalle,[12] calls Catholic feminist theologians to reconsider and refine their views. Any "deepening" of a theology of women *in the Church*[13] needs to keep in touch with this sort of debate.[14]

---

9 They may suppose that the reservation of priestly ordination to men is ultimately based on outdated and distorted perceptions of gender, perceptions that can be traced back to the theory of sexual complementarity.

10 See Michele M. Schumacher, "The Nature of Nature in Feminism, Old and New: From Dualism to Complementary Unity," in *Women in Christ: Toward a New Feminism*, ed. Michele M. Schumacher (Grand Rapids, MI: Wm. B. Eerdmans Publishing Co., 2004), 17-51.

11 See Tina Beattie, *The New Catholic Feminism: Theology, Gender Theory and Dialogue* (London and New York: Routledge, 2006).

12 See especially Nancy Dallavalle's essay "Neither Idolatry nor Iconoclasm: A Critical Essentialism for Catholic Feminist Theology," *Horizons* 25, no. 1 (1998): 23-42.

13 In "'Theology of Women in the Church' Only Beginning to Be Revealed," *National Catholic Register*, September 4, 2013, "new" feminist Pia de Solenni points out that the pope specifically intends to work out a new theology of "woman in the Church." See *http://www.ncregister.com/daily-news/theology-of-women-in-the-church-only-beginning-to-be-revealed*.

14 The response of Catholic feminists to the Congregation for the Doctrine of the Faith's *Letter to the Bishops of the Catholic Church on the Collaboration of Men and Women in the Church and in the World* (2004) also indicates topics that need to be considered. Along with Beattie's recent book, see Edward Col-

Promote a "Theology of Man" along with a "Theology of Woman"

In his "theology of the body," Pope Saint John Paul II considers man and woman together, in their common humanity and reciprocal complementarity.[15] In his 1988 apostolic exhortation *Christifideles Laici*,[16] he recommended developing "a more penetrating and accurate consideration of the *anthropological foundation for masculinity and femininity.*" In my opinion, any deepening of a theology of woman must include formal consideration of a "theology of man"—that is, the male—not only "in the Church," but also more generally. Feminist critics repeatedly ask why women, but not men, constitute a "problem" for the magisterium, and why the pope addresses a *Letter to Women*, thanking them for "being women," but does not address a corresponding *Letter to Men*, thanking them for "being men"! In the absence of specific attention to the dignity and vocation of men, the man—that is, the male human being—appears to function as the norm or default position for what it means to be human, and the woman appears as *the other*, with the result that she is valued only for her unique contribution(s).[17]

lins Vacek, "Feminism and the Vatican," *Theological Studies* 66 (2005), 159-177, for a review of this document and its reception.

15   See Pope John Paul II, *Man and Woman He Created Them: A Theology of the Body*, trans. Michael Waldstein (Boston: Pauline Books & Media, 2006). A helpful summary, with some development, of many themes in this work may be found in Chapter Two of the CDF *Letter on Collaboration*, note 14 above.

16   Pope John Paul II, post-synodal apostolic exhortation *Christifideles Laici* (On the Vocation and Mission of the Lay Faithful in the Church and in the World) (1988), 50, *http://www.vatican.va/holy_father/john_paul_ii/apost_exhortations/documents/hf_jp-ii_exh_30121988_christifideles-laici_en.html*.

17   This perception of the woman as "other" is what provoked Simone de Beauvoir's feminist manifesto, *The Second Sex* (New York: Vintage, 1952; French original, 1949), in the first place. In his allusions to this agenda so far, Pope Francis underlines women's tenderness, intuition, maternity, and fruitfulness. See his address to the International Union of Superiors General at *http://w2.vatican.va/content/francesco/en/speeches/2013/may/documents/papa-francesco_20130508_uisg.html*.

In Catholic teaching, the complementarity of the sexes reveals that both men and women have something positive to contribute to the family and to the human community. Their sexual difference is an invitation to collaboration and communion, not competition. Feminist critics who reject the "theory" of complementarity generally have in mind a theory that attributes different personality traits to men and women, and that concludes from these that men and women have different and mutually exclusive social roles. They are obliged to explain gender difference in terms of personality traits, because they fail to acknowledge the body, male or female, as an expression of the person. When Pope Saint John Paul II writes about complementarity, he is not thinking only of personality traits; he has in mind the two different ways of "being a body" that constitute a person as either a man or a woman. A person is a husband and a father, a wife and a mother, by means of the body. These two mutually exclusive roles, fatherhood and motherhood, are not stereotypes, or simply social roles, or reproductive role specializations. They are the vocations of persons. They are fundamental ways of fulfilling the vocation to love. Should not fatherhood and motherhood (understood as both physical and spiritual) serve as key factors in a theology of man and woman?[18]

---

18   To date, the magisterium has formulated the theological fittingness of reserving priestly ordination to men in terms of the nuptial symbolism of the body. See the Congregation for the Doctrine of the Faith, declaration *Inter Insigniores* (On the Question of Admission of Women to the Ministerial Priesthood) (1976), 5, and Pope John Paul II, apostolic letter *Mulieris Dignitatem* (On the Dignity and Vocation of Women) (1988), 25-26, and post-synodal apostolic exhortation *Pastores Dabo Vobis* (On the Formation of Priests in the Circumstances of the Present Day) (1992), 16-17, 22. See also Benedict M. Ashley, *Justice in the Church: Gender and Participation* (Washington, DC: Catholic University of America Press, 1996), 80, 97-111, and Carter Harrell Griffin's thesis on the Thomist theology of fatherhood as the perfection of masculinity, *Supernatural Fatherhood through Priestly Celibacy: Fulfillment in Masculinity. A Thomistic Study* (Rome: EDUSC, 2011).

Pope Saint John Paul II has sketched out the "feminine genius," but there needs to be a corresponding delineation of the "masculine genius." In *Mulieris Dignitatem*, the pope moves, quite tentatively, toward identifying the distinctive contribution of women when he says that "women are thought to be more capable than men of paying attention to another person," and that this constitutes a gift for humanity. He traces this gift to a woman's capacity for motherhood: "Motherhood *is linked to the personal structure of the woman and to the personal dimension of the gift.*"[19] A woman's unique contact with her child gives rise to this attitude toward all human beings; she has an "affective, cultural and spiritual motherhood."[20] What is the corresponding attitude of the man who becomes a father?

Magisterial documents sometimes contrast the *positive feminine* with the *negative masculine* in a way that does not respect men. For example, women are exhorted, "Hold back the hand of man who, in a moment of folly, might attempt to destroy human civilization,"[21] or are told that without the witness of their lives and values "humanity would be closed in self-sufficiency, dreams of power and the drama of violence!"[22] Surely it is necessary to construct a positive account of maleness and masculinity if the collaboration of the sexes is expected to enrich the Church with the distinctive gifts of each.[23]

---

19 Pope John Paul II, *Mulieris Dignitatem*, 18.

20 Pope John Paul II, *Letter to Women*, 9.

21 Pope Paul VI, *Address of Pope Paul VI to Women* (at the closing of the Second Vatican Council) (December 8, 1965), *http://www.vatican.va/holy_father/paul_vi/speeches/1965/documents/hf_p-vi_spe_19651208_epilogo-concilio-donne_en.html*.

22 CDF, *Letter on Collaboration*, 17.

23 For an evenhanded description of positive and negative masculine and feminine traits, see Giulia Paola di Nicola and Attilio Danese, "The Horizon of Reciprocity in the Family," in Pontifical Council for the Laity, *Men and Women: Diversity and Mutual Complementarity* (Libreria Editrice Vaticana, 2006), 151-173.

Distinguish the Economy of Salvation from the Situation Marked by Sin

Feminist theology, like other forms of liberation theology, begins with experience and proceeds by way of critical reflection on praxis. It arises, in fact, from the experience of women who become conscious of their situation of oppression or victimization by men and male-dominated structures.[24] In other words, it arises from a situation marked by sin,[25] the sin that feminists identify as patriarchy. Feminist theologians are self-described as women who have undergone a "conversion" in which they acknowledge and interpret their experience as victims of patriarchy, claim their power as active subjects, and seek to bring about social change that will foster the "full flourishing" of women. On the assumption that Christianity has until now lent support to patriarchal oppression, they proceed to evaluate its doctrines, symbols, and practices. They are determined to overcome the "massive distortion" it has undergone at the hands of men.[26] According to most feminist theologians, the theory of complementarity contributes to this distortion; they commonly suppose that difference implies inequality, and that acknowledging difference between the sexes invariably leads to their hierarchical ordering—to the advantage of men.[27] On this account, and reading the evidence from its "sin history,"[28] they reject complementarity

---

24   See Francis Schüssler Fiorenza, "Feminist Theology as a Critical Theology of Liberation," *Theological Studies* 36 (1975): 606-626.

25   CDF, *Letter on Collaboration*, 8.

26   See Anne E. Carr, *Transforming Grace: Christian Tradition and Women's Experience* (San Francisco: Harper & Row, 1988), 95, 162.

27   Some feminist theologians in the Catholic tradition insist that justice requires that women have access to the ministerial priesthood; others propose that it requires dismantling the hierarchical structure of the Church.

28   According to Schumacher ("The Nature of Nature in Feminism, New and Old," 28-33), the analysis provided by the "old" feminists shares with Martin Luther and other sixteenth-century Reformers the view that human nature

and other forms of "gender dualism." The remedies they envision are the feminist reconstruction of Christian doctrine and the demolition of patriarchy in the social order and the Church by means of political action and social and ecclesial legislation.

Pope Saint John Paul II does not deny that sinners and sinful social structures affect women in ways that prevent their full flourishing.[29] His Christian anthropology, however, has a different starting point—namely, the doctrine of creation. He distinguishes the order of creation ("original justice") from the situation after the Fall, and the order of redemption from that,[30] and then confidently proclaims that the grace of Christ can heal and transform the relations between the sexes that are wounded by sin. God's creation of man (the human race) as male and female is not a mistake, but a gift, and the restoration of the original harmony between the sexes belongs to the fundamental theme and promise of salvation as a covenantal or nuptial mystery. If the tension between the sexes is due to sin, the remedy lies not only in social legislation or women's access to new roles in decision-making, but in conversion. The remedy lies in the cultivation of a Christian way of life, a life of virtue, a life animated by love. The remedy for sin is conversion, the triumph of grace that moves a person beyond self-seeking to a life of self-giving love.

---

was not only wounded but corrupted by original sin. They call into question its natural orientation to the good and deny that justifying grace actually restores human freedom.

29   See Pope John Paul II, *Mulieris Dignitatem*, 10, and *Letter to Women*, 3-5.

30   See Pope John Paul II, *Mulieris Dignitatem*, 6-7, 9-12, 15-16, and CDF, *Letter on Collaboration*, 5-12. Pope Saint John Paul II brings forward this analysis of Edith Stein (Saint Teresa Benedicta of the Cross, OCD), found in her essay "The Separate Vocations of Men and Women According to Nature and Grace." See *The Collected Works of Edith Stein, Volume 2: Essays on Woman*, ed. L. Gelber and Romaeus Leuven (Washington, DC: ICS Publications, 1987), 57-85.

Distinguish the Question of Equality from the Question of Vocation

Since the Second Vatican Council, the Code of Canon Law has been revised. One of the principles guiding the revision was that the equality of all the Christian faithful (*Christifideles*), grounded in baptism, should be protected.[31] Any evidence of a bias against women was scrutinized and removed on the grounds that baptized men and women have the same basic rights and duties in the Church.[32] Canon 208 states: "From their rebirth in Christ, there exists among all the Christian faithful a true equality regarding dignity and action by which they all cooperate in the building up of the Body of Christ according to each one's own condition and function." This "true equality" tends to be misunderstood, however, because the baptized may have one or another *vocation* that affects their "condition" or "function." For example, in terms of the hierarchical constitution of the Church, the Christian faithful are either ordained (or sacred) ministers—that is, clerics—or laypersons.[33] Because the clerical vocation is reserved to males,[34] it may appear that men have different rights and responsibilities than women. In fact, the distinction between clerics and laypersons is not a distinction between men and women, for the vast majority of baptized men are not clerics; they have the same rights and responsibilities as baptized women,[35] all of

---

31   See Rose McDermott, "Woman, Canon Law on," *New Catholic Encyclopedia* 14 (2nd ed., 2003), 820.

32   See my essay, "Catholic Women and Equality: Women in the Code of Canon Law," *Feminism, Law, and Religion*, ed. Marie A. Failinger, et al. (Burlington, VT: Ashgate Publishing, 2012), 345-370.

33   Canon 207, §1, reads, "By divine institution, there are among the Christian faithful in the Church sacred ministers who in law are also called clerics; the other members of the Christian faithful are called laypersons."

34   Canon 1024.

35   No one, man or woman, however, has a "right" to be ordained. See CDF, *Inter Insigniores*, 6.

whom are laypersons. Considered from the perspective of the Church's "life and holiness," the Christian faithful are either "consecrated"[36] or they are not.[37] Consecrated persons are set apart for the service of God and the Church through the profession of the evangelical counsels; in particular, perfect continence in celibacy for the sake of the kingdom of God.

Members of the Christian faithful who have equal rights and responsibilities by virtue of their baptism, then, may have different vocations in the Church in accord with which they can (or may not)[38] exercise certain functions and may have certain additional rights and duties. The remarkable diversity of vocations in the Church, which extends far beyond these two canonical categories, of course, is the gift of the Holy Spirit for the building up of the Church (see 1 Corinthians 12:4-11). According to Pope Saint John Paul II, if women cannot be ordained to the priesthood, this is not prejudicial to their dignity, "provided that this diversity is not the result of an arbitrary imposition, but is rather an expression of what is specific to being male and female."[39] Similarly, if God does not

---

36 The "consecrated life" is a canonical state in the Church. Canon 207, §2, reads, "There are members of the Christian faithful from both these groups [clerics and laypersons] who, through the profession of the evangelical counsels by means of vows or other sacred bonds recognized and sanctioned by the Church, are consecrated to God in their own special way and contribute to the salvific mission of the Church."

37 The Second Vatican Council, in the Dogmatic Constitution on the Church (*Lumen Gentium*), 31, states, "The term laity is here understood to mean all the faithful except those in holy orders and those in the state of religious life specially approved by the Church." From this perspective, women religious are not "laywomen."

38 For example, clerics are not allowed to hold public office (Canon 285, §3).

39 Pope John Paul II, *Letter to Women*, 11. He goes on to say: "If Christ— by his free and sovereign choice, clearly attested to by the Gospel and by the Church's constant Tradition—entrusted only to men the task of being an *'icon' of his countenance as 'shepherd' and 'bridegroom' of the Church through the exercise of the ministerial priesthood*, this in no way detracts from the role of women, or for that matter from the role of the other members of the Church who are not ordained to the sacred ministry."

call all the baptized to the consecrated life, this does not mean that those not called are second-class Christians.

Vocations are not gender-free but are given to men and women according to their dignity as persons destined to be fulfilled through a gift of self.[40] These gendered vocations belong to the sacramental economy of the Church. The persons themselves are signs, not just functionaries. In recent years, the magisterium has appealed to the Covenant as a nuptial mystery in order to illustrate the fittingness of reserving priestly ordination to men: the priest acts in the person of Christ, Head and Bridegroom of the Church and Author of the New Covenant, vis-à-vis the Church, his Bride, when he offers the sacrifice of the Eucharist.[41] On the other hand, only a woman can receive the Consecration of Virgins (a sacramental, not a sacrament), for the consecrated virgin is an icon of the Blessed Virgin Mary and the Church as the Bride of Christ.[42] This is also the identity of women religious and women in other forms of consecrated life.

The feminine genius has traditionally been brought into the witness and workings of the Church as an institution by women religious, more often as "sisters" and "mothers" of the lay faithful than as "brides of Christ." It is imperative that women religious be consulted about a deeper theology of woman in the Church and about the advisability of restoring some sort of female diaconate.[43] Chapter Three in the *Letter on Collaboration* on how feminine values contribute to the social order provides a model for what might be attempted.[44] Com-

---

40   See Second Vatican Council, *Gaudium et Spes* (Pastoral Constitution on the Church in the Modern World) (1965), 24.

41   See Pope John Paul II, *Mulieris Dignitatem*, 25.

42   See Ashley, *Justice in the Church*, Chap. 4.

43   It is difficult, however, to imagine that women could receive the diaconate conferred by the Sacrament of Holy Orders, for which a baptized male is the sacramental sign.

44   Chapter Four is less persuasive. It instead asserts that since the Church herself is feminine and exhibits feminine values, women should see themselves

munities and associations of women should explore ways of contributing more effectively through the avenues for participating in decision-making that presently exist.[45]

Identify What Constitutes "Full Participation" in the Life of the Church

Many Catholic women have come to believe that only the clergy (thus, only men) have access to full participation in the Church and that they have been unjustly excluded. This perception seems plausible on some terms, but does it not betray a regrettable clericalism?[46] If full participation is equated with admission to the ministerial priesthood, then not just women but all non-ordained men—that is, all the lay faithful—are excluded from full participation! According to *Lumen Gentium*, all fully initiated Catholics who are "in communion" with the Church by the bonds of common faith, sacraments, and ecclesial government, and who possess the Holy Spirit, participate "fully" in the Church.[47] The ministerial charisms of women, expressed by women religious, single laywomen, and married women in their own families and in society, need to be recognized and celebrated as indispensable to the Church's life. Most of them need no further authorization than the sacraments of initiation, though for some ecclesial service a public ordering is appropriate. It is a

---

in her and take the Virgin Mary as a model of femininity.

45 Women trained in theology, philosophy, and canon law can contribute quite directly by publishing their research and their views and making them available to the appropriate dicasteries of the Holy See. According to Canon 228, §2, laypersons who meet certain criteria—not just academics or superiors of women religious, but women with diverse gifts and experience—can assist the Church's pastors as experts and advisers, "even in councils." Women have been invited to contribute to the past two General Synods of Bishops, not only as auditors but also as experts.

46 See my essay, "Women's Ordination: Three Questions," *Chicago Studies* 34:1 (April 1995): 75-88.

47 Second Vatican Council, *Lumen Gentium*, 14.

serious mistake to regard this service of women to the Lord and his Church as "second class."[48]

In any event, all of the baptized are called to holiness, the "perfection of charity." This is the goal of the Christian life, not admission to holy orders, and those in holy orders are called to serve this goal. Likewise, those in consecrated life are called to serve the rest as reminders of the fundamental values of the Gospel. "Full participation," in this understanding, is the prerogative of the saints. The goal of the Christian is not to be a priest but to be a saint.[49]

Pope Francis hopes for a "more incisive female presence in the Church,"[50] and he sees the importance of providing women with more opportunities to share in decision-making. Still, many Catholic women have some misgivings about the direction he intends to take in developing a deeper theology of woman in the Church. Surely he understands, however, that one way to allay their fears is to enlist the collaboration of women themselves in this project.

Sister Sara Butler, MSBT, STL, PhD, belongs to the Missionary Servants of the Most Blessed Trinity and has taught on seminary faculties for the past twenty-five years. She is professor emerita of Systematic Theology at Mundelein Seminary at the University of Saint Mary of the Lake, Mundelein, Illinois, in the Archdiocese of Chicago. Sister Sara served, by papal appointment, on the International Theological Commission and currently serves on the Pontifical Council for the Promotion of the New Evangelization. She is a consultant to the U.S. bishops' doctrine committee and is the author of many scholarly articles and several books, including The Catholic Priesthood and Women: A Guide to the Teaching of the Church *(Chicago: Hillenbrand, 2007).*

---

48   Is the perception that service is "second class" uncritically adopted from the feminist critique?

49   See CDF, *Inter Insigniores,* 6: "The greatest in the Kingdom of Heaven are not the ministers but the saints."

50   Pope Francis, *Evangelii Gaudium,* 103.

CHAPTER THREE

The Promise and the Threat of the "Three" in Integral Complementarity

Elizabeth R. Schiltz, JD

Inspired by the challenges posed by Pope Saint John Paul II in *Evangelium Vitae*[1] and by Pope Francis in *Evangelii Gaudium*,[2] many Catholic women are striving to articulate a new feminism and to discern an appropriate way to offer "a more incisive female presence in the Church." For many of us, a particularly helpful starting point has been the work by Sister Prudence Allen, RSM, PhD, professor of philosophy at Saint John Vianney Seminary in Denver, on the gender theory of complementarity.[3] Fundamentally, complementarity is the theory that there are differences between men and women that are not simply biological or socially constructed. Many contemporary feminists challenge this theory as fatally essentialist, inevitably relegating women to rigidly fixed roles centered on the private sphere of the family and

---

1 Pope John Paul II, *Evangelium Vitae* (On the Value and Inviolability of Human Life) (1995), 99, *http://www.vatican.va/holy_father/john_paul_ii/encyclicals/documents/hf_jp-ii_enc_25031995_evangelium-vitae_en.html*.

2 Pope Francis, apostolic exhortation *Evangelii Gaudium* (On the Proclamation of the Gospel in Today's World) (2013), 103, *http://w2.vatican.va/content/francesco/en/apost_exhortations/documents/papa-francesco_esortazione-ap_20131124_evangelii-gaudium.html*.

3 Sister Prudence Allen, RSM, was appointed to the International Theological Commission by Pope Francis in September 2014. She is the author of several significant works related to the theology of women. See note 7, infra.

subordinated to the authority of men. Sister Prudence offers an insightful corrective to this crude caricature of complementarity. Based on the solid foundation offered by centuries of philosophical reflection about women in the Western world and enriched by the modern philosophical schools of phenomenology and personalism, and by the theological insights of Pope Saint John Paul II, Sister Prudence calls her approach *integral complementarity*.

This understanding of complementarity as *integral* contrasts with a *fractional* understanding of complementarity. A fractional complementarity considers men and women as each being capable of contributing half (a fraction) of the totality of insights, viewpoints, and perspectives possible with respect to any situation. Only when the two fractions are added together do we have a whole perspective on the situation: $\frac{1}{2} + \frac{1}{2} = 1$. In contrast, an integral complementarity considers both men and women equally capable of making contributions to any situation. These contributions are whole and complete in themselves (thus integers, rather than fractions) but, when applied *together* in a particular situation, can be creatively amplified to result in something new, represented by the equation $1 + 1 = 3$.

The new "3" resulting from the combined insights of men and women working together is something that often has been suppressed, due largely to what Pope Saint John Paul II acknowledged as "the obstacles which in so many parts of the world still keep women from being fully integrated into social, political, and economic life."[4] Devising and implementing changes to cultural practices, legal systems, and economic structures to allow women to apply their particular insights in the public sphere without neglecting their responsibilities in the private sphere is a daunting task.

---

4   Pope John Paul II, *Letter of Pope John Paul II to Women* (1995), 4, *http://www.vatican.va/holy_father/john_paul_ii/letters/documents/hf_jp-ii_let_29061995_women_en.html.*

Some of the victories in the hard-fought battle for legal rec-ognition of women's equality were based on the premise that women will be seen as equal to men only if they become *like* men. Initiatives that reject this premise might appear to modern liberal feminists as retrenchments from a commit-ment to women's equality. But complementarity demands new cultural practices and legal and economic models that allow women to attain positions of influence in the public sphere without sacrificing or suppressing the very thing that makes their voice unique: a particular sensitivity to the truth about the human person. Men and women working together *qua* men and women, rather than *qua* men and imitation men, is required to achieve the synergetic "3"—a new world more properly oriented around the human person.[5]

Pope Francis applies this call for a more incisive fe-male presence to the structures of the Church, as well as to the political and economic structures of the world. This poses a challenge to many faithful Catholics that is just as difficult as changing legal and economic practices. Of course, throughout its history, the Church has celebrated many examples of extraordinary women who have made significant contributions to the Church, women such as Mary and the four female Doctors of the Church: Teresa of Ávila, Catherine of Siena, Thérèse of Lisieux, and Hilde-gard of Bingen. But the absence of women in any signifi-cant numbers in the institutional structures of the Church is undeniable. This absence worries Pope Francis, as evi-denced by his remarks at a press conference in 2013: "A

---

5   See my previous writings for a fuller discussion of this point. Elizabeth R. Schiltz, "Motherhood and Mission: What Catholic Law Schools Could Learn from Harvard about Women," *Catholic University Law Review* 56, no. 2 (2007): 405–450; Elizabeth R. Schiltz, "Should Bearing the Child Mean Bearing all the Cost? A Catholic Perspective on the Sacrifice of Motherhood and the Common Good," *Logos: A Journal of Catholic Thought and Culture* 10, no. 2 (2007): 15-33; Elizabeth R. Schiltz, "West, MacIntyre and Wojtyła: Pope John Paul II's Contri-bution to the Development of a Dependency-Based Theory of Justice," *Journal of Catholic Legal Studies* 45, no. 2 (2007): 369-414.

church without women is like the Apostolic College without Mary. The role of women in the church is not only maternity, the mother of the family, but it's stronger: It is, in fact, the icon of the Virgin, of Our Lady, the one who helps the church grow!... A woman's role in the church must not end only as mother, as worker, limited. No! It's something else...I think we must go further in making the role and charism of women more explicit."[6]

In this chapter, I argue that integral complementarity supports Pope Francis's call for a more incisive role for women in the Church, and it explains some of the challenges to answering this call. First, I will provide a short summary of the theological and philosophical insights that laid the groundwork for integral complementarity and describe some of the insights from Pope Saint John Paul II that Sister Prudence applies to develop this theory. Second, I will suggest some ways in which both particular aspects of women's voices that might be missing from the Church's conversations, as well as the creative dynamism of men and women working together, are essential to the work of the Church today. Third, I will describe some of the barriers to finding a place in the Church for a more incisive presence of women, focusing on obstacles that I argue arise from a fear of the unknown—a "fear of the three." Openly acknowledging our apprehensions about the unknown shape of the Church that would emerge from a more robust mix of male and female voices in the Church might help us confront the challenges facing the Church in today's world.

---

6   John L. Allen Jr., "Francis and Mary; Benedict the Reformer; India's Christians; and Ukraine," *National Catholic Reporter*, December 13, 2013, *http://ncronline.org/blogs/all-things-catholic/francis-and-mary-benedict-reformer-indias-christians-and-ukraine.*

Brief Description of Integral Complementarity

In a series of books and articles about the philosophy of women,[7] Sister Prudence describes the historical evolution of the theory of complementarity, enriched over the centuries by both philosophical and theological reflection. In this chapter, I can only briefly summarize the foundational elements of the theory, which I have described in greater detail in another work.[8] The theory of integral complementarity rests on two fundamental theological commitments of the Catholic faith: the *imago Dei* and the unity of the body and soul. It has been enriched over the past decades through insights from two modern philosophical schools: phenomenology and personalism. Even more recently, it has been significantly supplemented by the thought of Pope Saint John Paul II.

Two Theological Commitments

Integral complementary rests on two theological commitments of the Catholic Church. The first stems from a conviction that we are all created in the image of God. This means, of course, that men and women are fundamentally equal. The *Catechism of the Catholic Church* teaches: "Man and woman have been *created*, which is to say, *willed* by God: on the one hand, in perfect equality as human persons; on the other, in their respective beings as man and woman.... Man and wom-

---

7   See, for example, Prudence Allen, *The Concept of Woman: The Aristotelian Revolution, 750 B.C.—A.D. 1250* (Montreal and London: Eden Press, 1985); Prudence Allen, "Integral Sex Complementarity and the Theology of Communion," *Communio* 17, no. 4 (1990): 523-544; Prudence Allen, "A Woman and a Man as Prime Analogical Beings," *American Catholic Philosophical Quarterly* 66, no. 4 (1992): 465-482; Prudence Allen, "Can Feminism be a Humanism?" in *Women in Christ: Toward a New Feminism*, ed. Michele M. Schumacher (Grand Rapids, MI: Wm. B. Eerdmans Publishing Co., 2004); Prudence Allen, "Man-Woman Complementarity: The Catholic Inspiration," *Logos: A Journal of Catholic Thought and Culture* 9, no. 3 (2006): 87-108.

8   Elizabeth R. Schiltz, "A Contemporary Catholic Theory of Complementarity," in *Feminism, Law, and Religion*, eds. Marie A. Failinger, Elizabeth R. Schiltz, and Susan J. Stabile (Burlington, VT: Ashgate Publishing, 2013), 3-24.

an are both with one and the same dignity 'in the image of God.' In their 'being-man' and 'being-woman,' they reflect the Creator's wisdom and Goodness."[9] The second theological commitment is to the notion of hylomorphism—the unity of body and soul. "The unity of soul and body is so profound that one has to consider the soul to be the 'form' of the body; i.e., it is because of its spiritual soul that the body made of matter becomes a living, human body; spirit and matter, in man, are not two natures united, but rather their union forms a single nature."[10]

These two theological commitments constitute the foundation for the "new feminism" envisaged by Pope Saint John Paul II. It must be a feminism that rests in the firm conviction that men and women share equally in the dignity of being created in God's image. At the same time, though, it must rest in the equally firm conviction that the differences in the embodiment of men and women are not incidental biological attributes but are rather imbued with a metaphysical significance. The consequences of this conviction were appreciated and developed by a number of Catholic philosophers, offering correctives to some of the anthropological errors inherent in some modern versions of feminism.

Two Philosophical Influences

The commitment to hylomorphism contrasts sharply with the Cartesian separation of the "sexless" mind from the gendered body that underlies the development of many Enlightenment and post-Enlightenment secular philosophical movements dealing with gender relations.[11] René Descartes' arguments that the mind (which is sexless) can and should be considered the locus of a person's worth and identity, separate from the material body in which it is located, offered many early femi-

---

9   *Catechism of the Catholic Church* (New York: Doubleday, 1994), 369.

10   Ibid., 365; cf. Council of Vienne (1312); DS 902.

11   Prudence Allen, "Man-Woman Complementarity," 89-93.

nists an effective basis for asserting the equality of men and women in education and the political arena. As Sister Prudence points out, though:

> Cartesian dualism also spawned, especially among Protestants, an Enlightenment form of fractional complementarity, claiming that male and female are significantly different, but each provides only a fraction of one whole person. Woman was thought to provide half of the mind's operations (i.e., intuition, sensation, or particular judgments) and man the other half (i.e., reason or universal judgments). These two fractional epistemological operations, if added together, produced only one mind.[12]

Sister Prudence sees examples of this hidden polarity stemming from fractional complementarity in the philosophies of Jacques Rousseau, Immanuel Kant, Arthur Schopenhauer, Frederick Hegel, and Søren Kierkegaard.[13] She explains: "Fractional complementarity often left women feeling as though they had the smaller portion of the whole. For example, they were identified with a lower practical intuition, while men were identified with a higher theoretical reflection along with the highest creative intuition of genius in the arts and sciences. When this kind of differentiation happened, fractional complementarity really hid a more pervasive sex polarity."[14]

Phenomenologists such as Dietrich von Hildebrand and Edith Stein rejected both this dualism and this sex polarity. Using subjective, first-person experiences as a starting point for philosophical inquiry, they argued that the differences between men and women are more than merely biological; they are metaphysical. They asserted that the distinction between men and women "shows us two complementary types of the spiritual

---

12 Ibid., 90.

13 Ibid..

14 Prudence Allen, "Integral Sex Complementarity," 539.

person of the human species."[15] Indeed, Stein argued that "the soul has priority in gender differentiation."[16] The different bodily experience of life encountered as a man or as a woman shapes the mind and the soul. Each whole person—body and soul—is created in the image of God, thus equal in dignity. This means that neither portion of the body/soul composite—the body or the soul—is capable of being understood in isolation from the other portion, as proposed by Cartesian dualism. It also means that no person can be considered only a portion of a whole person, as proposed by fractional complementarity.

Existential personalists, such as Jacques and Raissa Maritain and Dietrich and Alice von Hildebrand, offered insights into the significance of gender differences that prevent complementarity from sliding into the rigid essentialism with which it is often associated. These personalists agree with the existentialists that human beings are all, to some extent, responsible for defining themselves. Applying this insight to the philosophy of gender, Sister Prudence explains:

> Free will decisions allow us to determine to some extent the kind of woman or man we want to be even within the constraints of the socially constructed aspects of our identity. We cannot change our genes, but we can, given modern technology, decide to change our anatomical structure, we can decide to chemically alter our hormonal balance, we can decide to incorporate or reject certain characteristics that our culture has identified as masculine or feminine, and we can decide how to interact as a man or a woman in relation to all these different aspects of our individual identity.[17]

It is this last act of free will that is of particular interest to the personalists—the decision about how to interact with

---

15 Prudence Allen, "Man-Woman Complementarity," 92.

16 Ibid., 93.

17 Prudence Allen, "A Woman and a Man as Prime Analogical Beings," 472.

others. Personalists propose that a person defines herself not by resisting any force that would constrain her freedom, as suggested by existentialists such as Jean-Paul Sartre, but rather by embracing others in relationship, without losing herself in the process. "The key factor in existential personalism is that the person actively creates his or her identity in a 'gift of the self to another.'"[18]

These ideas from these two schools of philosophy help explain the significance of the mathematical equation representing integral complementarity: 1 + 1 = 3. First, consider the significance of replacing the fractions (½) with integers (1). Sister Prudence explains, "The integral complementarity model... argues that each man and each woman is a complete person, in an ontologically important sense."[19] We can see the basis for this in both of these schools. Sister Prudence points out that the Hildebrands "emphasized that the fulfilling relationship of man and woman essentially requires that 'partners in marriage must remain independent persons.'"[20] But they require relationship to fully realize themselves as complete integers.

Second, consider the significance of the sum of the equation: 3. Not only do the man and the woman achieve a fuller realization of themselves as whole in relationship but also, Sister Prudence continues, "when [a man and a woman] enter into interpersonal relations, the effect is synergetic; something more happens in relationship than parts of a person adding up to one person; something new is generated."[21] This is not simply the 2 that would result mathematically if the two integers in the equation were identical—that is, if they were both men or both women. Only because the integers in this case are different can something new be generated—a child. The

---

18   Prudence Allen, "Integral Sex Complementarity," 538.
19   Prudence Allen, "Man-Woman Complementarity," 95.
20   Ibid.
21   Ibid.

principles of this model can be applied to all forms of human community, not simply the family. Sister Prudence explains:

> When there is a good balance of sameness and difference among the persons who are bonded together "for the other" in an intellectual community, a political community, or a spiritual community, then a new fertile reality can emerge which will be an analogous form of new life. These can take many forms such as a project, book, political reality, dynamic parish, and so forth. The fertile new life will always spring concretely from the persons bonding together in a specific community, just as a child emerges from the concrete context of his or her parents.[22]

Contributions of Pope Saint John Paul II

Sister Prudence traces the influences of phenomenology and personalism in the development of Pope Saint John Paul II's earliest writings.[23] She also describes how he proclaimed the groundwork for the theory of integral complementarity at the very beginning of his pontificate:

> Within the year of being elected on October 16, 1978, [he] gave a series of audiences in which he analyzed the structure of man-woman complementarity as revealed in Genesis. Asserting that God created man and woman equal as human beings and equal as persons, he defended the first principle of integral complementarity. Stating that man and woman are two significantly different ways of being persons in the world, he defended the second principle of integral complementarity. Demonstrating how a man and a woman are called by God into

---

22 Prudence Allen, "A Woman and a Man as Prime Analogical Beings," 477.
23 Prudence Allen, "Man-Woman Complementarity," 95-96.

a union of love in marriage, he proclaimed the vocational dimension of integral complementarity.[24]

Sister Prudence identifies one development in Pope Saint John Paul II's understanding of complementarity as constituting a particularly radical innovation for Catholic thinking about how men and women reflect the image of God. He challenged us "to consider the way in which the Trinity as a communion of divine Persons is being reflected in our communities of human persons and particularly in the complement relation of woman and man."[25] She cites Pope Saint John Paul II's *Mulieris Dignitatem*:

> The fact that man "created as man and woman" in the image of God means not only that each of them individually is like God, as a rational and free being. It also means that man and woman, created as a "unity of the two" in their common humanity, are called to live in a communion of love, and in this way to mirror in the world the communion of love that is in God, through which the Three Persons love each other in the intimate mystery of the one divine life.[26]

Sister Prudence is rightly cautious about the possible dangers of analogizing between "the human communion of persons and a Divine Communion of Persons."[27] She reminds us that the Trinity is one Being, "whereas a community of human persons is a relationship between distinct beings."[28] She cautions about the dangers of going from what is lesser known in the order of knowledge to what is better known, suggesting that "since the Trinity is so far beyond human knowledge

---

24   Ibid., 97.

25   Prudence Allen, "Integral Sex Complementarity," 543.

26   Ibid., citing Pope John Paul II, apostolic letter *Mulieris Dignitatem* (On the Dignity and Vocation of Women) (1988), 7.

27   Prudence Allen, "A Woman and a Man as Prime Analogical Beings," 479.

28   Ibid.

there is a sense in which we ought not to try to explain human community by appealing to an analogy with a Communion of Divine Persons."[29] She also warns against the temptation to engage in reflection about whether men or women are more like any one of the different Divine Persons in the Trinity, reflections that must founder on the ontic gulf between humans and God.[30]

Sister Prudence suggests that we must resist the temptation to focus on analogies between human persons and the Persons of the Trinity and focus instead on the analogies between *relationships* among human persons and the *relationships* among the Persons of the Trinity. For example, she suggests: "It...may be possible to learn something from a reflection on the way in which the Trinity is a community of Persons and then try to consider its application as a model for human community.... [I]t may be possible for a man or a woman to reflect on the way in which Jesus gave Himself to the Father in obedience to a mission and then to apply this model to an opportunity in his or her own life for 'self-gift' to another in obedience to a mission."[31] Or, she suggests, "If we think about the fact that God is relationship, and that this relationship is one perpetual offering of one Divine Person to another, of the Son to the Father, of the Holy Spirit to the Son and the Father, we can recognize that the relation of two persons in the form of mutual self-gift becomes the real basis for the communion of persons."[32]

And it is, perhaps, in precisely this sort of reflection, applied to the community of the Church, that the particular perspectives of women could be especially valuable.

---

29 Ibid.
30 Ibid., 480-481.
31 Ibid., 480.
32 Ibid., 481.

The Potential Value of a More Incisive Presence of Women in the Church

There are two different ways in which the more incisive presence of women in the Church—as called for by Pope Francis—might enrich the Church. It could be that there is something that women are particularly gifted at understanding or doing that is crucial to the future of the Church; without engaging women in its ongoing work, the Church will be simply less able to discern the best directions or approaches to particular challenges. Or it could be that the synergetic effect of men and women working together, rather than any particular insight of women, is what is being called for; without working together, neither men nor women will generate the fertile new reality that might result from more cooperative work for the Church. Most likely, of course, both effects would result. Let us consider both possibilities separately, though.

The Particular Genius of Women

Precisely what the particular gift, or "genius," of women might be is as difficult to pin down as what the particular gift, or "genius," of men might be. However, most attempts to describe the genius of women tend to revolve around what Pope Saint John Paul II describes as an innate and special sensitivity to the fact that each and every human being is entrusted to each and every other human being, and the truth of the human person that each of us exists to be loved.[33] This general sense that women have a particular aptitude for understanding relationships is criticized by some as being reductivist, essentialist, and the product of cultural biases rather than reality.

At the same time, though, it is a remarkably persistent result of research and studies, as well as the consensus of many

---

33 Pope John Paul II, *Mulieris Dignitatem*, 30. See also Elizabeth R. Schiltz, "Contemporary Catholic Theory of Complementarity," and Elizabeth R. Schiltz, "Learning from Mary: The Feminine Vocation and American Law," *Ave Maria L. Review* 8 (2009): 101.

feminists. As described by legal scholars June Carbone and Naomi Cahn, "the stereotypically feminine devotes greater attention to relational concerns, places a greater premium on inclusion and stability, is more attentive to interpersonal transactions, and contributes more to stability and productivity."[34] They contrast this to stereotypically masculine traits, which "involve the tendency to establish hierarchies, challenge the existing order when it enhances status to do so, prizes innovation and risk-taking, and resorts more readily to violence."[35]

It is important to note that, like Carbone and Cahn, Pope Saint John Paul II understands this particular genius of women to be something more than the ability to nurture children or vulnerable adult family members. It is also an intellectual or emotional capacity that is critical to transforming culture so as to reflect the truth about the human person.[36] Pope Francis expressed the same conviction, saying: "The role of women in the Church is not only maternity, the mother of the family, but it's stronger: It is, in fact, the icon of the Virgin, of Our Lady, the one who helps the church grow!"[37] Appreciating women's unique role as icons of Mary offers many possibilities for envisioning a more incisive role for women in the Church today. I have written elsewhere at greater length about two such possible roles women may be uniquely suited to play in the Church.[38] To summarize here briefly, two aspects of Mary's role could serve as models for reflection on the unique contributions women might offer the Church: her role as the human entrusted by God with mothering Jesus, and her role as prophet.

---

34   June Carbone and Naomi Cahn, "Behavioral Biology, the Rational Actor Model, and the New Feminist Agenda," in *Law & Economics: Toward Social Justice*, ed. Dana Gold (Bingley, England: Emerald Group Publishing Ltd., 2007), 189-235, 224.

35   Ibid., 224.

36   Elizabeth R. Schiltz, "Motherhood and Mission."

37   John L. Allen Jr., "Francis and Mary."

38   Elizabeth R. Schiltz, "Learning from Mary."

The Gift of Trust. In *Redemptoris Mater*, Pope Saint John Paul II stresses that Mary's motherhood of Jesus was "an extraordinary act of reciprocity between Creator and creature," in that God entrusted himself to Mary, "giving her his own Son in the mystery of the Incarnation."[39] Pope Saint John Paul II considered this act of "entrusting" extremely significant for the particular value of "womanhood as such." Indeed, he defined entrusting as "the response to a person's love, and in particular to the love of a mother." As the theologian Joyce Little points out, motherhood is not just uniquely female: it is also uniquely human. Noting that both Eve and Mary are designated in various ways as the mothers of all humanity, she argues: "The fullness of motherhood is properly found in women, whereas the fullness of fatherhood is found only in God ('Call no man your father on earth, for you have one Father, who is in heaven,' Matthew 23:9). The fullness of motherhood found in Mary corresponds to the fullness of fatherhood found not in Joseph, but in God the Father."[40]

Mary's fiat inaugurates the New Covenant, marked by the Incarnation, by God taking the form of a creature. Little points out that "the Father entrusted his Son to the *materia*, or materiality, of his creation in the only way he could be entrusted, by way of a *mater* or mother. Indeed, while it is true that Mary is unique because to her God entrusted his only-begotten Son, the fact remains that God entrusts to a mother every child he creates, for mothers provide the only entrance any child has into this world."[41] Neither our relationship with God the Father, nor our relationship with Christ the Son, can thus "supply the most basic instance of 'entrusting,' inasmuch as we must also necessarily trust our mothers before we are in a position to entrust

---

39   Pope John Paul II, encyclical *Redemptoris Mater* (On the Blessed Virgin Mary in the Life of the Pilgrim Church) (1988), 39.

40   Joyce Little, *The Church and the Culture War: Secular Anarchy or Sacred Order* (San Francisco: Ignatius Press, 1995), 148.

41   Ibid., 149.

ourselves to Christ. We must, in other words, be born of flesh and blood before we can be born of water and the Spirit. No one can enter into the New Covenant by way of baptism who has not first entered into the world by way of a woman."[42]

According to Little, this entrusting has two dimensions. First, each child is physically entrusted to a mother for survival during the months between conception and birth, and typically for the first few years after birth. Second, each child is entrusted to a mother

> in order that he might, through her, come to know the larger world into which he must himself someday go.… Children are entrusted to mothers in order that mothers might enable children to entrust themselves to others, initially their fathers, and, of course, ultimately their Eternal Father. And since not all people or things are trustworthy, children also depend on their mothers to inform them of and protect them from anyone or anything which might harm them. The child is entrusted to his mother in order that he might know, beyond her, what can and cannot be trusted.[43]

This particular expectation that mothers can be relied on to direct our trust was the reason the serpent approached Eve rather than Adam in the Garden of Eden. "The serpent's intent is to direct her trust away from God's command and toward his own interpretation of that command. She is seduced into concluding that the serpent is more to be trusted than is God, and Adam clearly relies on her judgment, to his grief and ours."[44] Mary, the new Eve, repairs this breach of trust.

> Mary, because she entrusted herself to the truth of God, was herself trustworthy. Hence, the Father was able to

---

42   Ibid., 150.
43   Ibid., 151.
44   Ibid., 152.

entrust his only son to her. Mary's *fiat*, however, was not an end in itself but was ultimately directed to the Son being able to entrust humanity to her, as our mother in the order of grace. For, as [Pope Saint John Paul II] points out, "This filial relationship, this self-entrusting of a child to its mother, not only has its *beginning in Christ* but can also be said to be *definitively directed toward him*. Mary can be said to continue to say to each individual the words which she spoke at Cana in Galilee: 'Do whatever he tells you.'"[45]

Mary's counsel to "do whatever he tells you" is an assurance that we can entrust ourselves to Christ, an invitation "to do what is, in the created order, the supremely female thing, namely to surrender ourselves to another."[46] This surrender to the truth of the person of Christ cannot be accomplished through abstract reason alone. "What we require is a different kind of knowledge, the kind which arises not out of abstract reasoning, but out of the intimacy of personal relationship. This knowledge, connatural as opposed to rational, is essential if we are to recognize the truth of Jesus Christ."[47] This is why "Christ requires the female mediation of his mother, for only a mother can offer us the assurance we require that we can not only believe what he says, but also safely entrust ourselves to the Person he is. For that reason, Mary's motherhood can be said to extend to all human beings, since all human beings require the assurance of this woman who is uniquely the Mother of God."[48]

If all women share in this ministry that Christ has entrusted to Mary, what might this mean concretely for women in the Church? Little suggests that "we live in a world situ-

---

45   Ibid., 152, citing *Redemptoris Mater*, 46.

46   Ibid., 153.

47   Ibid.

48   Ibid., 154.

ated between the suspicion of Eve and the trust of Mary. Indeed, it might plausibly be argued that today we are situated much more closely to the suspicion than to the trust."[49] In the twenty years since Little wrote these words, we have arguably moved even further toward the suspicion end of the spectrum.

Women clearly have a crucial role to play in restoring trust in both of the crucial dimensions of entrustment Little identified. First, the trustworthiness of women as protectors of life at its most vulnerable has been undermined at its core by the feminist movement's insistence on abortion as a fundamental right essential to women's equality. This trust cannot be restored without the engagement of women. Second, women must embrace their unique roles as reliable guides for their children, particularly with respect to teaching others to trust the Church. As Little reminds us, "Just as Mary's journey precedes that of the Church but finds its culmination in the Church, so every mother's relationship with a child precedes that child's relationship with the Church but find its culmination there."[50] In order for women to do both of these things, they must entrust themselves to the Church and then commit themselves to guiding others to the same.

Women invited into more active participation in the Church will be more effective in leading the charge on both of these fronts for a number of reasons. Particularly in light of the suspicions justifiably sown by the Church's sexual abuse crisis, the reassurance of women, who are most directly charged with the protection of children, is essential to restoring trust in the Church. If women are included in more visible roles in the administration of Church affairs, their arguments and their witness to the trustworthiness of the Church will have more credibility. Moreover, as insiders and participants in the formulation of the Church's response to this situation, women

---

49   Ibid.
50   Ibid., 158.

will be in a position to sort out justified concerns from unjustified attacks on the trustworthiness of the Church, and thus will be in a position to mount an informed and effective counteroffensive to the latter. These counteroffensives could be mounted in the public forum by female theologians or other laywomen trained in public discourse, or in the more private forum of women engaged in ministries of healing or teaching. In the former role, women could take as their models saints such as Catherine of Siena and Joan of Arc; in the latter, saints such as Thérèse of Lisieux and Elizabeth Seton. In any of these capacities, women can look to Mary for guidance.

As Little explains:

> Not only our children, but even the men of our society and our Church, look to women for guidance in what can and cannot be trusted. The servants at Cana sought out Mary, not because she could solve their problem, but because they trusted she would know where the solution could be found. Today our world is desperately looking for solutions to scores of problems. In this situation, what is required are women able confidently to advise, "Do whatever he tells you," and to point to the Church as the place where we learn what it is he asks.[51]

The Gift of Prophecy. The theologian Benedict Ashley argues that women (particularly contemplative consecrated virgins) may play a particular role for the Church as prophets. In developing his argument, he also invokes Mary as a model, noting that she gradually assumed a contemplative rather than an active role in the early Church. Even while actively participating in Jesus's ministry by bearing and raising him, she "constantly meditated on the mysteries which were the events of Jesus's life," pondering them in her heart. After Jesus began his active ministry, Mary retreated to contemplate Jesus's

---

51   Ibid., 161.

words and deeds and to pray with the apostles.[52] Ashley argues that this particular capacity for a contemplative life often nurtures a gift for prophecy, which he describes as "a special gift, usually, but not necessarily, given to persons advanced in holiness, the purpose of which is to build up the church not by some new public or even private revelation, but by arousing the Spirit of conversion, reform, or zeal in the church."[53]

Pope Emeritus Benedict XVI, writing as Cardinal Joseph Ratzinger, also recognized this connection between the contemplative life and prophecy, displayed by Mary in her "enduring attitude of openness to God's word.... [I]nasmuch as Mary hears in the very depths of her heart, so that she truly interiorizes the Word and can give it to the world in a new way, she is a prophetess."[54] Cardinal John Henry Newman also recognized Mary as the first theologian for her propensity to receive profound revelations and not merely accept them on faith, as it were, but to consider them and continue to ponder them in her heart.[55]

Ashley contends that this gift for prophecy can find expression in a particular ability to nurture faith, often displayed by women in roles such as mothers, theologians, spiritual teachers and writers, preachers of conferences and retreats, and spiritual directors. This gift is fostered by the contemplation for which Ashley argues women have particular aptitude. He argues that men are hampered in contemplative life by their...

---

52   Benedict M. Ashley, *Justice in the Church: Gender and Participation* (Washington, DC: Catholic University of America Press, 1996), 135-37.

53   Ibid., 144.

54   Joseph Ratzinger, "Hail, Full of Grace," in *Mary: The Church at the Source*, trans. Adrian Walker (San Francisco: Ignatius Press, 2005), 61-79, 72.

55   John Henry Newman, "The Theory of Development in Religious Doctrine," in *Fifteen Sermons Preached before the University of Oxford*, 3rd Edition. (1900), 312-14.

...tendencies to aggressive drive for power, their excessively logical (rationalistic) thinking, and their insensitivity in intimate relationships. Women, on the other hand, gifted with the nurturing, relational skills necessary for motherhood, often do not find it so difficult to do as Mary did, pondering the divine mysteries in their hearts, opening themselves up to the Holy Spirit. Consequently women who enter on the path of contemplation also open themselves to prophecy.[56]

Is it possible that women, as icons of Mary, can offer to the Church these two particular gifts—the motherly gift of understanding the trust we must place in God and the contemplative gift of prophecy—in a way that is particularly called for in the present age? An essay written by Joseph Ratzinger in 1980 seems to suggest so:

> In my opinion, the connection between the mystery of Christ and the mystery of Mary suggested to us... is very important in our age of activism, in which the Western mentality has evolved to the extreme. For in today's intellectual climate, only the masculine principle counts. And that means doing, achieving results, actively planning and producing the world oneself, refusing to wait for anything upon which one would thereby become dependent, relying rather, solely on one's own abilities. It is, I believe, no coincidence, given our Western, masculine mentality, that we have increasingly separated Christ from his Mother, without grasping that Mary's motherhood might have some significance for theology and faith. This attitude characterizes our whole approach to the Church. We treat the Church almost like some technological device that we plan and make with enormous cleverness and expenditure of energy. Then we are surprised when we

---

56 Benedict M. Ashley, *Justice in the Church*, 146.

experience the truth of what Saint Louis-Marie Grignion de Montfort once remarked, paraphrasing the words of the prophet Haggai, when he said, "You do much, but nothing comes of it" (Hag 1:6)! When making becomes autonomous, the things we cannot make but that are alive and need time to mature can no longer survive.

What we need, then, is to abandon this one-sided, Western activist outlook, lest we degrade the Church to a product of our creation and design. The Church is not a manufactured item; she is, rather, the living seed of God that must be allowed to grow and ripen. This is why the Church needs the Marian mystery; this is why the Church herself is a Marian mystery. There can be fruitfulness in the Church only when she has this character, when she becomes holy soil for the Word. We must retrieve the symbol of the fruitful soil; we must once more become waiting, inwardly recollected people who in the depth of prayer, longing, and faith give the Word room to grow.[57]

Just as with the role of entrusting, this would appear to be a gift that could be exercised most productively by women operating within the Church in some capacity, as theologians, teachers, or writers. As Ashley suggests, contemplative women religious might be in the best position to exercise this gift. However, laywomen could also offer significant contributions, sometimes informed and enriched by their encounters with the complexities of the world outside the Church. The Church could cultivate this gift in religious communities and in laywomen by consciously supporting initiatives to draw women into these fields, inviting women to learn with men in seminaries and schools of divinity, inviting women to

---

57   Joseph Ratzinger, "My Word Shall Not Return to Me Empty!" in *Mary: The Church at the Source*, 16-17.

be part of pontifical councils and institutes, and by incorporating the work of women into its pronouncements.

The Dynamic of Men and Women
Working Together for the Church

Ratzinger invokes the imagery of the Church as "the living seed of God" that requires "fruitful soil" from its people to "give the Word room to grow." This evokes Sister Prudence's arguments about the possibility of creating "a new fertile reality" through the interpersonal relationships between men and women. This, in turn, calls to mind Pope Saint John Paul II's invitation for us to, in the words of Sister Prudence, "consider the way in which the Trinity as a communion of divine Persons is being reflected in our communities of human persons and particularly in the complement relation of woman and man."[58] When we focus on the dynamism of the Church as the gathering of the people of God, we can, perhaps, see how it might be the synergetic effect of men and women working together that could be the most important consequence of a more incisive presence of women in the Church, rather than any particular attribute that women might possess.

The Church is catholic because, as the *Catechism of the Catholic Church* teaches, "she has been sent out by Christ on a mission to the whole of the human race."[59] Quoting *Lumen Gentium*, the *Catechism* continues:

> All men are called to belong to the new people of God. This people, therefore, while remaining one and only one, is to be spread throughout the whole world and to all ages in order that the design of God's will may be fulfilled: he made human nature one in the beginning and has decreed that all his children who were scattered

---

58 Prudence Allen, "Integral Sex Complementarity," 543.
59 *Catechism of the Catholic Church*, 831.

should be finally gathered together as one.... The character of universality which adorns the People of God is a gift from the Lord himself whereby the Catholic Church ceaselessly and efficaciously seeks for the return of all humanity and all its goods, under Christ the Head in the unity of his Spirit.[60]

This understanding of the Church as the gathering of all people scattered by original sin is rooted, according to theologian Henri de Lubac, in the *imago Dei*. Mankind's original state of unity is described by de Lubac as "a previous natural unity, the unity of the human race."[61] He explains that the Church Fathers located this unity in the idea of *imago Dei*, as expressed in the creation story of Genesis: "Was it not shown to them in Genesis, where it was taught that God made man in his own image? For the divine image does not differ from one individual to another: in all it is the same image. The same mysterious participation in God which causes the soul to exist effects at one and the same time the unity of spirits among themselves."[62] De Lubac thus insists that *imago Dei* means not only that each one of us, as an individual, reflects God's image, but also that it takes all of us together, collectively, to accurately reflect the fullness of God's image.

The Church Fathers, de Lubac continues, understood sin as disrupting not only man's relationship with God, but also man's relationship with his fellow man, ruining "that spiritual unity which, according to the Creator's plan, should be so much the closer in proportion as the supernatural union

---

60   *Catechism of the Catholic Church*, 831. See also Second Vatican Council, Dogmatic Constitution on the Church, *Lumen Gentium* (1964), 13, sections 1-2, *http://www.vatican.va/archive/hist_councils/ii_vatican_council/documents/vat-ii_const_19641121_lumen-gentium_en.html*; cf. Jn 11:52.

61   Henri de Lubac, *Catholicism: Christ and the Common Destiny of Man* (San Francisco: Ignatius Press, 1988), 25.

62   Ibid., 29.

of man with God is the more completely effected."[63] Original sin is characterized as the breaking up, the individualization, the scattering of mankind. Christ's redemptive sacrifice, then, is seen by the Fathers as a gathering back together of scattered mankind into the body of Christ: "Like the queen bee, Christ comes to muster humanity around him."[64] De Lubac characterizes redemption as something that Christ offers not just to each of us individually, but also to mankind collectively.[65] The mission of the Church is to "reveal to men that pristine unity that they have lost, to restore and complete it."[66]

No end of research from multiple disciplines demonstrates that men and women working together tend to reach different results than either men working alone or women working alone, and that these results tend to be better for whatever enterprise brought them together. This research is equally applicable for the Church, all the more so if we understand the Church as a dynamic gathering of people, and if we appreciate the particular understanding of and gift for relationship that women offer the Church.

Cahn and Carbone, for example, argue that recent game theory and neuroscience research demonstrates differences in how men and women make decisions that ought to be considered in challenging the "rational actor" assumptions of law and economics. They point to experiments in which magnetic resonance imaging shows that moral decision-making activates different parts of the brain in men than in women. Furthermore, they explain:

> Game theory experiments suggest that the interaction between men and women may change outcomes. In a carefully structured experiment, several economists found

---

63 Ibid., 33.
64 Ibid., 36.
65 Ibid., 39.
66 Ibid., 53.

that when charitable giving was anonymous, women gave significantly more than men. When charitable decisions were made in pairs, however, pairs consisting of one man and one woman give more than same-sex pairs, and all-male pairs give the least.... The authors concluded that, "men and women act more altruistically when in the presence of someone of the opposite sex suggesting that increased participation of women in economic affairs may lead people to behave more altruistically." These findings suggest that for the studies that attempt to tease out the elements of cooperation that make societies and markets function efficiently, gender matters and women do in fact display an ethic of care."[67]

Carbone and Cahn also discuss a 2001 World Bank Policy Research Report entitled *Engendered Development—Through Gender Equality in Rights, Resources, and Voice*. This report "found a correlation between the rights of women and the countries' economic and social well-being, and concluded that granting women more equal decision-making produced benefits for the society as a whole."[68] The report concluded that "greater gender equality correlates to better governance and less corruption. The empirical studies on which the report relied find that higher representation of women in the legislature went together with lower levels of corruption."[69] There is little research yet why this should be, but what there is suggests women "rarely succumb to authoritarian styles of behavior" and that "the presence of women in the higher echelons of the hierarchical structures exercises an extremely positive influence on the behavior of their male colleagues by restraining, disciplining, and elevating the latter's behavior."[70]

---

67   Carbone and Cahn, "Behavioral Biology," 41.

68   Ibid., 51.

69   Ibid., 52-53.

70   Ibid.

This intuition has motivated governments in countries such as Rwanda, Sweden, France, Italy, and Spain to institute gender quotas for various governmental bodies, and countries such as Norway, Spain, France, Netherlands, Italy, and Belgium to impose gender quotas on corporate boards of directors of publicly traded companies.[71] The potential benefits of men and women working together also have been noted in less formal communities, such as the L'Arche communities throughout the world, where people with and without disabilities live together. As Jean Vanier, founder of L'Arche, noted:

> To exercise authority one has to grow in wholeness, seeking continually to harmonize the masculine and the feminine. For many years I have exercised authority together with women. I have seen how we help each other. I had certain gifts which were less developed in them, as they had gifts which were less developed in me. It is good for men and women to exercise authority together.[72]

Returning, then, to our understanding of the Church as a gathering of the people of God, there are many reasons to think that both the particular gifts of women and the dynamic process of both men and women working together might be vital aspects of the missionary end of the Church.

Confronting the Barrier of Fear: Finding a Place in the Church for a More Incisive Presence of Women

The major challenge and obstacle to finding ways for men and women to work together in the Church, to obtain the benefits of that synergetic "3," seems to be fear. Just as a mother and fa-

---

71   Julie C. Suk, "Work-Family Conflict and the Pipeline to Power: Lessons from European Gender Quotas," *Michigan State Law Review* (Winter 2013): 1797.

72   Jean Vanier, *Community and Growth, 2nd rev. ed.* (Mahwah, NJ: Paulist Press, 1989), 259.

ther have no idea what a child growing in the mother's womb will look like, none of us knows what the Church—as the "3" that would result if women were given a more incisive voice— would look like, and the unknown is always frightening. Both the women who are called to provide this new female presence in the Church and the men currently in the Church need to be sensitive to this fear.

Challenges to Women

One set of fears arises from concerns that for women to have a more incisive role in the Church, they will have to assume the role and attributes of those currently in positions of authority in the Church—men. Most particularly, of course, some fear that women's quest for a more visible role in the Church is necessarily a quest for women's ordination. Women might help address those fears in two ways.

First, some women who hear the Church's call to offer their voice to the Church may tend to embrace that call as a thrilling opportunity to serve Christ in a way that reflects their unique gifts. The energy and enthusiasm with which women rush into this new opening can make it difficult for them to understand or sympathize with men who may see women's increased roles as a threat or a challenge. This suggests that women seeking a greater role in the Church must make efforts to better explain integral complementarity, making clear that the addition of women's unique perspectives and capacities is not intended to diminish the value of men's unique perspectives and capacities. This might help both men and women understand that what is sought is a new way to serve the Church, outside of ordination.

Second, women must resist the temptation to model their way of contributing to the Church on existing patterns of male contributions to the Church. Similarly, women must resist the temptation to measure their success by reference to male patterns and benchmarks of success. As with social conventions and legal and economic structures, women must not sacrifice or suppress the very things that make their voice unique and different as the price of gaining that voice.

Challenges to Men

The men (for the most part priests) who are called to work together with women in the Church also must face their fears directly. Men must understand that, although women might not aspire to assume men's unique roles in the Church, this does not mean that they might not raise some significant challenges to how men are serving that role. If women are to exercise a particular gift for prophecy for the Church, then women's incisive voices will not always be the comforting voices of the "spiritual motherhood" roles traditionally welcomed in seminaries, which ask women to "adopt" seminarians to pray for and mother them. The incisive voice of the woman is just as likely to be the challenging, prophetic voice of Mary's fiat, which was not at all comforting to Joseph. Vanier captures a dynamic that is unfortunately true of many men in dealing with women in the Church context:

> Men are in danger of fleeing from their own vulnerability and capacity for tenderness. They seek a wife-mother and then, very quickly and like small boys, they reject her because they want their freedom. They will throw themselves into the world of efficiency and organization and reject tenderness and true mutuality. But in doing that, they will cut themselves off from an essential part of their nature. Then they will either idealize women as pure virgins or denounce them as sirens, instruments of the devil and prostitutes, or else use them as servants. This is a rejection of sexuality, whether it is condemned as wicked or is denied. Either way, the man will reject any true relationship with a woman because he can see her only as a symbol of either purity or sin or as somebody inferior. A man has to grow into mature

relationships with women, to get beyond the stage of mother-child or seduction-revulsion.[73]

This might require increased sophistication in the human formation curricula of seminaries, with particular attention to forming mature, adult relationships with women. Perhaps intentional inclusion of religious and laywomen on seminary faculties, in positions of authority over them, including capacities related to human formation, could provide seminarians with models for women who are neither mothers who will baby them nor temptresses from whom they must flee.

A Mutual Challenge: Restoration of Trust between the Sexes

Two recent developments in the modern world already alluded to in this chapter represent significant sources of distrust between men and women; they must be overcome if the Church is to reap the benefits of the synergetic effect of men and women working together in the service of Christ. Both have resulted in unfounded generalizations that must be overcome by men and women cooperating to entrust themselves to the truth of our faith. One of these developments is the sexual abuse crisis; the other is the widespread acceptance of abortion. If the particular genius of women is a special sensitivity to the fact that each and every human being is entrusted to each and every other human being, men must accept the validity and the intensity of women's reactions to the sexual abuse crises—a situation that women may perceive as a particularly egregious abuse of trust by some priests and the hierarchy of the Church in their dealings with vulnerable children and adults. At the same time, though, women must accept the validity and intensity of men's reactions to abortion advocacy, which is presented as a prerequisite for women's equality—a

---

73   Ibid., 257-58.

situation that men may perceive as a particularly egregious abuse of trust by some women and secular equal rights organizations toward the most vulnerable, the unborn. Both men and women working together in the Church must trust each other enough to see beyond easy generalizations about blame for these tragedies.

Perhaps by openly confronting the fear of the unknown "3," a fear often rooted in such distrust, we can be more open to the invitation of Pope Francis to envisage a more incisive role for women in the Church. And perhaps we can gain courage for this task from the words of one of the Church's newly recognized saints, Pope Saint John Paul II, at the beginning of his pontificate:

> Brothers and sisters, do not be afraid to welcome Christ and accept his power. Help the Pope and all those who wish to serve Christ and with Christ's power to serve the human person and the whole of mankind. Do not be afraid. Open wide the doors for Christ. To his saving power open the boundaries of States, economic and political systems, the vast fields of culture, civilization and development. Do not be afraid.[74]

Professor Elizabeth Schiltz, JD, is the Thomas J. Abood Research Scholar and co-director of the Terrence J. Murphy Institute for Catholic Thought, Law, and Public Policy at the University of Saint Thomas School of Law. Professor Schiltz writes and speaks frequently on women, feminism, and the Church, and serves on the board of the National Catholic Partnership on Disability. Professor Schiltz and her husband are the parents of four children.

---

74 Pope John Paul II, *Homily of His Holiness John Paul II for the Inauguration of His Pontificate* (1978), 5, *http://www.vatican.va/holy_father/john_paul_ii/homilies/1978/documents/hf_jp-ii_hom_19781022_inizio-pontificato_en.html.*

Part Two

Theological Considerations

Toward a Richer Understanding of Complementarity

CHAPTER FOUR

Two Women and the Lord

The Prophetic Voice of Women in the Church and in the World

Sister Mary Madeline Todd, OP, STL

Although the explicit call for a deeper ecclesial reflection on women and their vocation was articulated by the Second Vatican Council,[1] this theme finds fresh impetus in the pontificate of Pope Francis. In his request for a more "profound theology of womanhood,"[2] Pope Francis highlights the need to express and implement "opportunities for a more incisive female presence"[3] in the Church and in the world. While some think that such a debate centers largely on questions such as the ordination of women to the Catholic priesthood,[4] there are more

---

1 See Second Vatican Council, *Gaudium et Spes* (Pastoral Constitution on the Church in the Modern World) (1965), 8, 9, 60, and *Apostolicam Actuositatem* (Decree on the Apostolate of the Laity) (1965), 9, in *Vatican Council II: The Conciliar and Post Conciliar Documents*, ed. Austin Flannery, rev. ed. (Northport, NY: Costello Publishing, 1988).

2 "Press Conference of Pope Francis during the Return Flight" (apostolic journey to Rio de Janeiro on the occasion of the XXVIII World Youth Day), July 28, 2013, *http://w2.vatican.va/content/francesco/en/speeches/2013/july/documents/papa-francesco_20130728_gmg-conferenza-stampa.html*.

3 Pope Francis, apostolic exhortation *Evangelii Gaudium* (On the Proclamation of the Gospel in Today's World) (2013), 103, *http://w2.vatican.va/content/francesco/en/apost_exhortations/documents/papa-francesco_esortazione-ap_20131124_evangelii-gaudium.html*.

4 See Anne Barbeau Gardiner, "Why Catholic Feminists Are Wrong about Women's Ordination," *New Oxford Review* 78, no. 9 (November 2011), *https://www.newoxfordreview.org/reviews.jsp?did=1111-gardiner*. In her review of Sister Sara Butler's book, *The Catholic Priesthood and Women: A Guide to the*

foundational questions at stake. The question of woman's identity and vocation[5] suggests a threefold inquiry concerning the specific aspects of the feminine genius, how women are liberated to discover and share these strengths, and how these gifts are exercised for the enrichment of the Church and the world. One method of approaching this question is through analysis of the lives of two women who exerted exceptional influence on the Church and the world: Mary of Magdala and Catherine of Siena.[6] Reflection on their lives illustrates how gifts associated with the feminine genius, enriched by the healing encounter with the Lord that liberates the human heart, en-

---

Teaching of the Church (Chicago: Hillenbrand Books, 2007), Gardiner cites and replies to some of the most vocal supporters of the ordination of women. They argue that women's ordination is key to promoting gender equality. She writes, "Among the feminist advocates of women's ordination, Elisabeth Schüssler Fiorenza has argued that Jesus's original intention was to form a 'discipleship of equals'; Sister Sandra Schneiders has argued that the glorified Christ is not 'exclusively male'; and Sister Elizabeth Johnson has argued that all the baptized can be Christ-like. Sister Sara answers each one, pointing out that all are called to be Christ-like and holy, but the priest alone acts *in persona Christi*, and that sexual complementarity on the divine plane is ordered to 'intimacy and fruitfulness.'" [Editor's note: In Chapter Two of this book, Sister Sara Butler outlines several factors that must be considered in any discussion about expanding women's presence in the Church.]

5   While the debate over diverse theories of gender and the possibility of speaking of specifically feminine or masculine traits is ongoing, this paper adopts the philosophical approach identified by Sister Prudence Allen as "integral gender complementarity," which acknowledges both the significant difference and the equal dignity of men and women. This philosophical position, as Sister Prudence demonstrates, harmonizes with the theological teaching of the Catholic Church. See Prudence Allen, "Man-Woman Complementarity: The Catholic Inspiration," *Logos: A Journal of Catholic Thought and Culture* 9, no. 3 (Summer 2006): 87-108.

6   The choice of these two women flows from the inclusion of both in *Mulieris Dignitatem*, by Pope Saint John Paul II. See apostolic letter *Mulieris Dignitatem* (On the Dignity and Vocation of Women) (1988) (Mary Magdalene, 15 and 16; Catherine of Siena, 27). Likewise, in order to reflect the universality of their gifts and vocations, it seems optimal to consider women of diverse periods and cultures (different millennia and continents), states in life (lay secular and consecrated), and types of encounter with Christ (historical and mystical).

able women to receive and proclaim a prophetic message that can transform the Church and the world.

The Feminine Genius Embodied

In his landmark apostolic letter on the dignity and vocation of women, *Mulieris Dignitatem*, Pope Saint John Paul II reflects on the constellation of women who encountered Jesus Christ during the years of his childhood and public ministry. He places particular emphasis on Mary, the Mother of Jesus, who best illustrates the fullness of the gifts of woman possessed by nature and perfected by grace. Mary has rightly been held as the exemplar of the gifts of the feminine genius. As one looks to the narratives of the Annunciation and the Visitation in the Gospel of Luke, the receptivity of Mary emerges. She is humbly open to God's plan for her life. Her "let it be to me according to your word" (Lk 1:38)[7] reflects a truthful understanding of herself as one who receives all from God. Thus she freely opens herself to receive the presence and work of the Holy Spirit, which bears fruit in the gift of new life, the gift of Christ himself.

Having received the Lord's gift, Mary is immediately concerned for her relative Elizabeth and goes on a journey to help her in her needs. This attentiveness to the person, which the pope links directly to the maternal character of woman,[8] enables her to notice and meet the needs of others in an exceptional way, such as Mary's intervention to assist the spouses who were running out of wine at their wedding feast in Cana. A profound implication of the other-centeredness of woman

---

7   Quotes from Scripture in this chapter are from *The Holy Bible, Revised Standard Version, Second Catholic Edition* (San Francisco: Ignatius Press, 2005).

8   Pope John Paul II, *Mulieris Dignitatem*. In Part VI, Pope Saint John Paul II observes, concerning biological motherhood, "This unique contact with the new human being developing within her gives rise to an attitude towards human beings...which profoundly marks the woman's personality" (18). He later explains that motherhood is not limited to the biophysical experience but is pre-eminently spiritual motherhood, which is exercised in many forms according to a woman's state in life.

is her compassion for those who suffer, which opens her to a courageous presence amidst those who are in situations of need or affliction. Reflecting on Mary's closeness to Jesus at the foot of the cross, the Holy Father states that "through faith [Mary] shares in the amazing mystery of her Son's 'self-emptying.'"[9] Pope Saint John Paul II notes that exceptional courage in the face of suffering was not limited to Mary, but rather was reflected in women in general at the hour of Jesus's death. He writes, "Women were in the forefront at the foot of the Cross...John was the only Apostle who remained faithful, but there were many faithful women...in this most arduous test of faith and fidelity the women proved stronger than the Apostles."[10]

Mary of Magdala, one of Jesus's disciples and the first recorded witness to his resurrection, illustrates the presence and diverse manifestations of the gifts of the feminine genius. Leaving aside the numerous debates about which of the women described in various narratives in the Gospels may be identified with Mary of Magdala,[11] one may easily discover, in the four scenes that explicitly refer to her by name and origin, her embodiment of the gifts associated with the genius of woman.[12] She is receptive to the Lord, as evidenced

---

9   Pope John Paul II, *Mulieris Dignitatem*, 19.

10   Ibid., 15.

11   See *Catholic Encyclopedia*, s.v. "St. Mary Magdalen." This article includes an overview of the diverse perspectives on the person of Mary of Magdala, both in the Latin and Greek traditions, as well as in later Protestant scholarship. Diversity of perspective principally flows from disagreement as to whether Mary of Magdala is also the woman who anointed Jesus in the house of Simon (see Lk 7:36-50), and Mary, the sister of Martha and Lazarus (Lk 10:38-42 and Jn 11).

12   Mary of Magdala is specifically named as: one of the women who provided for Jesus and the twelve out of their means (see Lk 8:2-30), a woman out of whom Jesus had cast seven demons (Mk 16:9 and Lk 8:1-3), and a faithful disciple present at the cross (Mt 27:55-56, Mk 15:40-41, Lk 23:49 and 55, and Jn 19:25) and resurrection (Mt 28:1-10, Mk 16:1-11, Lk 24:1-11, and Jn 20:1-18) of Jesus. Given the nature and scope of this paper, a formal-textual approach to the Scriptures concerning Mary of Magdala is not taken. While a consideration of the intentions of the Evangelists could be explored, here emphasis is on the link between the literal and spiritual senses of the Word of God, as highlighted in *Verbum Domini*, in which Pope Benedict XVI writes: "While acknowledging

by her openness to being healed by the casting out of the seven devils that plagued her. She is person-centered, a quality especially manifest in her eagerness to be present at the tomb in order to complete the anointing ritual for the body of Jesus, whom she loved tenderly. Reflecting on the encounter between Mary and Jesus at the tomb, Kyndall Renfro observes that this personal focus is essentially linked to Mary of Magdala's faith: "Mary's faith is awakened by an intimate and personal interaction: Jesus speaks her name. Doctrine or argument or physical proof does not convince her of the resurrection; a conversation, the sound of her name, a personal interaction does."[13] She is preeminently compassionate to Christ in his suffering, near him at the foot of the cross, courageously remaining present in the midst of the jeers and insults of other bystanders. Of her presence and that of the other women, Pope Saint John Paul II concludes, "In this moment of danger, those who love much succeed in overcoming their fear."[14]

In a far different historical context, Catherine of Siena likewise embodied the feminine genius amidst the political and spiritual tumult of the fourteenth century. As a young woman she consecrated herself to Christ as a Dominican tertiary. Never formally educated, she nevertheless became instrumental in ecclesial and political reform. Receiving every aspect of her vocation as a personal call from the Lord in prayer, Catherine was aware of her total dependence on God. In his biography of Catherine, Raymond of Capua recounts a

---

the validity and necessity, as well as the limits, of the historical-critical method, we learn from the Fathers that exegesis 'is truly faithful to the proper intention of biblical texts when it goes not only to the heart of their formulation to find the reality of faith there expressed, but also seeks to link this reality to the experience of faith in our present world.' Only against this horizon can we recognize that the word of God is living and addressed to each of us in the here and now of our lives" (37).

13   Kyndall Renfro, "Faithful Disciple, Feminine Witness: Mary Magdalene Revisited," *Review and Expositor* 110 (Winter 2013): 135.

14   Pope John Paul II, *Mulieris Dignitatem*, 15.

revealing conversation Catherine experienced in prayer with God the Father:

> Do you know, daughter, who you are, and who I am? If you know these two things you will be blessed. You are she who is not; whereas I am He who is. Have this knowledge in your soul and the Enemy will never deceive you and you will escape all his wiles; you will never disobey my commandments and will acquire all grace, truth, and light.[15]

Far from leading her to a passive or fearful paralysis, this reality of her creaturely dependence on a loving Creator opened Catherine to receiving in a radical way all of her being and action from the Lord. Her openness to the value of every person is manifested powerfully not only in her writings but also—and especially—in the many forms of charitable outreach to which she dedicated herself. She had a special love for the poor and the suffering, tending the sick whose wounds made them repulsive to most. She had tremendous compassion for those in trouble. So devoted was her care for the condemned criminal Niccolò di Toldo that he converted to Christ before his public beheading, dying with the names of Jesus and Catherine on his lips.[16]

While it is evident that women's gifts will take a different form and expression based on the uniqueness of each person and context, yet these qualities of receptivity, openness to persons, and compassion in adversity are notably present in women across temporal and cultural boundaries.

---

15 Blessed Raymond of Capua, *The Life of St. Catherine of Siena*, trans. George Lamb (London: Harvill Press, 1960), 79.

16 See Saint Catherine of Siena, *I, Catherine: Selected Writings of St. Catherine of Siena*, ed. and trans. Kenelm Foster, OP, and Mary John Ronayne, OP (London: Collins, 1980), 71-75. Catherine describes the execution of di Toldo in vivid detail in a letter to Raymond of Capua.

Encountering the Lord:
Liberation of Woman for Self-Gift

Asserting that such qualities are inherent to woman might readily prompt the question of why they are not more evident in the lives of every woman. As with the strengths of a just and holy man such as Joseph of Nazareth, virtues that can be associated with, although not limited to, masculine or feminine types seem far from universal in practice. The natural gifts of the human person, male or female, flourish and come to their fullness only with grace. In the cases of Mary of Magdala and Catherine of Siena, the rich gifts of their feminine persons came to maturity after their transforming encounters with Jesus.

While the Evangelists recount the details of the encounter between Mary of Magdala and Jesus only at his tomb after his resurrection, they imply a prior encounter in referring to his casting out of demons from her soul (see Mk 16:9 and Lk 8:1-3). Tradition attributes several explanations to the "seven demons" of Mary Magdalene.[17] Patristic sources, especially after the time and example of Saint Gregory the Great, often associated the combined references to Mary's demons and to her wealth with the profession of prostitution. Whether or not this was the situation of Mary of Magdala, her release from seven demons is clearly a dramatic spiritual liberation. The woman who follows Jesus and provides for the needs of the apostles out of her resources, and who later perseveres at Jesus's side at the place of his execution and even to the grave, is obviously

---

17   See Pamela Thimmes, "Memory and Re-Vision: Mary Magdalene Research since 1975," *Currents in Research: Biblical Studies* 6 (1998): 193-226. Thimmes traces the evolution of interpretation regarding Mary of Magdala in early Christian literature, noting an increasing tendency to emphasize her deliverance from evil and sin and a decreasing focus on her role as a witness to the Resurrection, stemming especially from "the composite/conflated characterization of her promulgated by the exegetical and homiletic work of ecclesiastical leaders from the early centuries of Christianity" (194). She notes that the explicit linking of Mary of Magdala, as one from whom demons were cast out, to the sinful woman of John's Gospel "achieves official ecclesiastical standing through the preaching of Gregory the Great" (221) by the late sixth century.

a free woman, a woman of immense strength and virtue. As Mary O'Driscoll reflects concerning Mary Magdalene, "Her healing was consequently also her call to discipleship."[18]

Catherine of Siena did not undergo the sort of radical conversion of Mary Magdalene, but she nevertheless received in her mystical encounters with Christ the self-knowledge and the confidence in the healing power of Christ's blood that enabled her to embrace the extraordinary calling she was given. At the age of six, Catherine saw Christ in a vision in which he asked her to dedicate herself to him. Christ raised his hand and blessed Catherine with the sign of the cross. Her biographer and spiritual director, Raymond of Capua, writes of this vision's effect, "At the sight of all this the little girl remained rooted to the ground, gazing lovingly with unblinking eyes upon her Lord and Saviour, who was revealing Himself to her in this way in order to captivate her love."[19] A year later, in 1354, at the age of seven, she made a private vow of virginity to bind herself to Christ her Spouse, asking Mary to "give me as Husband Him whom I desire with all the power of my soul, your most holy Son."[20]

As she grew, Catherine was aware of her own weaknesses. Sensitive to the unity of the members of the Body of Christ, she saw her personal failures in love as contributing to the corruption in the Church and society of her day. Among the themes that earned her recognition as a Doctor of the Church was her doctrine on self-knowledge in Christ. Catherine repeatedly emphasized the need for self-knowledge to prepare the soul for advancing in union with God. Raymond of Capua

---

18   Mary O'Driscoll, OP, "Mary Magdalene and Catherine of Siena: Dominican Sisters," *Dominican Ashram* 15, no. 2 (June 1996): 54. This article, based on a talk delivered to the Dominican family (gathering of priests, sisters, and laity) in New York in September 1995, offers a spiritual reflection on the lives of these two women that complements the approach taken here.

19   Blessed Raymond of Capua, *The Life of St. Catherine of Siena*, 25.

20   Ibid., 31.

recalls that she advised often, "Make yourself a cell in your own mind from which you need never come out."[21]

In a letter written to Alessa dei Saracini in 1377, Catherine describes the spiritual cell as one comprising two rooms in which one must simultaneously dwell to avoid the pitfalls of confusion or presumption. She warns that remaining only in the cell of self-knowledge leads the soul to confusion, brought on by awareness of its miseries. On the other hand, if one tries to dwell in knowledge of God's goodness without self-knowledge, the soul can succumb to presumption. When the two rooms are both entered, they become one. Self-knowledge leads to hatred of one's "selfish sensuality,"[22] a conversion that moves one's conscience to judge correctly and cultivates humility. This, in turn, strengthens the soul to suffer adversity with patience.

Catherine therefore makes the important distinction, as Thomas McDermott observes, that knowledge of truth requires not self-knowledge alone, but rather, as the Father teaches Catherine, self-knowledge united with the "knowledge of me in you."[23] In the greater and more perfect knowledge of God, Catherine tells Alessa: "You will discover the fire of divine charity, where you will find your pleasure on the cross with the spotless Lamb, searching out God's honor and the salvation of souls in continual and humble prayer. Herein lies all our perfection."[24] Thus for Catherine, knowing Christ and oneself in Christ is the necessary purification of the apostle. She writes to Costanza Soderini, a wife and mother: "I long to

---

21 Ibid., 43.

22 Saint Catherine of Siena, *The Letters of Catherine of Siena*, trans. Suzanne Noffke, OP, vol. 2 (Tempe, AZ: Arizona Center for Medieval and Renaissance Studies, 2001), 602. The letters of Saint Catherine have been published in four volumes, which are cited within this chapter according to the respective volume numbers.

23 Thomas McDermott, "Catherine of Siena's Teaching on Self-Knowledge," *New Blackfriars* 88, no. 1018 (2007): 639.

24 Saint Catherine of Siena, *Letters*, vol. 2, 602.

see your heart and affection divested of slavish fear and of all worldly love and attachments. I want you to be clothed only in Christ crucified. There put your faith and your trust."[25]

The Prophetic Voice of Women in the Church and in the World

Woman, endowed with natural and supernatural gifts and healed by the grace of encounter with Christ, is called by baptism to "share the priestly, prophetic and kingly office of Christ...[to] carry on the mission of the whole Christian people in the Church and in the world."[26] While these offices take many forms, which men and women fulfill in sometimes particular but nevertheless complementary ways, they are the call of all. Considering the interactions of Christ with the women of his time, there is evidence of an exceptional prophetic character in the call he extended to them. For example, the Samaritan woman whom Jesus encounters at the well is taught by Jesus directly and then goes to the village and proclaims his insight into her life and actions. Her testimony to him leads many to come and encounter Christ personally and to discover that he is indeed the "Savior of the world" (Jn 4:42).

Michele Schumacher, in a reflection on the prophetic vocation of woman, attests to the notable relational inclination in woman that opens her to bearing witness to God's love. She observes, "Beyond providing a natural foundation for the order of love through maternal self-giving, women, it may be argued, are especially suited for their prophetic vocation of witnessing to this order in virtue of their particular 'genius' (*Mulieris Dignitatem*, 30, 31) by which John Paul II means a certain 'womanly' attentiveness to the human person."[27] In

---

25   Ibid., 487.

26   Second Vatican Council, Dogmatic Constitution on the Church (*Lumen Gentium*) (1964), 31.

27   Michele M. Schumacher, STD, "The Prophetic Vocation of Women and the Order of Love," *Logos: A Journal of Catholic Thought and Culture* 2, no. 2 (Spring 1999): 169.

the lives of Mary of Magdala and Catherine of Siena, this attentiveness to persons enables them to receive and share the life-giving word of God's love, even in contexts where their very femininity poses a challenge to their cultural acceptance as witnesses.

In the life of Mary of Magdala, the prophetic vocation she receives arises from the express will and call of Christ. Because of her devotion to Jesus and her steadfast perseverance in remaining with him, she is a witness to the truth of his resurrection. She not only encounters the Risen Christ but also is sent to the apostles to testify to him. The Gospel of Mark tells of the apostles' mourning and refusal to believe her testimony (see Mk 16:10-11), to which the evangelist Luke adds that, "these words seemed to them an idle tale" (Lk 24:11). Jesus corrects the apostles for this closed attitude. As Mark records, "He upbraided them for their unbelief and hardness of heart, because they had not believed those who saw him after he had risen" (Mk 16:14).

In the Gospel According to John, Mary Magdalene is given the task to proclaim the message of the return of Jesus to his Father. Jesus directs her, "Go to my brethren and say to them, I am ascending to my Father and your Father, to my God and your God" (20:17). When Mary goes to the apostles, her first testimony is, "I have seen the Lord" (20:18). In his commentary on the Gospel of John, Thomas Aquinas writes of the unique prophetic vocation of Mary Magdalene:

> Note the three privileges given to Mary Magdalene. First, she had the privilege of being a prophet because she was worthy enough to see the angels, for a prophet is an intermediary between angels and the people. Second, she had the dignity or rank of an angel insofar as she looked upon Christ, on whom the angels desire to look. Third, she had the office of an apostle; indeed, she was an apostle to the apostles insofar as it was her task to

announce our Lord's resurrection to the disciples. Thus, just as it was a woman who was the first to announce the words of death, so it was a woman who would be the first to announce the words of life.[28]

In Mary Magdalene one sees how the exercise of her gifts led her to experience and to proclaim the living and life-giving presence of the Lord to the grieving, fearful apostles. In this fulfillment of her prophetic vocation, she awakens hope in the apostles who were called to lead Christ's Church. While the impact of her announcement of the resurrection of Jesus most explicitly affected the nascent Church, the news of Christ's resurrection transformed the world by its revolutionary testimony to life after death.

More than a millennium after the life and witness of Mary of Magdala, after a three-year period of prayer and seclusion in the home of her family, Catherine of Siena perceived a divine call to speak prophetically in the Church and the world, especially to call for purification, repentance, and peace. This was a call she perceived within the context of her love for Christ, her concern for the Church, her profound respect for the pope and clergy, and her zeal for the salvation of souls. She sought to support, not to oppose, Pope Urban VI in his role as Vicar of Christ. This she eloquently affirmed in a personal letter to him:

> You are the father and lord of the universal body of Christianity; all of us are under your holiness' wings. So far as authority is concerned you can do everything, but in terms of vision, you can see no more than one person can. So it is essential that your children single-heartedly, without any slavish fear, look out for God's

---

28 Saint Thomas Aquinas, *Commentary on the Gospel of John Chapters 9-21*, trans. Fabian R. Larcher, ed. Aquinas Institute, *Latin/English Editions of the Works of St. Thomas Aquinas* 36 (Lander, WY: Aquinas Institute for the Study of Sacred Doctrine, 2013), C. 20, L. 3, no. 2519, 470.

honor as well as your honor and welfare and that of the little sheep who are under your staff.[29]

Catherine, not unlike the prophets of every era,[30] hesitated to undertake this mission, aware of her own weaknesses and of the social norms of her day that made such a task seemingly impossible for a woman. Her objection to the task and the Lord's response are recorded in Raymond of Capua's biography. Catherine points out that both her personal frailty and her being a woman, a sex "not highly considered by men,"[31] make a preaching mission for the good of souls impractical. The Lord's response reflects divine wisdom, often at odds with human ways of thinking:

> Am I not He who created the human race and divided it into male and female? I spread abroad the grace of my spirit where I will. In my eyes there is neither male nor female, rich nor poor, but all are equal for I can do all things with equal ease...in these latter days there has been such an upsurge of pride, especially in the case of men who imagine themselves to be learned or wise, that my justice cannot endure them any longer...if they will come to their senses and humble themselves, I will behave with the utmost mercy toward them [when they] receive my doctrine, offered to them in fragile but specially chosen vessels, and follow it reverently.[32]

Thus Catherine came to understand that in order for both men and women to build up Christ's body, the Church, it was essential to walk in humility and truth. Christ crucified is the model for all believers, as Catherine reflected: "This dear

---

29 Saint Catherine of Siena, *Letters*, vol. 4, 217.

30 The prophets of the Hebrew Scriptures, such as Moses (cf. Ex 3:10-4:17), Isaiah (cf. Is 6:5-9), and Jonah (cf. Jon 1:1-3), were notable for trying to protest or flee from the prophetic task.

31 Blessed Raymond of Capua, *Life*, 108.

32 Ibid., 108-109.

master took the chair of the cross in order to give us a lesson grounded in truth. So we students ought to stand down below (in the lowliness of true humility, that is) to learn it."[33]

Sustained by God's choice and grace, Catherine began a public mission extraordinary for any man or woman in any period. Of this short but intense phase of her life, it is written, "She began to dispatch letters to men and women in every condition of life, entered into correspondence with the princes and republics of Italy, was consulted by the papal legates about the affairs of the Church, and set herself to heal the wounds of her native land by staying the fury of civil war and the ravages of faction."[34] What she learned in prayer and meditation, she freely and boldly proclaimed not only to fellow religious and family members, but also to princes and popes, politicians and prisoners. Catherine was tireless in calling for moral reform of individuals and of institutions. She is most noted for her intervention in ending the Avignon Papacy.

When one considers the depth of Catherine's love for Christ and his Church, it comes as no surprise that she directly intervened when the Church was threatened by division. One of the great crises of her time was the pope's absence from Rome and residence in Avignon. That the Bishop of Rome should be away from his see and subject to the political rivalries that plagued French and Italian politics was a heavy burden to Catherine's heart. She wrote a series of letters to Pope Gregory XI begging him to return to Rome and to make peace with the Italian factions. Addressing Pope Gregory as her dear father, Catherine implored: "If you can, come before September.... Pay no attention to any opposition, but like a courageous and fearless man, come!"[35] Under the persuasive influence of Catherine, Pope Gregory made plans to set out for Rome, but then he received word of a plot to poison him

---

33 Saint Catherine of Siena, *Letters*, vol. 3, 50.

34 *Catholic Encyclopedia*, s.v. "St. Catherine of Siena."

35 Saint Catherine of Siena, *Letters*, vol. 2, 191.

should he return. Emboldened by her zeal for the good of the Church, Catherine renewed her requests in September 1376: "I beg you in the name of Christ crucified not to be a timid child but a courageous man…if you are willing, he will give you (and us) the grace of making you strong and firm, unmoved by any wind or demonic illusion or advice from any devil incarnate."[36] Pope Gregory XI left by boat for Rome on September 13, 1376.

Reform, Rooted in Love and Truth

The connection between Mary of Magdala and Catherine of Siena is explicit in the letters of Catherine herself. She saw Mary Magdalene as a model disciple of Jesus and offered her as a sign of encouragement for other women to whom she wrote. To Monna Agnese and her spiritual daughters, Catherine wrote of her desire to see them be like "that loving apostle Magdalen. So great was her blazing love that she cared for nothing created."[37] Catherine saw in Mary of Magdala an exemplar of a love for Christ so total that it fosters fearless adherence and witness to Christ with utter confidence in his power to save souls.

In these two great women saints, a principle explored by Thomas Aquinas in his *Summa Theologica* becomes evident—namely, that "zeal, whatever way we take it, arises from the intensity of love."[38] Both Mary of Magdala and Catherine of Siena experienced the love the Lord had for them in union with God, in contemplative prayer. This love is foundational for becoming aware of the truth of who one is in Christ and of discerning rightly how to love and serve God and one's neighbor. The primacy of love is essential in the exercise of mission, including the prophetic role. As Thomas Aquinas continues, "For it is evident

---

36 Ibid., 247.

37 Saint Catherine of Siena, *Letters*, vol. 1, 3.

38 Saint Thomas Aquinas, *Summa Theologica*, trans. Fathers of the English Dominican Province (New York: Benziger Bros., 1947), I-II, Q. 28, Art. 4, resp.

that the more intensely a power tends to anything, the more vigorously it withstands opposition or resistance. Since therefore love is 'a movement toward the object loved,' as Augustine says (QQ. 83, qu. 35), an intense love seeks to remove everything that opposes it."[39] If women call for reform in the family, the political sphere, and the Church, they will be effective only if motivated by love and rooted in truth.

Both in the Gospels and in the history of the Church as embodied in the lives of the saints, it is clear that no division can be made between love and truth. In the life and writing of Catherine of Siena, it is evident that she found the guarantee of truth in obedience to the official teachings of the Church. When he named Catherine a Doctor of the Church, Pope Blessed Paul VI noted, citing the letters of Catherine: "The Virgin of Siena esteemed the Roman Pontiff as 'the sweet Christ dwelling on earth' (Letter 196), who must always be loved and obeyed. If anyone should not be obedient to the earthly Christ, since he is the same as the heavenly Christ, such a one does not share in the fruit of the Blood of the Son of God (Letter 206)."[40] Essential to discernment in every age is fidelity to Christ, who continues to guide his Church by the wisdom of the Holy Spirit.

If, like these great models, women today were to know themselves in Christ and bring to the Church and the world the gifts that are especially associated with the feminine genius, what might emerge? How would a spirit of receptivity affect often-competitive models of business and leadership? How might a person-centered approach transform political, economic, and social policies? What would a courageous voice that defends the poor, weak, and suffering offer to public debates? The prophetic proclamation, by Mary Magdalene, of

---

39   Ibid.

40   Pope Paul VI, *Mirabilis in Ecclesia Deus* (October 4, 1970), 3, accessed at *http://www.drawnby love.com*. As noted in the document, "No official English translation was ever published of this work. This translation was done by the late Father W.B. Mahoney, OP, Aquinas Institute of Theology, Dubuque, Iowa. The official Latin text is found in *Acta Apostolicae Sedis* (*AAS*), 1970, pp. 672+."

the risen Lord moved the apostles from fear to hope, from hiding to action. This transformation was essential to the foundation of the Church. The Church of today has no less need to be moved to proclaim the gospel of life in the face of a growing culture of death. The prophetic voice of Catherine of Siena challenged the pope to courage, princes to consider peaceful resolutions to conflict, and many individuals to turn from selfishness to reliance on Christ for the grace of self-giving love, a call whose need never ceases.

Mary of Magdala and Catherine of Siena offer a paradigm for women today: Their receptivity to God's love and his word and their proclamation of that prophetic word, in diverse historical circumstances, exerted an influence for the transformation of the Church and the world. For women to have the impact on the Church and the world today, flowing from the very gifts they possess, they must first encounter Christ in prayer. In Christ, one discovers the truth that sets one free (see Jn 8:32), especially by pondering God's word, participating in the sacramental life of the Church, and discerning his or her authentic vocation in the light of magisterial teaching. It is essential that within this knowing of themselves in Christ women rediscover and embrace the gifts of the feminine genius. Receptivity is necessary to welcome the truth of God's word and the gift of each person. In a time of increasing attempts to manipulate and reject human life, to select who is "wanted" or "worthy to live," such openness is needed more than ever. A person-centered approach is central to efforts to counter materialistic ideologies that put profits and power above persons and service. If persons are seen as central, "progress" has a humane measure that rejects novelty at the expense of the individual or common good. Compassion for those who suffer in body or spirit is foundational for awakening a hunger for justice and, ultimately, for a society built on solidarity rooted in genuine charity.

Pope Saint John Paul II, in his address at World Youth Day 2000 in Rome, made a statement so captivating that it has echoed ever since. To the crowd of over two million, he called out: "From Rome, from the City of Peter and Paul, the Pope follows you with affection and, paraphrasing Saint Catherine of Siena's words, reminds you: 'If you are what you should be, you will set the whole world ablaze!' (cf. Letter 368)."[41] In order for women today to have a "more incisive presence," we need not deny our femininity nor reject the gifts that have been entrusted to us. Rather we must "be what we are," with deep faith that, with God's grace and strength and in whatever sphere to which we are called, our contributions can set the world ablaze.

Sister Mary Madeline Todd, OP, STL, is a doctoral candidate at the Pontifical University of Saint Thomas Aquinas (the Angelicum) in Rome. She holds an MA in English literature from the University of Memphis and an MA in theology from the Franciscan University of Steubenville. After eleven years of teaching, Sister Mary Madeline went to Sydney, Australia, to serve as assistant to Bishop Anthony Fisher in preparation for World Youth Day 2008. In Sydney, she also worked for the University Chaplaincy Team and spoke extensively on the dignity of women, pro-life issues, and various theological themes. Her interviews and articles have been featured in the Sydney Morning Herald, *ABC's* 7:30 Report, The Catholic Weekly *and other publications, including the website for the Pontifical Council for the Laity. Sister Mary Madeline completed her STL in moral theology in Rome at the Angelicum and is currently residing in Washington, D.C., writing her doctoral dissertation on a Christ-centered theological anthropology of women.*

---

41   Pope John Paul II, *Closing of World Youth Day: Homily of the Holy Father John Paul II* (August 20, 2000), *http://www.vatican.va/holy_father/john_paul_ii/ homilies/documents/hf_jp-ii_hom_20000820_gmg_en.html.*

CHAPTER FIVE

The Feminine Genius and Women's Contributions in Society and in the Church

Margaret Harper McCarthy, PhD

Hans Urs von Balthasar once wrote:

> The Catholic Church is perhaps humanity's last bulwark of genuine appreciation of the difference between the sexes. In the dogma of the Trinity, the Persons must be equal in dignity in order to safeguard the distinction that makes the triune God subsistent love; in a similar way the Church stresses the equal dignity of man and woman, so that the extreme oppositeness of their functions may guarantee the spiritual and physical fruitfulness of human nature. Every encroachment of one sex into the role of the other narrows the range and dynamics of humanly possible love, even when this range transcends the sphere of sexuality, birth and death and achieves the level of the virginal relationship between Christ and his Church.[1]

Mindful of the "difference between the sexes," this chapter addresses the recent call of Pope Francis that women actively carry their profile forward.[2] "The feminine genius," he wrote, "is needed in all expressions in the life of society...

---

1   Hans Urs von Balthasar, "Women Priests," in *New Elucidations*, trans. Mary Theresilde Skerry (San Francisco: Ignatius Press, 1986), 195-196.

2   "Press Conference of Pope Francis during the Return Flight" (apostolic journey to Rio de Janeiro on the occasion of the XXVIII World Youth Day), July

the workplace, and in the various other settings where important decisions are made, both in the Church and in social structures."[3]

This chapter, then, addresses the presence of women in the workplace, both in the Church and in society, but of necessity begins with a cautionary note. We should be wary of letting any deliberations about women (or the laity) be guided or motivated simply by pressures coming from the dominant culture, especially where its notion of equality is concerned. Liberalism has *no* resources for looking at two complementary dimensions, involving mutually exclusive tasks, as anything other than a play between a superior and an inferior.[4] The "equality" of liberalism knows no other differences. One need only look at the *Lean In* phenomenon (book, movement, and foundation, not to mention Facebook presence), which came swooping down on former State Department official Anne-Marie Slaughter, who dared to suggest that there was a *natural reason* why women "can't have it all": that they have a different relation to their children than their husbands, and therefore a different (not inferior!) relation to outside work.[5] Catholic Christians who *do* have those resources have no reason to capitulate to this cultural orthodoxy, much less to minimize or apologize for recognizing sexual difference in society or the understanding of the spousal nature of the Church. On

---

28, 2013, *http://w2.vatican.va/content/francesco/en/speeches/2013/july/documents/papa-francesco_20130728_gmg-conferenza-stampa.html*.

3 Pope Francis, apostolic exhortation *Evangelii Gaudium* (On the Proclamation of the Gospel in Today's World) (2013), 103. Pope Francis opens up consideration of "the possible role of women in decision-making in different areas of the Church's life, " *Evangelii Gaudium*, 104. "It is necessary to broaden the opportunities for a stronger presence of women in the church." See Antonio Spadaro, SJ, "A Big Heart Open to God: The Exclusive Interview with Pope Francis," *America*, September 30, 2013, *http://americamagazine.org/pope-interview*.

4 See Martha C. Nussbaum, "The Feminist Critique of Liberalism," *Sex and Social Justice* (Oxford: Oxford University Press 1999), 55-80.

5 Anne Marie Slaughter, "Why Women Still Can't Have It All," *The Atlantic*, July/August 2012. See also Sheryl Sandberg, *Lean In: Women, Work, and the Will to Lead* (New York: Alfred A. Knopf, 2013).

the contrary, Catholics must be proud of the Christian novelty of *equality in difference* (which derives from the Trinity). We must show, moreover, that this difference is the *only guarantor* of the "spiritual and physical fruitfulness of human nature" (and the Church), as Balthasar suggested.

The proper pride that accompanies this novelty moves us to communicate the truth regarding the relationship between man and woman. However, given the complex nature of the culture we inhabit, this messaging must be approached with great care. We want, of course, to communicate—but to communicate always that which is true. For truth is what the heart most deeply desires, even if it is met with incomprehension and ridicule,[6] even violence, as it was with Jesus (and before him Socrates). In other words, as we shape a message for the Church and for the world regarding the contribution of women, we must not let cultural pressures set the terms of the conversation or dictate our way of thinking about the question itself. We must not, therefore, assume the inferiority complex that always lurks behind the dominant egalitarian thinking, where—in this case—the home (vis-à-vis society) and the laity (vis-à-vis the hierarchy) always get short shrift, and where "solutions" tend in professional and clerical directions.

Of course, cultural pressures *are* in some way pushing the Church to deal with the "problem of women." Pope Francis has them clearly in mind when he says, "Demands that the legitimate rights of women be respected...present the Church with profound and challenging questions which cannot be lightly evaded."[7] Thus, keeping in mind the signs of the times, this chapter offers some considerations on the contribution of women in society and in the Church.[8]

---

6   In this vein we note Pope Francis's awareness of the culture's consistent ridicule of the Church's teaching on abortion, presenting her position "as ideological, obscurantist and conservative." See *Evangelii Gaudium*, 213.

7   Pope Francis, *Evangelii Gaudium*, 104.

8   It should be made clear that to speak about women first in society and then in the Church is not to imply that they are two separate spheres. Indeed,

Feminine Genius—What Is It and Why Is It Needed?

Pope Francis has called for a greater presence of the "feminine genius" in society and in the Church—so we must first understand *what* this feminine genius is. Let's consider its *scope,* its *nature,* its *character,* and why it was invoked by Pope Saint John Paul II in the first place and now, as we see, by Pope Francis.

Scope, Nature, and Character

By feminine genius, Pope Saint John Paul II referred to a talent or intelligence *specific to women,* something she has by virtue of her specific difference with respect to a man. This particular genius does not, of course, exclude other forms of genius (in fields such as mathematics, science, literature, and so forth), geniuses that belong to humanity as such, the common humanity the woman shares with the man. At the same time the feminine genius is not simply one genius among others. It is the *specific* genius—distinct vis-à-vis the man—through which she bears all the others, just as her specific—that is, different—body is the way in which she bears the bodily humanity she shares in common with man. Therefore, this genius, analogous to the genius of man, penetrates to the core of what it is for her to be human without compromising the continuity of their shared nature. Balthasar expresses the phenomenon thus:

> Each possesses the whole of human nature but each has a different manner of being human. And this manner touches each to their very core: The male body is male throughout, right down to each cell of which it consists, and the female body is utterly female; and this is also

---

there is a true distinction between the spheres, but because the Church touches everything, there is a true interpenetration. To understand the contribution of women in both spheres can only enhance and further inform our understanding of her contribution to the world as a whole.

true of their whole empirical experience and ego-consciousness. At the same time both share an identical human nature, but at no point does it protrude, neutrally beyond the sexual difference, as if to provide neutral ground for understanding.[9]

What *is* the feminine genius? As Pope Saint John Paul II understood it, the feminine genius is an intelligence or sensitivity tied to the fact that a woman is *apt for maternity* through her spousal gift of self. By virtue of that fact, a woman is able to welcome the child, making room, and enabling him or her to grow. The woman *qua* mother is able to *let the child be,* respecting the child in his or her otherness,[10] and is therefore entrusted with the human being "in a special way."[11] The woman has a "special openness to the...person"[12] tied to the fact that the human being finds a home in her.[13]

We should make two caveats here. The first is that this genius does not depend on a woman actually—that is, physically—being a mother. It depends on *the kind of being she is,* a being apt for motherhood. The second point reinforces the

---

9   Hans Urs von Balthasar, *Theo-Drama, II: Dramatis Personae: Man in God,* trans. Graham Harrison (San Francisco, Ignatius Press, 1990), 365.

10   Pope John Paul II, *Evangelium Vitae* (On the Value and Inviolability of Human Life) (1995), 99. Pope Francis also insists on the woman's "sensitivity and intuition for the other, the weak and the defenseless." John L. Allen Jr., "Pope Wants 'Capillary and Incisive' Role for Women in Church," *National Catholic Reporter,* January 25, 2014, *http://ncronline.org/blogs/francis-chronicles/pope-wants-capillary-and-incisive-role-women-church.* See also VIS, "Pope Francis Receives the Italian Women's Centre: Broaden the Space for Women in the Church," Official Vatican Network, January 25, 2014, *http://www.news.va/en/news/pope-francis-receives-the-italian-womens-centre-br.*

11   Pope John Paul II, apostolic letter *Mulieris Dignitatem* (On the Dignity and Vocation of Women) (1988), 30.

12   Pope John Paul II, *Mulieris Dignitatem,* 18.

13   It is crucial to see that this special openness or sensitivity proper to women is intimately tied to the *specificity* of the woman. In other words, as we saw with Balthasar, if it is true that what is distinct about man and woman penetrates to their core, then their self-giving to each other, and to their children, will be informed by their specific difference.

first point precisely because, as Pope Saint John Paul II says, aptness for physical motherhood is itself iconic of something deeper.[14] The vocation to virginity is a revelation of this "something deeper" that reveals the depth of the motherhood (actual or not) of every woman[15]—a "letting be" of the human being according to the horizon of the *new generation* that has been introduced into the world through the Virgin Mary. Pope Francis's desire for woman to be a presence in the world and in the Church means, in the first place, being present in terms of her motherhood, in its full depth. As the pope explains, "The role of women in the Church is not simply that of maternity, being mothers, but much greater: it is precisely to be *the icon of the Virgin, of Our Lady, what helps make the Church grow!*"[16]

One of the characteristics of this feminine genius is its *hiddenness.* Its first sphere of action is the womb, then the home. As Pope Saint John Paul II said: "In [the social and ethical dimensions of progress in society], which often develops *in an inconspicuous way* beginning with the daily relationships

---

14 Pope John Paul II, *Letter of Pope John Paul II to Women* (1995), 11, http://www.vatican.va/holy_father/john_paul_ii/letters/documents/hf_jp-ii_let_29061995_women_en.html.

15 On this point see Pope John Paul II, *Mulieris Dignitatem*, 17-22: "[O]ne can say that the profile of marriage is found spiritually in virginity. And does not physical motherhood also have to be a spiritual motherhood, in order to respond to the whole truth about the human being who is a unity of body and spirit?" See also Pope John Paul II's *Letter to Families*: "Human fatherhood and motherhood are rooted in biology, yet at the same time transcend it. The Apostle, with knees bowed 'before the Father from whom all fatherhood in heaven and on earth is named,' in a certain sense asks us to look at the whole world of living creatures, from the spiritual beings in heaven to the corporeal beings on earth. Every act of begetting finds its primordial model in the fatherhood of God.... When a new person is born of the conjugal union of the two, he brings with him into the world a particular image and likeness of God himself: *the genealogy of the person is inscribed in the very biology of generation.*" See also Pope John Paul II, *Gratissimam Sane* (Letter to Families) (1994), 9, http://www.vatican.va/holy_father/john_paul_ii/letters/documents/hf_jp-ii_let_02021994_families_en.html.

16 "Press Conference of Pope Francis," July 28, 2013.

between people, especially within the family, society certainly owes much to the 'genius of women.'"[17] The work tied to the feminine genius is made up of hundreds and thousands of small, repetitive actions that often appear insignificant and fruitless. This work is not performed by someone with a "position" or some other form of public recognition. And it does not garner a salary. But for all this, the work of the feminine genius is not less important work. We might say that it is more important, that it is ranked with the highest kind of work, which cannot be compensated because it is work that is good in itself. And as we shall see in forthcoming sections, the hidden work of cultivating a home is visibly fruitful in several ways.

Why the "Feminine Genius" Is Invoked

Now *why* is the feminine genius invoked? Pope Saint John Paul II usually invoked the feminine genius alongside his concerns regarding certain cultural tendencies that make the world "un-homelike": tendencies in modern technology and science that "[push] others to the edges of society"[18]—especially the most vulnerable. These tendencies in social organization and management crush the *humanum* under the criteria of efficiency and productivity.[19] All of this "can also lead to a gradual *loss of*

---

17   Pope John Paul II, *Letter to Women*, 9. "Spousal love—with its maternal potential hidden in the heart of the woman as a virginal bride—when joined to Christ, the Redeemer of each and every person, is also predisposed to being open to each and every person," citing *Mulieris Dignitatem*, 21.

18   Pope John Paul II, *Mulieris Dignitatem*, 30. David L. Schindler, drawing on Wendell Berry, explains how the technological ontology of modernity perpetuates the "un-homelike," or rather, *homeless* structure of our culture. "Homelessness…consists of an abstract and mechanistic pattern of being, thinking, acting, and producing that makes human beings rootless in a world stripped of its intrinsic creaturely order." David Schindler, "Homelessness and the Modern Condition: The Family, Community, and Global Economy," *Communio* 27.3 (Fall 2000), 415. Moreover, it is precisely this mechanistic ontology that "furthers an undomesticated view of space and time in a way that favors a consumerist, as distinct from genuinely communional, notion of the human person." David Schindler, "Homelessness," 159. This aspect will be further discussed in the section addressing the relationship between home and society.

19   Pope John Paul II, *Letter to Women*, 4.

sensitivity for man…for what is essentially human."[20] Two texts from Balthasar speak to the depth of the *homelessness* in modernity:

> [W]henever the relationship between nature and grace is severed…the whole of worldly being falls under the dominion of "knowledge." And the springs and forces of love immanent in the world are overpowered and finally suffocated by science, technology and cybernetics. The result is a world without women, without children, without reverence for love in poverty and humiliation—a world in which power and the profit-margin are the sole criteria, where the disinterested, the useless, the purposeless is despised, persecuted and in the end exterminated—a world in which art itself is forced to wear the mask and features of technique.[21]
>
> Where positivistic, technology-oriented thinking succeeds in reigning supreme, the female element also vanishes from the attitude of the man. There is no longer anything that maternally embraces the human being's existence: under the power of the human spirit, nature has descended to the level of mere material… natural things and conditions mean above all material for manufacturables.[22]

Then, too, when a culture places no value on those things to which women are most attuned, *women themselves* jettison their genius and jump on board to be where the action is, valuing only those activities which are publicly recognized and reimbursed. Women are often the first to jettison their own genius. Now *everyone* becomes a go-getter, and the culture has no brake. The desire for power, as Pope Francis

---

20   Pope John Paul II, *Mulieris Dignitatem*, 30.

21   Hans Urs von Balthasar, *Love Alone*, trans. and ed. Alexander Dru (New York: Herder and Herder, 1969), 114-115.

22   Hans Urs von Balthasar, "Women Priests," 189.

notes, may become a surreptitious motivation for both men and women, even within the Church. Balthasar makes a similar point:

> "Power" is so often unobtrusively behind many contestations and movements, supposedly on behalf of justice, equality and so forth, that, precisely in the case of the theme under consideration here [women in the Church], extreme caution and the most precise discernment of spirits are necessary. Both sexes, each in its own way, aspire to "power," and use the most varied methods to gain it. Power is connected subterraneously with humanity's original sin and concupiscence and, naturally, also makes itself felt as a motive within the Church. It is by no means a prerogative of men.[23]

In sum, the feminine genius is invoked as a *counterbalance* to disturbing trends that are ultimately the expressions of a less human world, a "world without women and children." The genius of women is needed because it recalls us to the essentially human. And thus, as Pope Saint John Paul II wrote, "our time in particular *awaits the manifestation* of that 'genius' which belongs to women, and which can ensure sensitivity for human beings in every circumstance: because they are human!"[24]

Women and Society—Ways to Be More Present

Given these general comments on the feminine genius, what does it mean to say women must be more present in society? Let us first recall the two temptations Pope Francis asks us to avoid. On the one hand, the temptation of egalitarianism promotes "a kind of emancipation that, in order to fill areas that have been taken away from the male, deserts the feminine at-

---

23 Ibid., 197.
24 Pope John Paul II, *Mulieris Dignitatem*, 30.

tributes with all it precious characteristics."[25] This temptation would reduce the question of women in society to a merely statistical one rather than a question of women present in society *as such*. The second temptation goes in the opposite direction. It places great value on the feminine genius but "sets the woman and her potential aside" so that woman's gifts have little formative influence in society at large.[26] Keeping in mind these temptations, let me now note three considerations regarding the presence of women.

Valuing and Privileging the Work Specific to Women

Let us begin with an obvious but fundamental point, one that is often shunted aside in discussions about women and society: Society must *value and privilege* the work specific to a woman, the work tied to her conceiving, bearing, nursing, and raising children, work that is made of thousands of small repetitive actions performed out of public view, all of which is done *gratis*.[27] G. K. Chesterton captured the significance of this work profoundly and in his uniquely quotable way:

> [W]hen people begin to talk about this domestic duty as not merely difficult but trivial and dreary, I simply give up the question. For I cannot with the utmost energy of imagination conceive what they mean. When domesticity, for instance, is called drudgery, all the difficulty arises from a double meaning in the word. If drudgery only means dreadfully hard work, I admit the

---

25 Pope Francis, "Address of Pope Francis to Participants in a Seminar Organized by the Pontifical Council for the Laity on the Occasion of the 25th Anniversary of 'Mulieris Dignitatem,'" October 12, 2013, http://w2.vatican. va/content/francesco/en/speeches/2013/october/documents/papa-frances-co_20131012_seminario-xxv-mulieris-dignitatem.html.

26 Ibid.

27 As Pope John Paul II said: "[I]t is…necessary that the man be fully aware that…he owes a special debt to the woman. No programme of 'equal rights' between women and men is valid unless it takes this fact fully into account." See *Mulieris Dignitatem*, 18.

woman drudges in the home, as a man might drudge at the Cathedral of Amiens or drudge behind a gun at Trafalgar. But if it means that the hard work is more heavy because it is trifling, colorless and of small import to the soul, then as I say, I give it up; I do not know what the words mean.... I can understand how this might exhaust the mind, but I cannot imagine how it could narrow it. How can it be a large career to tell other people's children about the Rule of Three, and a small career to tell one's own children about the universe? How can it be broad to be the same thing to everyone, and narrow to be everything to someone? No, a woman's function is laborious, but because it is gigantic, not because it is minute.[28]

Valuing the work specific to women also means *privileging* it. Having and raising a family affect a woman differently than a man and require, on the part of the woman, time—and not just "quality time," but *quantity time*.[29] Cardinal Joseph Ratzinger took this consideration seriously in

---

28 G. K. Chesterton, *What's Wrong with the World* (San Francisco: Ignatius Press, 1910), 94-95.

29 The privileging of the mother's presence in the home is a consistent teaching of the Catholic Church's social doctrine: "[C]hildren, especially the younger among them, need the care of their mother at home. This domestic role of hers must be safely preserved." Second Vatican Council, *Gaudium et Spes* (Pastoral Constitution on the Church in the Modern World) (1965), 52. It is further reinforced by the Church's advocacy for the *family wage*—see Pontifical Council for Justice and Peace, "Compendium on the Social Doctrine of the Church" (2004), 250, *http://www.vatican.va/roman_curia/pontifical_councils/justpeace/documents/rc_pc_justpeace_doc_20060526_compendio-dott-soc_en.html*—and tax structures that make it more possible for women to stay home with their young children, as opposed to the current trends that *discourage* the presence of mothers in the home in favor of the ideal two full-time career household. John Rawls, for example, advocates that the social system not "make it rational and less costly for husband and wife to follow a gendered division of labor in the family," on his assumption that this division of labor is a key suspect in the forms of "injustice" toward women. See "The Idea of Public Reason Revisited," in *The Law of Peoples: With the Idea of Public Reason Revisited* (Cambridge, MA: Harvard University Press, 2001), 471-472.

the Congregation for the Doctrine of the Faith letter to the bishops, "On the Collaboration of Men and Women in the Church and in the World."[30] The CDF suggested that society ought to privilege women's work in the family by making it economically possible for women to dedicate themselves entirely to it and by recognizing the distinct relation women have with any outside work:

> It cannot be forgotten that the interrelationship between...family and work...has, for women, characteristics different from those in the case of men. The harmonization of the organization of work and laws governing work with the demands stemming from the mission of women within the family is a challenge. The question is not only legal, economic, and organizational; it is above all a question of mentality, culture, and respect. Indeed, a just valuing of the work of women within the family is required. In this way, women who freely desire will be able to devote the totality of their time to the work of the household without being stigmatized by society or penalized financially, while those who wish also to engage in other work may be able to do so with an appropriate work schedule, and not have to choose between relinquishing their family life or enduring continual stress, with negative consequences for one's own equilibrium and the harmony of the family.[31]

30 Congregation for the Doctrine of the Faith, *Letter to the Bishops of the Catholic Church on the Collaboration of Men and Women in the Church and in the World* (2004), *http://www.vatican.va/roman_curia/congregations/cfaith/documents/rc_con_cfaith_doc_20040731_collaboration_en.html*.

31 CDF, *Letter on Collaboration*, 13. See also the Message of Pope John Paul II for the XXVIII World Day of Peace (1995), *http://www.vatican.va/holy_father/john_paul_ii/messages/peace/documents/hf_jp-ii_mes_08121994_xxviii-world-day-for-peace_en.html*. On this point, Edith Stein wrote: "Many of the best women are almost overwhelmed by the double burden of family duties and professional life. Always on the go, they are harassed, nervous, and irritable. Where are they to get the needed inner peace and cheerfulness in order to offer

Thus the first consideration in any discussion about the presence of women in society is the need for society to value and privilege women and the work specific to them.

Relation between Home and Society

Next, it is vital to recognize that women are *already in society* through their specific work—of giving life a home. Indeed, women *generate* society, since the family is society's "first and vital cell."[32] Here it is important to take seriously how much our understanding of the "public" sphere (Rawls's "basic structure") rests on contrary assumptions, to the point that the family is marginalized—even more, held under suspicion as the "school of despotism," at odds with liberal democracy and its principles, and therefore at best *tolerated,* only on condition that one has only a *voluntary* relation to it.[33] Then, too, we must reckon with the economic expression of this marginalization, beginning with the Industrial Revolution. At that time, the home became a mere "haven in the heartless world," cut off from the "real world," and then, in time, utterly absorbed by it, especially by its new economy driven by consumerism.[34]

---

stability, support, and guidance to others?... Often the home and children are abandoned either to themselves or to domestics, strangers who are no more conscientious than the mothers themselves." Edith Stein, "Ethos of Women's Professions," *The Collected Works of Edith Stein*, vol. 2, eds. L. Gelber and R. Leuven, trans. Freda Mary Oben (Washington, DC: ICS Publications, 1987), 53.

32 Pontifical Council for Justice and Peace, *Compendium of the Social Doctrine of the Church* (2004), 211. On the positive relation between the family and society, see the *Compendium*, 213-14, *http://www.vatican.va/roman_curia/pontifical_councils/justpeace/documents/rc_pc_justpeace_doc_20060526_compendio-dott-soc_en.html.*

33 This is guaranteed especially by easy access to divorce (cf. John Rawls, *Justice as Fairness: A Restatement* [Cambridge, MA: Harvard University Press, 2001], 164.)

34 That economy, as Christopher Lasch describes it, has "no other object than to keep people at work and thus to sustain the national 'capacity to consume'... all without reference to the intrinsic quality of the goods and services produced or the intrinsic satisfaction of the work that went into them." Christopher Lasch, *Haven in a Heartless World: The Family Besieged* (New York: W.W. Norton & Company, 1995), 110.

To deal with the question of women in society, we have to deal, then, with the question of the place of the home in society, with a keen awareness of the strong cultural trends that have already emptied and marginalized the home. Here Dorothy Sayers's response to men who accuse women of "wanting to do men's work" is relevant:

> At this point, somebody is likely to say: "...[men] don't force their way into the household and turn women out of their rightful occupations." Of course they do not. They have done it already. Let us accept the idea that women should stick to their own jobs—the jobs they did so well in the good old days...it is a formidable list of jobs: the whole of the spinning industry, the whole of the dyeing industry, the whole of the weaving industry. The whole catering industry...the whole of the nation's brewing and distilling. All the preserving, pickling and bottling industry, all the bacon-curing. And...a very large share in the management of landed estates. Here are the women's jobs—and what has become of them? They are all being handled by men. It is all very well to say that woman's place is the home—but modern civilization has taken all these pleasant and profitable activities out of the home, where the women looked after them, and handed them over to big industry, to be directed and organized by men at the head of large factories. Even the dairy-maid in her simple bonnet has gone, to be replaced by a male mechanic in charge of a mechanical milking plant.[35]

Valuing the feminine genius for society, then, requires us to recover the vitality of the home as well as women's role in

---

35   Dorothy Sayers, *Are Women Human? Penetrating, Sensible, and Witty Essays on the Role of Women in Society* (Grand Rapids, MI: Wm. B. Eerdmans Publishing Co., 2005), 23-24.

domesticating the world.[36] It is clear enough that a home with a *maternal presence in it* (or not) is no small matter for society, especially when it comes to its next generation.

In this light, then, the truest test of whether we have successfully "brought women into society" should not be how visible or statistically represented she is in the workplace, or some other public place, but rather how well these places are transformed—domesticated—by a revitalized home, thanks to woman's specific relation to it.[37]

---

36   Cf. David L. Schindler on this point in "Catholic Theology, Gender, and the Future of Western Civilization," *Communio* 20 (Summer 1993): 232, and David Schindler, "Homelessness and the Modern Condition: The Family, Community, and Global Economy," *Communio* 27 (Fall 2000): 411. The point that the home first generates society is made by the *Compendium of the Social Doctrine* with respect to the economy: "The home has been for a long time—and in many regions still is—a place of production and the centre of life. The dynamism of economic life, on the other hand, develops with the initiative of people and is carried out in the manner of concentric circles, in ever-broader networks of production and exchange of goods and services that involves families in continuously increasing measure. The family, therefore, must rightfully be seen as an essential agent of economic life, guided not by the market mentality but by the logic of sharing and solidarity among generations." Pontifical Council for Justice and Peace, *Compendium of the Social Doctrine of the Church*, 248.

37   This is the exact opposite of what is being proposed in the dominant discourse about women and work, represented most recently by the book/movement *Lean In.* Cf. Margaret McCarthy, "A Woman's Work Is Never Done!" *Humanum* (Spring 2013): "While one of the currents in early feminism tied a more active entry of women into public life to 'social housekeeping,' namely the domestication of the public arena—plagued as it was by the abuse of power in the form of slavery, drunkenness, immorality, etc.—what seems to be more in view in the recent discussion is a workplace that will *un-domesticate the home*.... But, if the home is effectively empty, what is it that we are working for? And for whom, we might add, are we working, other than for ourselves? What is striking in [Sheryl] Sandberg's book is how she thinks about her work, her career. It is tautological. The reason to have a career is to have a career, or, at the very most, to 'effect change' so that other women can have a career. Nothing is said substantively about the reason for work—about what, or whom, it serves. There's no mention even of just making a living for one's own family. Work isn't in relation to anything.... Now that the world of work has absorbed the home, Sandberg would take one of the initial feminist projects of domesticating the world to its polar opposite: every woman for herself." McCarthy, "A Woman's Work Is Never Done!", 5-7.

Presence of Women in Society

The role of the woman in society, however, is not reduced to the question of whether a woman stays in the home. As David L. Schindler maintains, the point "is not that all women need to remain always in the home, as mothers, but that they should retain their intrinsic relation to home and maternity even as (if) they enter the culture and engage its ('public') activities."[38] The point is that a woman is always a *mother,* whether physically or spiritually,[39] and that all of her activity, private and public, ought to be pursued *from the point of view of her motherhood,* her "genius."

Here then, we can turn to the value of the presence of women in society in the more specific (though limited) sense; the specific reason in modernity for turning so urgently to the feminine genius is "the establishment of economic and political structures ever more worthy of humanity"[40] and to make them *more homelike.* Edith Stein notes, "the participation of women in the most diverse professional disciplines could be a blessing for the entire society, private or public, precisely if the specifically feminine ethos would be preserved."[41] Indeed, she continues, women would provide "a blessed counter-balance precisely here where everyone is in danger of becoming mechanized and losing his humanity."[42] This kind of presence is sorely needed not because of the lack of women in public, but because a great proportion of today's "public women" perpetuate the un-homelike character of the world through their actions directed against the family and its home.[43]

---

38   David Schindler, "Catholic Theology and Gender," *Communio* 20 (Summer 1993): 232.

39   Pope John Paul II, *Mulieris Dignitatem*, 17-22.

40   Pope John Paul II, *Letter to Women,* 2.

41   Edith Stein, "Ethos of Women's Professions," 50-51.

42   Ibid., 50.

43   Cf. note 37, above.

We might here recall the work of the "Maternalists," a group of women who filled the ranks of the administration of President Franklin D. Roosevelt, and who in various ways fought for social reforms that had in mind not abstract citizens, but men and women as actual or potential mothers and fathers.[44] Fighting against the strong opposition of the National Association of Manufacturers, the Maternalists resisted the industrialist push for equality, because it was blind to the specific responsibilities and needs of men and women. In that vein they championed countless efforts (the family wage, "mother's pensions," home economics education, maternal and infant health education, and so forth) to strengthen the family bonds, not weaken them by providing substitutes for them. These women offer a great example of what Pope Francis is calling for when he asks for "the effective presence...[of women] in so many ambits of public life, in the world of work and in the venues where the most important decisions are adopted, [who] at the same time *maintain a presence and a preferential attention...in and for the family.*"[45]

Women and the Church

In light of all that has been discussed so far regarding the feminine genius, we can now ask what a "more incisive female presence in the Church"[46] might be. We note three considerations (analogous to the ones above).

---

44   The "Maternalist" group included women such as Frances Perkins, Secretary of Labor (the first woman to hold a cabinet-level position); Molly Dewson, member of the Social Security Board; Grace Abbott, member of the Council on Economic Security; Katharine Lenroot, head of the Children's Bureau; and Mary Anderson, of the Labor Department's Women's Bureau, to name a few. See Allan Carlson's discussion of the Maternalists in *The "American Way": Family and Community in the Shaping of the American Identity* (Wilmington, DE: ISI Books, 2003), 58-59, 149-69.

45   John L. Allen Jr., "Pope Wants 'Capillary and Incisive' Role for Women"; Pope Francis, "Italian Women's Centre," emphasis added.

46   Pope Francis, *Evangelii Gaudium*, 103.

Valuing and Privileging the Feminine Church

First, we must recognize and value the Church in its feminine reality, in what has been called the "Marian Dimension."[47] Balthasar, following certain openings in the ecclesiology of the Second Vatican Council, in particular, did much to draw out this dimension of the Church, which to some degree had been left hanging after the First Vatican Council. (The council, having been brought to a close prematurely, concentrated entirely on the "Petrine Dimension"—the magisterium—in its statement about papal infallibility.) Drawing out the feminine dimension, Balthasar wished to resituate the Petrine dimension in the larger reality to which it belonged, the reality that *preceded* it and formed its raison d'être. He notes the simple chronological priority of the Marian dimension established at the Annunciation, thirty years prior to the commission of the apostles, a priority that remained and deepened in significance when Mary was given to them (at the cross) as their Mother. Pope Francis alludes to this when he says: "a woman, Mary, is more important than the bishops,"[48] or "a Church without women is like the college of the apostles without Mary.... The Church is feminine...bride...mother."[49] Now the Marian Church—the laity or "common priesthood"—beginning in Mary, is the dimension that bears Christ in the world, making the world a home for him, by allowing him to be in it. It is that *secular* dimension that makes the Church grow by making it "present and operative in those places and circumstances where only through them [the laity] can it become the

---

47   Hans Urs von Balthasar, *Theo-Drama, III: The Dramatis Personae: the Person in Christ,* trans. Graham Harrison (San Francisco: Ignatius Press, 1992), 353ff.; Hans Urs von Balthasar, *The Office of Peter and the Structure of the Church,* trans. Andrée Emery (San Francisco: Ignatius Press, 1986), 204ff.; Hans Urs von Balthasar, "Who Is the Church?" in *Explorations in Theology II: Spouse of the Word* (San Francisco: Ignatius Press, 1991), 157ff.

48   Pope Francis, *Evangelii Gaudium,* 104.

49   Press Conference of Pope Francis, July 28, 2013.

salt of the earth."[50] It is also that more *hidden* dimension—hidden in discrete actions and relations—though not for that any less worthy or fruitful. Considering its feminine character, we could say that it is the dimension that makes the world home-like in a new way, by helping the world "to be" and to grow according to its deepest calling.

Naturally, the Marian dimension does not exist without the Petrine dimension, since it is not the source of its own life. The "Petrine Dimension," for its part, "embodies Christ who comes to the Church to make her fruitful," and thus "guarantees the constant flow of life from [Christ] to her."[51] In addition, the Petrine dimension confronts and judges what is foreign to the Church—anything "outside the Marian center of love"[52]—such as sin (which it knows only too well) and heresy.[53] But this Petrine (masculine) function emerges from within the Marian dimension (always remaining in it as a member[54]) and serves it. The Petrine dimension is always, therefore, a *"transmission* of a vital force that originates outside itself and leads beyond itself—a share in a fruitfulness (before the Eucharist, she gave birth to Christ) and purity (she was absolved from all eternity) belonging non-officially to the perfect feminine Church."[55]

The Relation between the Marian and the Petrine Church

From the perspective of this *polar* understanding of the Church, we note (as before when speaking about the relation

---

50 Second Vatican Council, Dogmatic Constitution on the Church (*Lumen Gentium*) (1964), 33. See also Pope John Paul II, *Mulieris Dignitatem*, 27, which states how all the baptized share in the priesthood of Christ by giving "witness to Christ in every place, and...an explanation to anyone who asks the reason for the hope in eternal life that is in them (cf. *1 Pt 3:15*)."

51 Hans Urs von Balthasar, *Theo-Drama, II*, 354.

52 Hans Urs von Balthasar, *The Office of Peter*, 209.

53 Ibid,, 214.

54 Ibid., 210.

55 Hans Urs von Balthasar, "Women Priests," 193.

between home and society) that being a member of the Marian dimension of the Church one is *already in the Church and a full participant therein.* Thus to speak about the presence of women in the Church, insofar as these are "icons" of the Marian lay dimension,[56] we have to resist certain tendencies toward clericalism, which gives women—or any layperson for that matter—ecclesial busy work so as to make them feel more involved, *as if they were not already.* Such clericalist assumptions drain the very energy the laity should be spending on its specific vocation to make a home for Christ in the world. It curtails the openness of the Church to the world and the fruitfulness it can bear in it—the very thing the Petrine dimension exists to serve. The presence of women/laity in the Church, then, is first secured by their "staying in place," in the Marian dimension at the heart of the world.

Presence of Women in the Church

Finally, there is a place for laity to be called "in various ways to a more direct form of cooperation in the apostolate of the Hierarchy. This was the way certain men and women assisted Paul the Apostle in the Gospel, laboring much in the Lord" (cf. Phil 4-3; Rom 16:3ff.).[57] Insofar as members of the *laity* are consulted in an official capacity by the hierarchical church, there is really nothing novel—even if hitherto rare—about women being consulted. Because women are members of the laity, there is no need to justify why women could participate in certain specifically ecclesiastical functions and decision-making if laymen do. However, if we consider the participation of laywomen *as such,* we can put our finger on what essential purpose such involvement might have beyond, again, including everyone.

---

56 "Press Conference of Pope Francis," July 28, 2013.

57 Second Vatican Council, *Lumen Gentium,* 33. *Mulieris Dignitatem* speaks to the many women who played *"an active and important role in the life of the early Church,* in building up from its foundations the first Christian community—and subsequent communities—*through their own charisms and their varied service."* See Pope John Paul II, *Mulieris Dignitatem, 27.*

Analogous to the public role of women in society *as women*, the greater presence in the Church of women *as women* "wherever we make important decisions" could be a humanizing force, correcting the tendencies toward bureaucratic clericalism and careerism. To *see* the feminine Church is to remember what can easily be forgotten by the Petrine dimension—that it owes itself to something other than itself, and that it is in *her* service, "leading from the last place."[58]

Indeed, it seems that Pope Francis invokes the need for the feminine genius precisely in these terms, as a counterweight, that is, to the problem of *clericalism and careerism* in the hierarchy, where "sacramental power is too closely identified with power in general,"[59] and results in an "ideology of machismo."[60] Our culture in general cannot read authority in any terms other than *power*. Even *within the Church* there is a temptation to identify sacramental power with power as domination.[61] In his book *The Flight from Woman*, Karl Stern notes that this temptation models itself on the modern tendency to privilege (male) *organization* over (female) *organism,* to which the former belongs. Noting this temptation in the Church, he says: "The Mystical Body is, as the name implies, first an organism and only secondarily an organization. I believe that scandals in the history of the church occurred whenever the sense of organization prevailed over the sense of organism. Although the organizational everywhere implies a temptation of power, it is needed as a complement, as it were, to the organismic."[62]

In other words, prioritizing organization over the organismic ultimately leads to a priority of the parts over the whole, and of one part only. This inversion sees "organization" as the

---

58   Hans Urs von Balthasar, "Women Priests," 196.

59   Pope Francis, *Evangelii Gaudium,* 104.

60   Antonio Spadaro, SJ, "A Big Heart Open to God," *America,* September 30, 2013, *http://www.americamagazine.org/pope-interview.*

61   Pope Francis, *Evangelii Gaudium,* 104.

62   Karl Stern, *The Flight from Woman* (New York: Farrar, Straus, and Giroux, 1965), 283.

whole itself rather than a *part of a whole,* which precedes it. It is here where the tendency toward power arises.

Keeping in mind the relation between the temptation toward power—be it bureaucratic, clerical, careerist, or otherwise—and the forgetfulness of the feminine, one can see the legitimacy of a desire for a more "capillary and incisive" presence of women at the institutional level where "decisions are made" (congregations, for example). A feminine presence *as such* could remind "Peter" of what he *belongs to* and what he *serves.* It could remind "Peter" that his decisions are made within a prior decision, the fiat of Mary, as Cardinal John Henry Newman had said.[63]

Naturally, though, bringing forward the profile of women would exclude any suggestion that women are gradually moving toward those offices that are specifically and exclusively *male,*[64] as that would eliminate their presence *as women* and expand the clericalism it is meant to correct. In addition, it would perpetuate the inferiority complex of the Marian/lay dimension itself.[65]

---

63 John Henry Newman, "On Consulting the Faithful in Matters of Doctrine," *Rambler* (July 1859). Noting the interrelation of the two ecclesial dimensions in the "decision" of dogma, Balthasar writes: "Tradition and the instinct of faith are of the essence of the whole (Marian-Petrine) Church. But the episcopal office has to guard the authenticity of the 'prophetical' sense of faith that is alive in the whole people; it must evaluate it and keep it pure. On the other hand, the episcopal office, for that very reason, has to pay attention to this 'prophetical' office of the whole Church, and when necessary it must learn from it (as when the Beloved Disciple tells Peter, 'It is the Lord,' John 21:7). For Newman, on his journey toward the Catholic Church, had a crucial insight: during the Arian crisis of the fourth century, while a number of holy bishops did put forward the orthodox position, it was primarily the ordinary faithful, rather than the episcopate, who proclaimed and maintained the divine tradition entrusted to the infallible Church." See also Balthasar, *Theo-Drama, III,* 358.

64 "The reservation of the priesthood to males, as a sign of Christ the Spouse who gives himself in the Eucharist, is not a question open to discussion." *See* Pope Francis, *Evangelii Gaudium,* 104.

65 Pope Francis's warning about "feminine machismo" is relevant here, especially when it comes to the question of "more active roles" for women in the Church: "I am wary of a solution that can be reduced to a kind of 'female *machismo,*' because a woman has a different make-up than a man. But what I

Conclusion

Mindful of the pressures of the dominant culture when addressing the question of woman's contribution to society and to the Church, we have attempted to focus this question through the lens of the "difference between the sexes," as the only "guarantee of the spiritual and physical fruitfulness of human nature."[66] We have argued that any consideration of the question must take seriously the woman *as such,* as a being apt for motherhood (spiritual and/or physical), who makes a home for the human being in the deepest sense, that this is *already* societal (and ecclesial), and that the value of the woman as such stepping out or stepping forward in a more publicly recognizable way is to make the world (and the Church) *more* homelike, not less so.

Finally, although we have focused our reflections on the question of the feminine genius in society (and the Church), this discussion cannot be complete without thinking about the "male genius." For it is only in respect to *both* geniuses that the "range and dynamics of humanly possible love" can break open modern egalitarian functionalism and achieve proper fruitfulness in the home, in the Church, and in the world.

Margaret Harper McCarthy, PhD, is an assistant professor of theological anthropology at the John Paul II Institute for Studies on Marriage and Family, Washington, D.C. She serves on the editorial board of Humanum, *a quarterly review of family, culture, and science, and on the editorial board of the international journal* Communio. *Professor McCarthy is also the author of a forthcoming book on children and divorce. She and her husband are the parents of three teenagers. Research assistant Hannah Hudspeth, a graduate student at the John Paul II Institute, contributed to the final version of this chapter.*

hear about the role of women is often inspired by an ideology of *machismo.*" See Antonio Spadaro, SJ, "A Big Heart Open to God."

66   Hans Urs von Balthasar, "Women Priests," 195-196.

CHAPTER SIX

The Genius of Man

Deborah Savage, PhD

Pope Francis's recent call for the development of a "theology of women" is the next step in a trajectory the Church has been following since the latter half of the twentieth century. It constitutes a development of thought that, while grounded in the teachings and example of Christ, reflects more contemporary concerns regarding the place women occupy in the Church and in society. Although every pontiff since Pope Pius XII has given voice to this issue, the Church's teaching has found its fullest expression to date in the work of the late Pope Saint John Paul II.

Pope Saint John Paul II's reflections on women are unprecedented in their scope and significance—pointing to new landscapes yet to be fully explored. They are remarkable for many reasons, but perhaps, above all, because they introduce into the Catholic tradition an entirely new category in the Church's understanding of the human person: the "feminine genius."[1] This quality or characteristic, ascribed universally to all women and epitomized most perfectly by the person of Mary the Mother of God, has become an integral part of the Church's magisterial teaching.[2] The genius of women, as well

---

1 I have argued elsewhere that Pope Saint John Paul II uses this phrase as primarily a rhetorical device to describe a phenomenologically accessible reality, and that it was not his intention to supplant the word "charism" or argue that this represents a newly discovered power of the soul.

2 Pope John Paul II, apostolic letter *Mulieris Dignitatem* (On the Dignity and Vocation of Women) (1988), *http://www.vatican.va/holy_father/john_paul_ii/apost_letters/documents/hf_jp-ii_apl_15081988_mulieris-dignitatem_en.html*. See also Pope John Paul II, *Letter to Women* (1995), *http://www.vatican.va/holy_father/john_paul_ii/letters/documents/hf_jp-ii_let_29061995_women_en.html*.

as the complementarity that characterizes the relationship of man and woman, are now tenets of Catholic doctrine.[3]

Certainly these are important developments, especially in light of the contemporary context. Indeed, the Church's teaching on women and the "new feminism" has proven to be a critical means of engaging the culture in the New Evangelization, helping men and women alike to rediscover Catholicism in all its depth and beauty. Her vision of the place women occupy in human history, her affirmation of woman *qua* woman, reflect a profound grasp of woman's dignity and significance.

But the argument at the heart of this chapter is that any further exploration of the "genius" of woman cannot properly take place without a concomitant investigation into the "genius" of man. In fact, it can be argued that the genius of woman cannot be understood apart from that equally significant reality. In his apostolic exhortation on the mission of the laity, *Christifideles Laici*, Pope Saint John Paul II himself makes it categorically clear: "The condition that will assure the rightful presence of woman in the Church and in society is a more penetrating and accurate consideration of the *anthropological foundation for masculinity and femininity* with the intent of clarifying woman's personal identity in relation to man, that is, a diversity yet mutual complementarity."[4]

If the Church and her theologians are to take the next step in this investigation, it must be with the full realization

---

3   The *Compendium of the Social Doctrine of the Church* makes frequent mention of both complementarity and the feminine genius. See, for example, Pontifical Council for Justice and Peace, *Compendium of the Social Doctrine of the Church* (2004), 146, 147, 295, just to name a few. See *http://www.vatican.va/roman_curia/pontifical_councils/justpeace/documents/rc_pc_justpeace_doc_20060526_compendio-dott-soc_en.html*.

4   Pope John Paul II, post-synodal apostolic exhortation *Christifideles Laici* (On the Vocation and Mission of the Lay Faithful in the Church and in the World) (1988), 50, italics in original, *http://www.vatican.va/holy_father/john_paul_ii/apost_exhortations/documents/hf_jp-ii_exh_30121988_christifideles-laici_en.html*.

that a one-sided emphasis on the *feminine* genius would reflect its own kind of gender polarity (where one sex is considered superior to the other) and would almost certainly risk distorting our vision of the complementarity that characterizes the reciprocal relationship of man and woman. Given the current crisis of understanding of masculinity, femininity, and gender in Western culture, it is urgent that we affirm and communicate to the world at large that it is this very uni-duality that gives man and woman their *mission,* for "to this 'unity of the two' God has entrusted not only the work of procreation and family life, but the creation of history itself."[5]

And so we come to the aim of this chapter. It should be considered an initial investigation into the nature of what I will term the "masculine genius." My thesis is that man's genius originates in his embodiment as the active principle, both as an ontological reality and in terms of his bodily composition; Adam's creation as the first man, his solitude before God prior to woman's appearance, and the tasks he is given in the state of original solitude are central to this thesis. The headship of Adam finds its origin here, in the particular nature of his relationship with the Creator.[6] His genius is revealed when he is asked by God to name the goods of creation. It is further illuminated when, as it says at Genesis 2:15, he is put in the

---

5 Pontifical Council for Justice and Peace, *Compendium of the Social Doctrine,* 147. Quoting Pope John Paul II, *Letter to Women,* 8.

6 The question of the "headship" of the father in a family is a disputed one, and rightly so in many cases, given the way it is articulated and understood, particularly in some Protestant circles. Though a full treatment of this issue is beyond the scope of my work here, I believe I can demonstrate that Scripture reveals that, since the man is first in the order of creation, he is responsible particularly as protector of the family. The problem with the usual interpretation is that it is focused on the nature of man's authority, understood as a type of power over the family. That is not the interpretation at work here. The question may be whether we wish to reclaim the word "headship" or find another one that renders intelligible the unique role of the father in family life.

garden "to till it." Adam is given dominion over things—and his calling is to care for them.[7]

This account relies first of all on my exegesis, developed more fully elsewhere,[8] of the two creation accounts found in Genesis 1 and 2; this exegesis provides an initial framework within which the genius of the original man and woman, as well as their equality and difference, can be understood. My intent is to demonstrate here, briefly, that it is possible to derive both the masculine "genius" and feminine "genius" from these passages; I will then turn to the primary purpose of this chapter: a fuller consideration of the genius of man, including the proposal that Joseph, Mary's spouse, is representative of this masculine genius in a way analogous to Mary's embodiment of the feminine.

Genesis 1 and 2 Revisited

Pope Saint John Paul II makes a complex and profound argument concerning the nature of the feminine genius, an argument I do not dispute or take issue with in any way.[9] However, grounded as it is in the undeniable fact that all women have the potential to be mothers, his work is vulnerable to the criticism that it risks a kind of biological determinism regarding the role that women can and ought to play in human society.[10] Obviously, this was neither his meaning nor his intention. I will argue that there is actually a prior point of departure for an account of the feminine genius, one unencumbered by such

---

7 Scriptural references in this chapter are from the *Catholic Edition of the Revised Standard Version of the Bible* (San Francisco: Ignatius Press, 1966).

8 This chapter summarizes briefly my previous research: Deborah Savage, "The Nature of Woman in Relation to Man: Genesis 1 and 2 through the Lens of the Metaphysical Anthropology of Thomas Aquinas," *Logos: A Journal of Catholic Thought and Culture* (Winter 2014). Where necessary, I will refer to the key elements of that exegetical framework as we proceed.

9 Pope John Paul II, *Mulieris Dignitatem*, 4, 29.

10 See, for example, Elizabeth A. Johnson, "Imaging God, Embodying Christ: Women as a Sign of the Times," in *The Church Women Want: Catholic Women in Dialogue*, ed. Elizabeth A. Johnson (New York: Crossroad, 2002).

criticisms. And though Pope Saint John Paul II does not treat the possibility of a masculine genius in any explicit way, I will show that this point of departure also permits us to ground the genius of man in the creation narratives found in Genesis 1 and 2.

Our starting place is in the opening pages of *The Theology of the Body*.[11] In these pages, the late Holy Father argues that we can derive the meaning of man first as an objective reality created in the image of God and, second, in the aspect of his subjectivity, from the two distinct creation accounts found in Genesis 1 and 2.

Pope Saint John Paul II states that the "powerful metaphysical content" hidden in Genesis 1 has provided "an incontrovertible point of reference and a solid basis" for metaphysics, anthropology, and ethics and been a source of reflection throughout the ages for those "who have sought to understand 'being' and 'existing.'"[12] But in Genesis 2, he goes on to say, the depth to be uncovered in this second (though historically earlier) creation account has a different character; it "is above all subjective in nature and thus in some way psychological." Here we find man in the concrete, as a subject of self-understanding and consciousness; here the account of the creation of man refers to him "especially in the aspect of his subjectivity."[13]

These two categories, being and existence, on the one hand, and personal subjectivity, on the other, are foundational to the thought of Karol Wojtyla/John Paul II. Throughout his writings, this philosopher pope frequently contrasts the philosophy of being and the philosophy of consciousness and seeks ways to reconcile and synthesize their claims. His own anthropology attempts a creative completion of the Aristotelian-Thomistic account of man, which, he argues, though it pro-

---

11   Pope John Paul II, *Man and Woman He Created Them: A Theology of the Body*, ed. Michael Waldstein (Boston: Pauline Books & Media, 2006).

12   Pope John Paul II, *Theology of the Body*, 2:4.5, 136-37.

13   Ibid., 3:2.1, 138-39.

vides the necessary "metaphysical terrain" in the dimension of being and paves the way for the realization of personal human subjectivity, leaves out an adequate investigation of lived human experience, and thus lacks an essential component of what it means to be an actual living person.[14] The thrust of his effort is to capture the meaning of human personhood in light of both the objective nature of the person and his lived experience as the subject of his own acts.[15]

This claim found at the beginning of the *Theology of the Body*—that the two creation accounts provide the scriptural basis of an account of man *qua* man and man in his subjectivity—is an important and intriguing one. However, Pope Saint John Paul II himself does not fully exploit his own claim, stating that his intent is not to pursue this more metaphysical account of the soul in union with the body but to focus instead on the "meaning of one's own body."[16]

Nonetheless, as I have shown elsewhere,[17] a careful analysis of these two creation accounts, when considered in light of Aquinas's metaphysical account of the soul, does support Pope Saint John Paul II's claim: They reveal the meaning of both man in the abstract—that is, man *qua* man—and man in the concrete, created as male and female. Both are human, since both are an embodiment of a substantial form common to the spe-

---

14   Karol Wojtyla (Pope John Paul II), "Subjectivity and the Irreducible in the Human Being," *Person and Community: Selected Essays,* trans. Theresa Sandok (New York: Peter Lang, 1993), 212. See also my paper, Deborah Savage, "The Centrality of Lived Experience in Wojtyla's Account of the Person," *Roczniki Filozoficzne* LXI, no. 4 (John Paul II Catholic University of Lublin, 2013).

15   See in particular Karol Wojtyla (Pope John Paul II), *Love and Responsibility,* rev. ed. (San Francisco: Ignatius Press, 1993); Karol Wojtyla (Pope John Paul II), *The Acting Person* (New York: Springer, 1979); see also several essays in Karol Wojtyla (Pope John Paul II), *Person and Community* (1993), as well as Pope John Paul II, encyclical *Fides et Ratio* (On the Relationship Between Faith and Reason) (1998), *http://www.vatican.va/holy_father/john_paul_ii/encyclicals/documents/hf_jp-ii_enc_15101998_fides-et-ratio_en.html.*

16   Pope John Paul II, *Theology of the Body,* 7:1-2.

17   Deborah Savage, "The Nature of Woman." See note 8.

cies *humanum*.[18] Both must be seen to be distinct instantiations of the species, made as they are of different matter and animated by souls that are commensurated or adapted to their individual person.[19] This commensuration reflects both the universal structure of male and female and the personal structure of any one particular man or woman. Gender is not reducible to matter; it has an ontological component since gender is the type of accident that is attributed to the subject *qua* subject—that is, to the whole composite of soul and body that constitutes the subject as a unity.[20] But there is no risk to the equality of men and women in understanding their nature in this way. Woman and man are equal but different, a fact immediately discernible in human experience and accessible to scientific analysis.[21]

---

18   This is clear from an analysis of Genesis 1, in which the Hebrew word *adam* can be understood to refer to man in the collective sense. Strictly speaking, there is no equivalent for man per se in the Semitic language, but it is most certainly plausible to equate the use of *adam* with man in the abstract sense. See Deborah Savage, "The Nature of Woman."

19   In the creation account found in Genesis 2, we are no longer speaking of man in the abstract, but of individual persons. At this point, matter (dust, man's rib) enters the picture. And, Aquinas states, thus we enter the realm of accident. Aquinas explains gender as a type of (inseparable) accident. See Thomas Aquinas, *De Ente et Essentia* (On Being and Essence), trans. Armand Maurer, 2nd ed. (Toronto: Pontifical Institute of Medieval Studies, 1968), 68.

20   See Thomas Aquinas, *Summa Contra Gentiles: Book II: Creation*, 81, 8. Though it does not deal directly with the distinction between genders but with the individuation of the human soul and its continuing individuation after it is separated from the body at death, it is here that Aquinas introduces the notion of the commensuration of each soul to each body. Commensuration is a term that means literally to have the same measure. Aquinas means here that each body is adapted or accommodated, even interpenetrated in an equal measure by the soul intended for it.

21   Though it will not be possible to include it here, it should also be noted at the outset that scientific research regarding what distinguishes men and women supports many of the conclusions found in the work of Pope John Paul II as well as in this paper. See Steven E. Rhoads, *Taking Sex Differences Seriously* (San Francisco: Encounter Books, 2005), 22-26; Anne Moir and David Jessel, *Brain Sex: The Real Difference Between Men and Women* (New York: Dell Publishing, 1991), 68-112. For additional sources and a critique of brain organization theory as a whole, see Rebecca Jordan-Young, *Brain Storm* (Cambridge, MA: Harvard University Press, 2010). The author's general argument is that there

Though it is certainly a matter disputed by some, the Church, in her core teachings, has always affirmed the equality and dignity of man and woman.[22] The example set by Jesus Christ and the truth about man revealed by sacred Scripture affirms that men and women are both equal and different.

Genesis 1:27 and 2:22 Taken Together

This admittedly foreshortened analysis of Genesis 1 and 2 does establish both the equality of men and women and their difference. But there is more to be found in these texts. Considered together, Genesis 1 and 2 illuminate more fully the meaning of the second creation account and its significance for our question here.[23] In Genesis 1, the sacred author seems to lay out a particular hierarchical order in which God creates. God be-

---

are risks associated with attributing sex differences to hormones and that brain organization theory (found in these other sources) cannot account for all of them. I agree with her critique. Philosophy and theology must make their contribution.

22   Certainly some feminists have disputed this point, and not without reason. The error can be traced to Aristotle's argument that woman is a defective male whose capacity for reason is inferior to man's. Aquinas does not fall entirely into this trap, but the flawed biology of Aristotle has made its way into the Western intellectual tradition in various ways. I offer a corrective to these errors in my paper "The Nature of Woman." (See note 8.) On the specific question of the Church's teaching on the role of women, please see Sister Sarah Butler, "Catholic Women and Equality: Women in the Code of Canon Law," and Elizabeth R. Schiltz, "A Contemporary Catholic Theory of Complementarity," in *Feminism, Law, and Religion,* eds. Marie A. Failinger, Elizabeth R. Schiltz, and Susan J. Stabile (Burlington, VT: Ashgate Publishing, 2013), 345-370 and 3-24, respectively.

23   These two Genesis accounts of creation are clearly very different, with male and female created seemingly simultaneously in the first chapter, but sequentially in the second. Scripture scholars have long argued that this seeming contradiction can be attributed to the "Documentary Hypothesis," viz., that the two accounts were written at different times by different authors. See Antony F. Campbell, SJ, and Mark A. O'Brien, OP, *Sources of the Pentateuch: Texts, Introductions, Annotations* (Minneapolis, MN: Fortress Press, 1993), 1-20. This is an interesting theory and perhaps even true, although there is a certain turning away from this hypothesis now. See Thomas B. Dozeman and Konrad Schmid, eds., *A Farewell to the Yahwist?: The Composition of the Pentateuch in Recent European Interpretation,* Symposium Series 34 (Atlanta: Society of Biblical Literature, 2006). However, it has never satisfied the systematic theologian's need

gins with the heaven and the earth, then light. He then divides the waters, then creates dry land, then vegetation, day and night. He goes on to create swarms of living creatures: birds, monsters, cattle, and things that creep. This all culminates in the creation of *adam*, human nature created male and female. This is clearly a hierarchy that is on its way *up*, from lower life forms to higher.

In the second account we read at 2:7 that a particular man (*'ish*) is made from the dust of the earth. When, at Genesis 2:18, God sees that Adam is alone, God forms every creature and brings them to Adam to be named. Then God, realizing that none of the creatures correspond to Adam's own being, and that it is not good for Adam to be alone, decides it is necessary to make a fitting helper (*ezer negdo*) for him[24]—then puts him into a deep sleep and forms the woman (*'issah*) from Adam's rib. Adam says, "This at last is bone of my bones and flesh of my flesh." As Pope Saint John Paul II points out, Adam recognizes in Eve another *person*, a being equal to himself, a someone, not a something—a someone he can love, to whom he can make of himself a gift and who can reciprocate in kind. This seems fairly straightforward.

But there are several additional and important points to glean from considering these two chapters together. First, only when we come to the making of Eve do we see the final significance of the order introduced in the first account and brought to completion in the second. Adam is made from the earth

---

to reconcile the meaning intended by what is ultimately and arguably a decision inspired by the Holy Spirit to juxtapose these two accounts in this way.

24   The word *ezer* is translated in many different ways: a "suitable helper," or a "suitable partner." Perhaps the best is found in the Jewish Tanak—a "fitting helper." This point is also made by Cardinal Joseph Ratzinger in the Congregation for the Doctrine of the Faith's *Letter to the Bishops of the Catholic Church on the Collaboration of Men and Women in the Church and in the World* (2004), 6, when he points out that "the term here does not refer to an inferior, but to a vital helper." See *http://www.vatican.va/roman_curia/congregations/cfaith/documents/rc_con_cfaith_doc_20040731_collaboration_en.html.* See also note 5 in this chapter.

(*adama*), but Eve is made from Adam. Though it has troubled feminists forever—and is arguably the root of the historical misinterpretation of this passage—the fact that Eve is created second is not to make her subservient. She is, in fact, made on the way *up*—the last creature to appear, a creature made, not from earth, but from Adam—that is, from something that arguably *already* contains a greater degree of actualization than dust or clay. It does seem as though she is made of "finer stuff." Because of the order suggested by reading the accounts together, Eve can be seen as the pinnacle of creation, not as a creature whose place in that order is subservient or somehow less in stature than that of Adam.

This proposition is reinforced when we consider that the Hebrew word usually translated as "helper" is *ezer,* which does not mean servant or slave.[25] When this word is used elsewhere in Scripture, it *has the connotation of divine aid.*[26] Used here to express helper or partner, it indicates someone who is most definitely NOT a slave or even remotely subservient—there is the sense of an equal, a partner, help sent by God.[27] But it is essential to note the full text: it is *ezer negdo; negdo* is a preposition that means "in front of," "in the sight of," "be-

---

25   I am using the word here as it is usually meant—as someone who occupies a lower rung on the ladder in any particular context. A different interpretation of the word "servant" is associated with being a follower of Christ, which, at this point in salvation history, cannot be invoked. But I do not mean to imply that woman is not to serve man. As Saint Paul says in Ephesians 5, both men and women are to submit to one another out of reverence for Christ. The question of the headship of the man in the family is not under scrutiny here, however, and is a topic for further research.

26   Excellent examples can be found in the Psalms: e.g., Psalm 30:10, "O LORD, be thou my **helper** [*'ezer*]," or Psalm 121:1, "I lift up my eyes to the hills, from whence does **my help**[*'ezri*] come?" The name of the great scribe Ezra of the restoration of Israel under the Persians, namesake of the biblical book, seems to be the Aramaic masculine form of the same word.

27   In his very fine translation of these texts, Robert Alter translates *ezer negdo* as "sustainer" rather than "helper," a word with a much closer meaning, in my opinion, to that intended by the sacred author. I refer here to "helper" because that is the more traditional term used in most translations and makes my dispute with the usual interpretation more precise.

fore" (in the spatial sense). Thus Eve is not to be Adam's servant—a different word would have been used if that were the intention—but someone who can help him to live. Eve is not "below" Adam in the order of creation; nor is she above him. She stands in front of him, before him, meeting his gaze as it were and sharing in the responsibility for the preservation of all that precedes them. At Genesis 1:28, both male and female are given the command to subdue the earth and fill it.

Thus woman and man are equal, and both constitute the "other" for each other. Eve's place in the order of creation reveals her true nature and mission—that of help sent by God. And thus is another misunderstood element in the tradition— that woman is subservient to Adam, sent to be merely his slave—set right.

A Preliminary Remark Concerning the Genius of Man and Woman

The preceding analysis allows us to derive something significant and quite distinct about the "genius" attributable to both man and woman. Though I will treat the genius of man more substantively shortly, I will offer, first, a preliminary observation about the genius attributable to Eve, in order to demonstrate that both the masculine and feminine genius can be derived from the same Scripture passages and to contrast Eve's genius with that of Adam.

Apart from his special relationship with the Creator, Adam's first contact with reality is of a horizon that otherwise contains only lower creatures, what we might call "things" (*res*). It is this fact that leads God to conclude that Adam is incomplete and alone, and ultimately leads to the generation of Eve. In contrast, and of special significance for any consideration of the feminine genius, is the quite legitimate claim that, because Eve comes into existence after Adam, her first contact with reality is of a horizon that, *from the beginning*, includes Adam—that is, it includes persons. One can imagine Eve (whom we have argued is a person also endowed with reason and free will), who, upon seeing Adam, recognizes another like her, an equal, while the other creatures and things around her appear only on the periphery of her gaze. This exegetical insight seems to provide a starting place in Scripture for the equally well-documented phenomenon that women seem more naturally oriented toward persons.[28]

So, while we can affirm Pope Saint John Paul II's argument in *Mulieris Dignitatem*—that is, that the feminine genius is grounded in the fact that all women have the capacity to be mothers—and that this capacity, whether fulfilled in a physical or spiritual sense, orients her toward the other, toward persons—it seems that there is a broader principle at work. Although Eve is certainly the mother of all mankind, in addition to her capacity to conceive and nurture human life, indeed *prior to it*, her place in the order of creation reveals that—from the beginning—the horizon of all womankind includes persons, includes the other. Perhaps this explains why girls and women seem to know—from the beginning—that they are meant for relationship. Human experience seems to confirm that it takes men a bit longer to look up and realize that they are lonely for something they only just realized was missing—and to look for the one who can complete them.

And so, in these brief sketches, we see the outline of what might constitute a starting place for both the genius of man and of woman. Scripture, like science and experience, suggests what differentiates men and women: Men seem more oriented toward things; women seem more oriented toward persons. These claims do not in any way preclude men attending to persons or women having dominion over things. But Genesis 3 offers further evidence, as we learn that man and woman will suffer particular and distinct

---

28   See Steven E. Rhoads, *Taking Sex Differences Seriously*; and Anne Moir and David Jessel, *Brain Sex: The Real Difference Between Men and Women*.

forms of alienation as punishment for the Fall.[29] Adam will now fight with creation; Eve will encounter disorder in her relationship to man. These seem to confirm that, in their original innocence, Adam and Eve were in a right relationship to things (Adam) and persons (Eve). I will return to these elements shortly but turn now to explore the masculine genius.

The Genius of Man

In what follows, I provide an exegesis and interpretation of several passages from Genesis 2, laying the groundwork for the subsequent discussion of what might constitute the genius of man. As this is but an initial investigation into the meaning of these passages, I have limited myself to what I believe are the essential elements in an account of man's genius. Much more work remains to be done to fully exhaust the meanings found in the first three chapters of Genesis on these questions. In addition, it is important at this point to spell out more explicitly why an account of the masculine genius is so needed at this time in history.

At least in the West, relationships between men and women are characterized by confusion and disorder. In the United States in particular, the radical feminist movement that marked the latter half of the twentieth century, while not solely responsible for the situation, has left men and boys in a quandary about who they are and what is expected of them. Dr. Meg Meeker, author of *Boys Should Be Boys,* states that "you can't have a revolution without casualties, and in the feminist revolution the casualties were boys."[30]

Consider the following facts: Compared with girls, boys are less likely to graduate from high school, less likely to go to college, more likely to be diagnosed with a learning disability.

---

29 Gn 3:16-19.
30 Emily Stimpson, "Why We Must Let Our Boys Be Boys," *Our Sunday Visitor,* May 31, 2009, 5.

Boys are more likely to attempt suicide, use illegal substances, and engage in risky sexual behavior. Their struggle is due in part to attempts by well-intentioned feminists to help girls get ahead—not a bad thing in itself—leading educators to change the way they teach in the classroom and to establish school schedules that favor female learning.[31] But by far the biggest factor is the absence of men from young boys' lives. Half of all boys grow up without a father in the home. They have fewer male teachers and fewer real heroes. More than 30 million children in the United States do not have a father living with them; 90 percent of all runaway and homeless children are from fatherless homes, as are more than 71 percent of high school dropouts. At least 85 percent of all youths in prison grew up in fatherless homes.[32]

We live at a time when boys are told over and over that men are responsible for all the evils in the world. All the great heroes have been deconstructed, and boys have few real-life and historical male role models. In the absence of such models, they turn elsewhere and open themselves up to misdirection from male peers, gang leaders, and worse. Fathers, and men in general, are disinvesting in family structures and the persons within them, even though evidence shows that such involvement provides men with a way toward real perfection and happiness.[33]

---

31 Center for Disease Control, "Youth Risk Behavior Surveillance," 2005 and 2007, quoted in Dr. Meg Meeker, *Boys Should Be Boys: 7 Secrets to Raising Healthy Sons* (New York: Ballantine, 2009).

32 David Popenoe, *Life Without Father: Compelling New Evidence That Fatherhood and Marriage Are Indispensable for the Good of Children and Society* (Boston: Harvard University Press, 1999). These data are no doubt somewhat out of date, but the situation has only deteriorated since this text was published.

33 David Blankenhorn, *Fatherless America: Confronting Our Most Urgent Social Problem* (New York: Harper Perennial, 1995), 25-38. Timothy Fortin, "Fatherhood and the Perfection of Masculine Identity: A Thomistic Account in Light of Contemporary Science," *Dissertationes, Pontificia Universita della Santa Croce* 26 (EDUSC, 2008), 442-455. Fortin's research and that of Father Carter Griffin bear further investigation of fatherhood as perfective of masculinity in both the natural and priestly sphere. Carter Harrell Griffin, *Supernatu-*

Even in this abbreviated account, we can recognize that humanity urgently needs a deeper understanding of the genius of men.

The Scriptural Foundations

To grasp what might constitute the genius of man, we return, once again, to the opening chapters of Genesis, beginning with Genesis 2:7-9 and the creation of the first man, '*ish*. It reveals that man's—that is, the male person's—proper place is in the midst of creation:

> ...then the LORD God formed man of dust from the ground, and breathed into his nostrils the breath of life; and man became a living being. And the LORD God planted a garden in Eden, in the east; and there he put the man whom he had formed. And out of the ground the LORD God made to grow every tree that is pleasant to sight and good for food.

The next passage of significance for our question provides an insight into Adam's personal mission as well as his role in the Fall. At Genesis 2:15-17, we read:

> The LORD God took the man and put him in the garden of Eden to till it and keep it. And the LORD God commanded the man, saying, "You may freely eat of every tree of the garden; but of the tree of knowledge of good and evil you shall not eat, for in the day that you eat of it you shall die."

This particular passage has profound meaning for our understanding of human work since, clearly, Adam is placed in the garden to do exactly that. But it also reveals that the instruction not to eat the fruit of the tree of knowledge is

ral Fatherhood through Priestly Celibacy: Fulfillment in Masculinity: A Thomistic Study (CreateSpace Independent Publishing Platform, 2011).

given directly to the man. We will come back to these themes shortly.

Finally, at Genesis 2:18-23, we learn that the man is tasked with naming all the living creatures, including the one made a "helper" (*'ezer*) for him:

> Then the LORD God said, "It is not good that the man should be alone; I will make a helper fit for him." So out of the ground the LORD God formed every beast of the field and every bird of the air, and brought them to the man to see what he would call them; and whatever the man called every living creature, that was its name.

Having given names to every beast, yet still not encountering a fitting helper, God puts the man into a deep sleep and fashions the woman (*'issah*) out of the rib of the man. When she is brought before him by the Lord God, the man declares: "This at last is bone of my bones and flesh of my flesh; she shall be called Woman, because she was taken out of Man" (Gn 2:23).

These passages reveal several important things about the masculine genius. First, although we have already established that woman does not occupy a subservient role simply because she comes into existence after him, man is clearly first in the order of creation. He is first to know God and, when woman is brought to him, both the man and the Lord God recognize her for who she is—a person, and his partner. The man's prior relationship with God prepares him in a special way to introduce the woman to God and to the things of creation. The origin of man's role in the family can be traced to this fact, as well as to the revelation that woman is herself created out of man. In a sense, man provides the material for the generation of woman and, it could be said, thus establishes his place as the active or generative principle.

But the heart of my hypothesis concerning the masculine genius is found in Genesis 2:15-23. Here we learn that man's place is in the midst of the created order and, further, that his task is to care for it. He is put in the garden to till it. Though it is not insignificant that, in the first account, both woman and man are instructed to "fill the earth and subdue it," to have dominion over the earth, only *'ish* is given a specific task. And man's task is to work, to care for the things found in God's creation. This becomes more evident when we consider that, as God searches for a partner for the man, he brings to him all the things of creation to see what *he will name them.* One by one, the man gives each a name—that is, *he takes dominion over them.*[34]

In order to name things well and have dominion over them, man would have to gain some kind of direct knowledge of them and to possess a certain familiarity and sophistication with things. And it is here that we come to the core of what I propose is man's genius: He learns that he excels at discovering what things are, how they are to be distinguished from one another, and what they are for. This is his gift.

From this account we are justified in at least proposing that man's capacity to name things, to determine what can be predicated of something and what cannot, and an ability to arrive at a systematic way of judging the matter, might be said to be the gifts men bring to the tasks of human living.[35] When considered along with the fact that man's mission is to work in

---

34 Indeed, Saint Thomas Aquinas argues that Adam received an additional preternatural gift, infused knowledge, in order to be able to name all the animals brought before him. *Summa Theologica* I, Q. 94, Art. 3. And though it is from an entirely different tradition, I find it so interesting to consider that one of Lao-tzu's more famous aphorisms is: "The beginning of wisdom is to call things by their right names."

35 See Zenit interview with Anthony Esolen, "Finding the Masculine Genius," Zenit.org, April 23, 2007, *http://www.zenit.org/en/articles/finding-the-masculine-genius.* Though Professor Esolen admits he doesn't exactly have a theory, his thinking is very helpful. He adds: "Without this literal discernment, I mean the clear separation of what may be predicated of a thing and what may not, with systematic means for judging the matter, there can be nothing so intricate as law, the government of a city, higher learning, a church—not to mention philosophy and theology."

the Garden, to care for God's creation, we are able to draw a further conclusion: that the genius of man is found in his capacity to know and to use the goods of the earth in the service of authentic human flourishing.

Three further points must be made in this regard. First, it is equally important to point out that the first man's capacity to know and use things does not mean that he is *only* oriented toward things. In truth, his first contact with reality includes the Lord God. He is, in the first instance, aware of his dependence upon his Creator, and he is truly marked by that relationship forever after. It is within this context that he encounters the woman. Until the woman is brought to him, both to name and to love as he can love no other, he has no "other" like himself. He knows immediately that the woman is *not* a thing; she is a person. Without hesitation he declares that she is "bone of my bones and flesh of my flesh." And, while he can and does name her, he cannot have dominion over her in the same way he has dominion over everything else. She represents for him his highest good, the greatest gift God has given him and, as a consequence, the value of all the rest of creation is abrogated. From and through Adam's encounter with the woman, the Lord God reveals to him the nature of the reciprocal relationship of the gift of self. And he must realize as well that his own gift—that of caring for and using the goods of creation—is a gift to be exercised in service to her authentic good.

Second, man's prior relationship with the Lord God and his sophistication with things reveals something rather important about the Fall. In relation to man, woman is rather unsophisticated about "things"; she has heard that they are not to eat of the tree at the center of the Garden, but it was man who heard it directly from God. And it is worth noting that man appears to be more or less at her side at the critical moment of decision at Genesis 3:6. It is in this passage that we see man fail in what will be an essential element of his charism—that of protector. He knows firsthand what God has instructed; he has superior knowledge of things, at least at this moment in the narrative. The serpent has approached the woman because he suspects she will have influence over the man. And, of course, we know what happens next. But man's guilt in the Fall is thus exposed. His mission is to ensure that the goods of creation are used for woman's *good*; he failed to exercise dominion over creation at a critical moment in salvation history.

Last, the rather well-documented proclivity of men to attend more to things than to persons is often criticized, in many cases legitimately so, distorted as it can be by the effects of original sin. Nonetheless, I maintain that we are justified in seeing it as a reflection of man's genius, once it is established that it is in virtue of this gift that man contributes to the good of humankind. But a further proposition is required to support this claim: We must recall that the goods of creation, like persons, have ontological status also. They are created by God, held in existence by God, endowed with a *telos* that orders them toward a final end according to God's design.[36] Thus, though the constant moral context of all human action is the fact that the highest value is and always will be the authentic good of human persons—the only creatures created for their own sakes—man's orientation toward "things" is also an orientation toward creatures. In fact, it is this orientation that makes him most properly their steward.

Properly understood, the particular genius of man has proven throughout history to be an essential gift in sustaining families and creating social order—indeed, it has been the key to the very building up of civilizations.[37] Of all the creatures

---

36   Please see my paper: Deborah Savage, "The Metaphysics of Creation as a Foundation of Environmental Stewardship and Economic Prosperity," *Nova et Vetera* 12 (Winter 2012), 233-52.

37   Even a well-known mainstream feminist seems to agree with this point. See Camille Paglia, "It's a Man's World, and It Always Will Be," *Time*, December 16, 2013, *http://ideas.time.com/2013/12/16/its-a-mans-world-and-it-always-will-be/*.

in the material world, humans are the only ones who actually have to work to master their environment and create conditions that support human flourishing.[38] Without the specific genius of man, the human species would not have survived.[39] We owe men a debt of gratitude even if we must also remember that all of us—man and woman alike—are forever under the sway of the effects of original sin. It is the logic of sin that confuses us, that "needs to be broken [so that] a way forward can be found that is capable of banishing it from the hearts of sinful humanity."[40] But as our faith reveals, self-knowledge is an important weapon in our constant battle with the forces that seek to defeat us. To understand the masculine genius in this way is to equip man with the knowledge he needs to strengthen his own struggle with the effects of original sin, which now can be seen in a new light.

And so, we must take up one last passage if we are to arrive at a satisfactory, albeit preliminary, account of the mascu-

---

38   Mieczyslaw A. Krapiec, *I-Man: An Outline of Philosophical Anthropology* (New Britain, CT: Mariel Publications, 1983), 29-38. Father Krapiec points out that of all the creatures on earth, man is actually a kind of alien in his environment. He does not possess fangs or a pointed snout that would permit him to smell out and tear apart his food. He does not have fur to protect him from the harshness of his surroundings. This analysis is also reflected in Thomas Aquinas, *Summa Theologica* I.76.a.5. In short, as Pope John Paul II illuminates so beautifully in the introduction to his encyclical On Human Work: "Man is made to be in the visible universe an image and likeness of God himself, and he is placed in it in order to subdue the earth. From the beginning therefore he is *called to work. Work is one of the characteristics that distinguish* man from the rest of creatures, whose activity for sustaining their lives cannot be called work. Only man is capable of work, and only man works, at the same time by work occupying his existence on earth." See Pope John Paul II, *Laborem Exercens* (On Human Work) (1981), *http://www.vatican.va/holy_father/john_paul_ii/encyclicals/documents/hf_jp-ii_enc_14091981_laborem-exercens_en.html.*

39   There is an interesting connection to be made and explored between this aspect of the genius of man and Cardinal Angelo Scola's argument that the father introduces the child to the "law of exchange (work) as the law of growth in life." See Angelo Cardinal Scola, *The Nuptial Mystery (Ressourcement: Retrieval & Renewal in Catholic Thought)* (Grand Rapids, MI: Wm. B. Eerdmans Publishing Co., 2005), 242.

40   Congregation for the Doctrine of the Faith, *Letter on Collaboration*, 8.

line genius. We cannot leave out the significance and meaning found in the story of the Fall. In Genesis 3:17-19, the man is told that because he listened to his wife, "cursed is the ground because of you; in toil you shall eat of it all the days of your life; thorns and thistles it shall bring forth to you; and you shall eat the plants of the field. In the sweat of your face you shall eat bread till you return to the ground."

The man's sin has now brought struggle to the specific feature that characterized him in his original innocence. His natural relationship to the things of creation is now fraught with difficulty: It will be forever after burdened by confusion and backbreaking work. That he is told, specifically, that as a result of his sin he will have to struggle with creation only confirms the uniqueness of man's relationship to the things of creation. In contrast, the woman's punishment will be the pain of childbirth and a desire for her husband. Even though he seeks to dominate her, hers is a struggle with disordered relationships and thus a distortion of her equally personal gift: a natural orientation toward persons.

Thus the scriptural account reveals that the very things that had been the natural charisms of man and woman are now the source of suffering and struggle. They are both our greatest weaknesses and our path to redemption.

In sum, the masculine genius is grounded in the scriptural account of the first man, which reveals that his fundamental gift is to know creation and to discover in it the goods that will permit him to contribute to the good of his family and of all humankind. He thus is oriented toward generative activity that leads him to create things *outside of himself,* things that can be brought to bear on man's highest good, that of human flourishing. But because he is marked by the burden of original sin, he often forgets that his donation of self—the act of making of himself a gift—is something that can only be given to another person. One cannot make of oneself a gift to a bottom line or a project, no matter how important; on the other end of the donation of self is *always* another self. It becomes woman's task to remind man of this reality by affirming and expressing what she understands through her own genius: that all human activity must be ordered toward the good of persons.

Though many men fail to live up to the potential found in their own genius, surely an equal number of women fail as well. This is not surprising. Both the masculine and the feminine genius are in fact supernatural realities that, though they can be spoken of on the level of nature, require participation in the life of grace to reach their full expression. The men, the fathers in our lives, are quite often engaged in superhuman efforts to lead, protect, and support their families. We should all be grateful for the masculine genius.

Saint Joseph as an Icon of the Masculine Genius

It is fitting to conclude this initial investigation into the nature of the masculine genius by looking to Mary's spouse, Saint Joseph, as an example of its embodiment in a concretely existing human person. For just as Mary is the perfect reflection of the feminine genius, Jesus's earthly father, Saint Joseph, reflects the genius of man. Though limitations of space do not permit an extended treatment of Saint Joseph, Pope Saint John Paul II's apostolic exhortation on Joseph, *Redemptoris Custos*,[41] points us toward that particular manifestation of the masculine genius found in fatherhood—a role that both reflects and serves to perfect his masculine nature.[42]

---

41 Pope John Paul II, apostolic exhortation *Redemptoris Custos* (On the Person and Mission of Saint Joseph in the Life of Christ and of the Church) (August 15, 1989), 5, *http://www.vatican.va/holy_father/john_paul_ii/apost_exhortations/documents/hf_jp-ii_exh_15081989_redemptoris-custos_en.html*. (Editor's note: For a more extensive discussion of Saint Joseph, fatherhood, and the resulting implications for women, see Chapter Seven of this book, "The Dignity and Vocation of Men: Why Masculinity and Fatherhood Matter to Women," by Theresa Farnan, PhD.)

42 The work of Timothy Fortin and Father Carter Griffin will be important in pursuing this proposal.

Pope Saint John Paul II is quick to point out that Saint Joseph is not a mere bystander in the events surrounding the Incarnation. Mary is already betrothed to Joseph at the time of the Annunciation, and Joseph is "the first to be placed by God on the path of Mary's 'pilgrimage of faith.'"[43] He is chosen to ensure fatherly protection for the child when, as Mary's spouse, he is introduced to the mystery of Mary's motherhood by the messenger in his own "annunciation." It is to Joseph that the messenger returns, "entrusting to him the responsibilities of an earthly father with regard to Mary's Son."[44] Joseph thus becomes, together with Mary, the first guardian of this divine mystery.[45] Joseph is "called by God to serve the person and mission of Jesus directly through the exercise of his fatherhood," and his entire life is lived in service to the mystery of the Incarnation.[46] But since salvation comes through the *humanity* of Christ, it is theologically significant to note that this humanity is revealed in Joseph's assumption of fatherly responsibility over his son. Joseph is the overseer of Jesus's birth and the guardian of his private, hidden life.

Thus Joseph would have had to possess the genius of man to a greater degree than most. For Mary would have encountered Joseph as a *person* and, since she was unencumbered by any hint of blindness due to original sin, would have recognized in Joseph—albeit unconsciously perhaps—a man whose very being mirrored the qualities worthy of her sinless state. He is an icon of the masculine genius, and his example bears further investigation.[47]

---

43 Pope John Paul II, *Redemptoris Custos*, 5.

44 Ibid., 3

45 Ibid., 5.

46 Ibid., 8.

47 Saint Joseph's role as Mary's "most chaste spouse" and Jesus's earthly father also suggests that his embodiment of the masculine genius is in some way analogous to Mary's embodiment as Virgin and Mother. This bears further exploration, especially in light of Father Louis Bouyer's very interesting analysis of the distinctions between the "virginity" of men and of women and the nature of

For now, I will simply point to several aspects of Joseph's role in the life of the Holy Family that correspond in concrete ways to the account of the masculine genius proposed in this paper. First, the generations listed at the beginning of Matthew's Gospel are according to the genealogy of Joseph; it is from Joseph's line that we understand the connection with the heritage of David and with the many prophesies associated with the coming of the Messiah. And of special significance in light of our previous analysis, it is Joseph who is told to name the child, the first of the new creation, just as the first man named everything of the old.[48]

But above all, Joseph obeyed, and in silence. The Gospels do not record a single word he may have spoken. At his own "annunciation" he says nothing; he simply does what the angel tells him to do. And, Pope Saint John Paul II tells us, this became the beginning of "Joseph's way," a way marked by his silent witness to the meaning of the just man.[49] In this regard, Joseph's signature quality reflects that of the first man: He was a man who *worked*. This word, Pope Saint John Paul II says, "sums up Joseph's entire life," revealing at the same time the possibilities of sanctifying the quotidian rhythms of daily life.[50] Joseph makes of himself a total gift of self, of his life and work; he "turns his human vocation to domestic love into a superhuman oblation of self."[51]

This necessarily brief treatment reveals that the figure of Saint Joseph embodies and personifies the masculine genius in ways that approach its full expression. His example reflects the courage, loyalty, and tireless efforts of many men

---

fatherhood. See Louis Bouyer, "Woman and God," *Woman in the Church* (San Francisco: Ignatius Press, 1979), 29-39.

48   Pope John Paul II, *Redemptoris Custos*, 7.

49   Ibid., 17.

50   Ibid., 22-24.

51   Ibid., 8.

who serve their families and populate our communities. And for them, we give thanks.

Conclusion

This chapter offers an initial proposal of what might constitute the masculine genius. I have indicated several points of contact between this framework and the additional research that can be done to develop the proposal further. Clearly much work remains to fully explore the nature of masculinity as a human perfection, the significance of fatherhood as an ontological and biological reality, and the place spiritual fatherhood has in the life of the Church. As women can be both physical and spiritual mothers, men can be both physical and spiritual fathers. A thorough investigation of the masculine genius is needed, one that will permit a full consideration of the role of men and fathers in contributing to the family and the common good—and to building up the Body of Christ.

Deborah Savage, PhD (religious studies), is professor of philosophy and theology and director of the master's program in Pastoral Ministry at Saint Paul Seminary, University of Saint Thomas, Saint Paul, Minnesota. Professor Savage is also the co-founder and a member of the advisory board of the Siena Symposium for Women, Family, and Culture at Saint Paul Seminary. Her scholarship focuses on the philosophy of Pope Saint John Paul II, the role of the laity, and the Church's teachings on women. She and her husband are the parents of one daughter.

CHAPTER SEVEN

The Dignity and Vocation of Men

Why Masculinity and Fatherhood Matter to Women

Theresa Farnan, PhD

Pope Francis's call for a "deeper theology of women" has prompted women and men to reexamine the Church's teachings on women.[1] In *Mulieris Dignitatem*, Pope Saint John Paul II used the insights of Genesis 1 and 2 to illuminate certain truths about the dignity and vocation of women, including the truth that men and women, both created in the image of God, need each other in order to discover and confirm their own humanity. The subsequent study of the dignity and vocation of women, and the particular focus on the genius of women, has borne much fruit. Even as the Church continues to develop its teaching on women, however, the need to develop a corresponding teaching

---

1 "Press Conference of Pope Francis during the Return Flight" (apostolic journey to Rio de Janeiro on the occasion of the XXVIII World Youth Day), July 28, 2013, *http://w2.vatican.va/content/francesco/en/speeches/2013/july/documents/papa-francesco_20130728_gmg-conferenza-stampa.html*. See also Antonio Spadaro, SJ, "A Big Heart Open to God," *America*, September 30, 2013, *http://www.americamagazine.org/pope-interview*. For examples of reactions, see Adelaide Mena, "Pope's Remarks on Women in the Church Call for Deeper Theology, Says Expert," *National Catholic Register*, July 31, 2013, *http://www.ncregister.com/daily-news/popes-remarks-on-women-in-the-church-call-for-deeper-theology-says-expert/*; and Megan Fincher, Colleen Dunne, "Women Resistant to Pope Francis' Call for New Theology," *National Catholic Reporter*, November 4, 2013, *http://ncronline.org/news/women-resist-call-new-theology*.

on the dignity and vocation of men—illuminating the masculine virtues and fatherhood—has become critical.

Although women have made great advances in education, employment, and civil rights, the well-being of women, children, and the family increasingly has been undermined by confusion over sexual difference, reflected in societal distortions not only of women and motherhood, but also of masculinity and fatherhood. These distortions of masculinity and fatherhood have created a new set of problems for women.

Social science offers an important contribution when it identifies the pathologies that result from the distortion of fatherhood and the resulting difficulties for mothers and children. However, it cannot offer the anthropological explanation of the human person necessary to understand why these distortions so negatively impact women. Only Christian anthropology can do so. Women in the Church, and in society as a whole, need the Church's teaching on the person—specifically, the dignity and vocation of women and men—to illuminate fatherhood and its relationship to the dignity of women and motherhood. The fundamental anthropological principles in *Mulieris Dignitatem* and the rich vision of masculine virtue and faithful fatherhood found in *Redemptoris Custos,* Pope Saint John Paul II's apostolic exhortation on the person and mission of Saint Joseph, provide a promising framework for such a task. Read together, these documents provide the opportunity to examine motherhood and fatherhood as inseparable, complementary, and irreplaceable for human flourishing.

In the following pages, I will use these documents to reflect on several themes in particular that highlight the value of masculine presence and virtues and the vocation of fatherhood. This is by no means an exhaustive reflection, as masculine virtue and fatherhood offer rich opportunities for reflection on divine fatherhood, the spiritual fatherhood of Jesus, and the spiritual fatherhood of the priesthood. Instead, this work is intended to highlight the importance of fatherhood for women and children. If women are to have an incisive presence in the life of the Church, they need men of virtue as husbands, fathers, and colleagues supporting them in their work. This is the practical implication of the complementarity of the sexes.

The Problems of Women Are Inseparable from the Problems of Men

Distortions of fatherhood and masculine virtue have serious, lasting consequences for women and the family. In authoritarian societies and relationships, for example, women suffer from the actions and attitudes of men who distort masculine virtue and fatherhood into domination and abuse of power. This takes many forms, ranging from denied opportunities for education and political participation to cultural practices such as genital mutilation, polygamy, bride-burning, and child marriages.[2] Even in countries where these practices would seem to be unthinkable, women still suffer from domestic violence at the hands of men who view masculinity as authoritarian.[3] The high rate of gender-selection abortions, dubbed by one demographer as the global war on baby girls, and the silence

2   See, for example, Rahul Bedi, "Indian Dowry Death on the Rise," *The Telegraph*, February 27, 2012, *http://www.telegraph.co.uk/news/worldnews/asia/india/9108642/Indian-dowry-deaths-on-the-rise.html*; Jamie Dettmer, "Britain's Part Time Wives," *The Daily Beast,* August 5, 2013, *http://www.thedailybeast.com/witw/articles/2013/08/05/britain-s-muslim-communities-see-rise-in-multiple-marriages-as-career-women-seek-part-time-husbands.html*; Institute for Marriage and Public Policy, "British Columbia: The Case Against Polygamy," *iMAPP Research Brief* 4, no. 8 (December 2011), *http://www.marriagedebate.com/pdf/iMAPP.Nov2011.Polygamy.pdf*; Media Centre, "Child Marriages: 39,000 Every Day," *World Health Organization* (March 7, 2013), *http://www.who.int/mediacentre/news/releases/2013/child_marriage_20130307/en/*; and "Female Genital Mutilation/Cutting: A Statistical Overview and Exploration of the Dynamics of Change," *UNICEF,* July 2013, *http://www.unicef.org/media/files/FGCM_Lo_res.pdf*.

3   "Facts and Figures: Ending Violence against Women," *UNWomen* (United Nations Entity for Gender Equality and the Empowerment of Women). *http://www.unwomen.org/en/what-we-do/ending-violence-against-women/facts-and-figures*.

of many governments on this issue indicates that the devaluing of women is widespread.[4]

Conversely, in societies where women enjoy great freedom and opportunity, men are increasingly absent from the family, abandoning masculine virtues and the responsibilities of fatherhood. In the United States, more than 40 percent of all children are born outside of marriage. Among some ethnic groups, the percentage of children born outside of marriage is greater than 60 percent.[5] Sociologists have noted that while the census bureau tracks this number according to ethnic groups, it actually reflects the socioeconomic reality that marriage increasingly belongs to those who are well educated and financially prosperous. Moreover, single motherhood increases the risk of poverty for women and their children, creating a spiral of poverty.[6]

In addition, in Western culture, gender theorists have promoted an aggressive denial of difference between men and women. This denial of difference has tended to reduce father-

---

4   Nicholas Eberstadt, "The Global War against Baby Girls," *New Atlantis* no. 33 (Fall 2011), *http://www.thenewatlantis.com/publications/the-global-war-against-baby-girls*.

5   Centers for Disease Control and Prevention, *National Vital Statistics Reports, Births: Final Data for 2012* (December 30, 2013), *http://www.cdc.gov/nchs/data/nvsr/nvsr62/nvsr62_09.pdf* (see pages 8 and 9 in particular). Nonmarital birthrates for non-Hispanic black women (72 percent) and Native American women (67 percent) were especially high, while Hispanic women had a nonmarital birthrate of 54 percent.

6   See, for example, University of Virginia/The National Marriage Project and the Institute for American Values, "When Marriage Disappears: The Retreat from Marriage in Middle America" (2010), *http://stateofourunions.org/2010/when-marriage-disappears.php*; Jason DeParle and Sabrina Tavernise, "For Women Under 30, Most Births Occur Outside Marriage," *New York Times*, February 17, 2012, *http://www.nytimes.com/2012/02/18/us/for-women-under-30-most-births-occur-outside-marriage.html?_r=2&ref=us*; and Princeton University Center for Research on Child Wellbeing and Center for Health and Wellbeing and Columbia University's Columbia Population Research Center and the National Center for Children and Families, "Fragile Families and Child Wellbeing Study Fact Sheet," *Fragile Families and Child Wellbeing Study* (2010), *http://www.fragilefamilies.princeton.edu/documents/FragileFamiliesand-ChildWellbeingStudyFactSheet.pdf*.

hood and motherhood to a set of gender-neutral functions within the family, disconnected from essential notions of femininity, masculinity, and relationship.[7] According to this view, family structure is tied to personal and sexual preference of the adults involved, and the well-being of children necessarily follows from the free exercise of gender and sexual preference by adults. This has had a disproportionate impact on the presence of men in the family. As reproductive technology makes it possible for women to have babies without the presence of fathers, and as other socioeconomic forces make men's financial contributions less valuable, fathers are vanishing from the family.[8]

Both of these distortions of masculinity and fatherhood—domination or absence—can have dramatic, dire consequences. The negative consequences of men abusing or devaluing women are self-evident—one does not need a social scientist to know that physically harming or denying an education to a young girl is objectively bad for her, for example. But the absence of a father has measurably harmful effects on girls and boys as well. Girls who grow up without a father are more likely to be sexually active at an early age and more likely to become teen mothers, while boys who grow up without fathers are at greater risk for incarceration. Children of both sexes who grow up without their fathers are at greater risk for

---

7   Gender feminists propose that gender is a set of socially constructed roles detached from the body and from biological sex, and that true gender freedom lies in the choice of gendered roles without any cultural or biological restrictions. See, for example, Judith Butler and Fina Birulés (interviewer), "Gender Is Extramoral," *Barcelona Metropolis*, Summer 2008. *http://www.egs.edu/faculty/ judith-butler/articles/gender-is-extramoral/*.

8   Discussions of the absence of men include Hanna Rosin, "The End of Men," *The Atlantic*, July/August 2010, *http://www.theatlantic.com/magazine/ archive/2010/07/the-end-of-men/308135/*; Kate Bolick, "All the Single Ladies," *The Atlantic*, November 2011, *http://www.theatlantic.com/magazine/ archive/2011/11/all-the-single-ladies/308654/*; and Isabel Hardman, "Save the Male! Britain's Crisis of Masculinity," *The Spectator*, May 3, 2014, *http://www .spectator.co.uk/features/9197481/the-descent-of-man/*.

child abuse, substance abuse, behavioral and educational difficulties, and poverty.[9]

Accordingly, any attempt to develop an authentic understanding of the genius and vocation of women must include serious study of the irreplaceable role of men as fathers and husbands, both for women and for the family. It is not enough simply to reject the false philosophies that either place men in opposition to women or discount their importance. Instead, any endeavor to understand the genius and vocation of women should avail itself of the resources offered by Christian anthropology to discover the genius and vocation of men, affirm the complementarity of men and women, and explore the rich, practical implications of complementarity for women, men, and the family.

Complementarity—Not Just of Men and Women, but of Their Vocations

Complementarity is at the heart of Pope Saint John Paul II's work and is the cornerstone of Christian anthropology. Crude caricatures of the relationship between the sexes rely on a fractional understanding of complementarity. Sister Prudence Allen[10] describes fractional understanding of complementarity as resting on a sense of deficiency in the other. According to popular caricatures, men are stupid and need a woman to tell them what to do, or women are helpless and need a man to order their lives. In contrast, Pope Saint John Paul II's understanding of complementarity proposes an integral model

---

9   See National Fatherhood Initiative, "Father Facts," *fatherhood.org, http://www.fatherhood.org/father-absence-statistics*; Ellis, Bates et al., "Does Father Absence Place Daughters at Special Risk for Early Sexual Activity and Teenage Pregnancy?", *Child Development* 74, no. 3 (May 2003): 801-821, *http://www.ncbi.nlm.nih.gov/pmc/articles/PMC2764264/*; and Cynthia C. Harper and Sara S. McLanahan, "Father Absence and Youth Incarceration," *Journal of Research on Adolescence* 14, no. 3 (September 2004), 369-397.

10   Sister Prudence Allen, RSM, an authority on the vocation and role of women, was appointed by Pope Francis to the International Theological Commission for a term through 2019.

of complementarity, a collaboration of two whole persons, neither of whom is deficient, that is creative precisely because of the masculine/feminine dynamic. The creative dimension of the relationship between a man and a woman is illustrated most vividly, but not exclusively, by the creation of a child. However, integral complementarity cannot be reduced only to procreation but occurs anytime men and women collaborate at home, in the workplace, or in the church, as husbands and wives, brothers and sisters, colleagues and friends.[11]

Complementarity is not something that occurs only occasionally, as an intentional act of cooperation. Rather, all of human history unfolds in the context of this call to live as man and woman in interpersonal communion, integrating their masculinity and femininity into all of their interactions with other persons. This interpersonal communion enables men and women to "discover" and "confirm" their humanity through their relationships with each other.[12] When Adam encounters Eve in the Garden of Eden, he immediately recognizes that she is like him. As another human being, Eve can provide the companionship and love that Adam is seeking, overcoming the loneliness that he experienced without her.[13]

The unity of two, Adam and Eve, made in the image and likeness of God, not only mirrors the communion of love of the Trinity, but also signifies an ethical duty. Men and women are called to live in communion with each other, to exist mutually for each other through the free and total gift of self that

---

11 Prudence Allen, "Man-Woman Complementarity: The Catholic Inspiration," *Logos: A Journal of Catholic Thought and Culture* 9, no. 3 (Summer 2006): 87-108. Available at the philosophy page of the Pontifical Council for the Laity, *http://www.laici.va/content/dam/laici/documenti/donna/filosofia/english/man-woman-complementary-the-catholic-inspiration.pdf.* See also Elizabeth R. Schiltz, "A Contemporary Catholic Theory of Complementarity," in *Feminism, Law, and Religion*, eds. Marie A. Failinger, Elizabeth R. Schiltz, and Susan J. Stabile (Burlington, VT: Ashgate Publishing, 2013), 3-24.

12 Pope John Paul II, apostolic letter *Mulieris Dignitatem* (On the Dignity and Vocation of Women) (1988), 7.

13 Ibid., 6.

occurs as a result of integral complementarity. Pope Saint John Paul II refers to this as the spousal characteristic of the person—not only that a person can only "find" himself or herself through total gift of self, but also that men and women have an intrinsic desire for "spousal love whereby the woman's 'sincere gift of self' is responded to and matched by a corresponding 'gift' on the part of the husband."[14]

The spousal characteristic of the person is key to understanding the dimensions of vocation and the importance of complementarity to that vocation. Created as male or female, we are called to live the gift of self as an integral unity of body and soul, existing in communion with other persons. Pope Saint John Paul II identified the two dimensions of vocation for women as virginity and motherhood.[15] Correspondingly, in men, the two dimensions of vocation are virginity (celibacy) and fatherhood. But masculine and feminine vocations do not exist side by side, so to speak; instead they complement each other in a way that enables the person to discover the richness of his or her humanity. Man finds and confirms the meaning of his humanity in his fatherhood, spiritual and/or physical, and in woman's spiritual and/or physical motherhood. Woman finds and confirms the meaning of her humanity in her motherhood, spiritual and/or physical, and in man's spiritual and/or physical fatherhood. One's encounter and interaction with the vocation of the opposite sex, beginning with the interaction of infants with their mothers and fathers, adds richness and depth not only to a person's own vocation, but also to that person's very being.

Masculinity, Fatherhood, and Responsibility for Others

Just as in Mary virginity and motherhood acquire full meaning and value, similarly, in Saint Joseph, a celibate husband who became the father of Jesus, celibacy and fatherhood ac-

---

14   Ibid.,10.
15   Ibid.,17.

quire full meaning and value. Mary discovered and confirmed the meaning of her humanity through both her physical and spiritual motherhood, but also through her lived interaction with Joseph's fatherhood. Similarly Joseph discovered and confirmed the meaning of his humanity not only through his vocation as Mary's husband and Jesus's father, but also through his interaction with Mary's motherhood. Joseph's total gift of self united both dimensions of a man's vocation, fatherhood and celibacy, in his loving guardianship of Mary and Jesus, such that "one did not exclude the other but wonderfully complemented it."[16]

Saint Joseph illustrates that fatherhood requires the free and loving acceptance of responsibility for the child *and his or her mother*, prenatally and postpartum. As motherhood absorbs the physical energies of the woman, it gives a man a "focus for"—he devotes his intellect, will, talents, and energy to the service of the mother and child. For man, learning to protect and cherish his child and the child's mother develops a uniquely masculine mode of living a virtuous life, a code of conduct that includes justice, magnanimity, generosity, courtesy, courage, industry, perseverance, and other virtues exemplified by Saint Joseph.

Pope Saint John Paul II proposes that a man "learns" his fatherhood from the mother.[17] At first glance a literal reading of this passage seems fairly straightforward—the mother literally shows the father how to care for an infant, indeed how to act like a father. Yet a literal reading—women teach men how to be fathers—is problematic. Fatherhood then is reduced to a set of roles or chores, alien to the man, disconnected from his physical desire and capacity for fatherhood. Or, alternatively, it seems to suggest that, as a relationship, fatherhood does

---

16 Compare with *Mulieris Dignitatem,* 17.

17 "The man—even with all his sharing in parenthood—always remains 'outside' the process of pregnancy and the baby's birth; in many ways he has to *learn* his own *'fatherhood' from the mother*" (emphasis in original). Pope John Paul II, *Mulieris Dignitatem,* 18.

not come naturally to men. In either case, then, only women would have the two dimensions of their vocation inscribed upon their nature, suggesting a radical disconnection between man's capacity to physically father a child and the emotional, psychological, and spiritual way of relating to another that we think of as fatherhood.

Taking this passage literally suggests that although women display an intimate unity of body and soul, whereby their capacity for receiving another person creates the openness and sensitivity to the other that is the genius of women, men lack a similar unity of body and soul. Such a literal reading undercuts Pope Saint John Paul II's understanding of the body as signifying metaphysical truths about the person and calls into question the possibility of the spiritual fatherhood of the priesthood. In what sense would priests "learn" their spiritual fatherhood from women? And from which women would priests "learn" their spiritual fatherhood? Moreover, reading this passage literally tempts the reader to look at fatherhood only from a woman's perspective, reinforcing stereotypes of men as incompetent and emotionally disconnected, in need of direction from women in order to function as fathers.

However, if we understand this phrase in the context of men and women discovering and confirming their own humanity through their relationship with each other *and each other's vocations*, then we resolve these problems and encounter a richer meaning of fatherhood. Joseph learns, *discovers*, his fatherhood through his relationship with Mary as mother. Mary's pregnancy, her vulnerability and need for his masculine gifts and presence, evoke Joseph's fatherly gifts. His protective instincts toward Mary as a mother prepare him for protecting and guarding his child as well. Joseph's desire to protect Mary from scandal, even before he realized from the angel's message that this child was to be his gift and responsibility, indicates that the mere fact of a women's pregnancy should evoke a paternal protective response from men. Reading this passage in this way also provides an explanation for other paternal responses and masculine virtues. The vulnerability and need for protection of those most helpless evoke a paternal response in men, explaining why men are drawn to military, police, and rescue services often before they have any children of their own. This is part of the masculine gift of self—acceptance of responsibility for another person.

Original Sin and Distortions in Relationships between Men and Women

Unfortunately, original sin brings disruption not only in the human person's relationship with God and nature, but also in the relationships between men and women.

> Sin brings about a break in the original unity which man enjoyed in the state of original justice: union with God as the source of unity within his own "I," in the mutual relationship between man and woman (*"communio personarum"*) as well as in regard to the external world, to nature.[18]

This occurs through the radical misuse of freedom. The desire to appropriate to himself the power to decide what is good and evil specifically leads men to the desire for domination with no regard for what is objectively good for him or for other persons.[19] Male domination is especially problematic for women, who are physically and emotionally vulnerable as they reach the age of sexual maturity. Human trafficking, rape, child marriage, and coerced or forced abortion are particularly horrifying examples of the consequences of male domination over women.

Yet Genesis does not only warn women that sin will tempt men to domination and abuse of power. In it, God warns Eve that the disruption of the relationship between men and women will affect her as well, telling her, "I will

18   Ibid., 9.
19   Ibid., 10.

intensify your toil in childbearing; in pain you shall bring forth children. Yet your urge shall be for your husband, and he shall rule over you."[20] This phrase—"he shall rule over you"—suggests that original sin causes a disorder in the way women seek to relate to men as well. The weakness of original sin leads women to desire to please men above all else, even if it results in disordered affections or conduct. This by no means excuses the sins of men, but suggests a shared moral responsibility in situations where women have a choice, when they are choosing between living virtuously or giving in to sinful behavior. The Eve/Mary comparison offers additional insights into this dynamic. In the Garden of Eden, Eve not only sinned but drew Adam into her sin as well. In contrast, when the angel appeared to Mary, she chose to put God's will first, certainly knowing that this would cause a rift in her relationship with Joseph. Her free assent to God's will set in motion the events that led to Joseph's sanctification.

Accordingly, an honest assessment of the effects of original sin on the relationship between men and women should include a discussion of not only the masculine tendency to dominate, but also the feminine desire to please, each of which becomes disordered by sin. Examining these tendencies will give a clearer understanding of how men and women can help each other live according to a standard of virtue and integrity.

The example of Saint Joseph and Mary illustrates how men and women help each other grow in holiness and virtue. Although burdened with the concupiscence of original sin, Joseph, through his relationship with Mary and grace of communion with Jesus, is able to order his daily actions to God's will and fulfill his responsibilities to respect and love his wife and child, and serve them through his daily work.

---

20   Gn 3:16 (*New American Bible, Revised Edition, referenced throughout this chapter*).

His example shows how every man is called to intimacy with Christ—the only way to overcome sin and live a life of masculine virtue.

Consider the woman caught in adultery, a story featured prominently in Pope Saint John Paul II's meditation on Christ's interaction with women. Pope Saint John Paul II uses this event in Jesus's life to teach directly about the dignity of women and the responsibility and dignity of men:

> A woman is left alone, exposed to public opinion with "her sin," while behind "her" sin there lurks a man—a sinner, guilty "of the other's sin," indeed equally responsible for it. And yet his sin escapes notice, it is passed over in silence: he does not appear responsible for "the other's sin"! Sometimes, forgetting his own sin, he even makes himself the accuser, as in the case described. How often, in a similar way, *the woman pays* for her own sin (maybe it is she, in some cases, who is guilty of "the other's sin"—the sin of the man), but she alone pays and she pays *all alone*! How often is she abandoned with her pregnancy, when the man, the child's father, is unwilling to accept responsibility for it?[21]

Jesus's response displays his profound awareness of the relationship between men and women from the beginning. In reminding the men who would stone her of their own sinfulness and gently admonishing the adulterous woman not to sin, Jesus emphasizes that while a woman is responsible for her own moral situation, men must not exploit vulnerable women. This applies especially to instances of promiscuity, prostitution, and pornography—even if a woman makes herself available for exploitation, men are never justified in using her as an object of gratification:

---

21   Pope John Paul II, *Mulieris Dignitatem*, 14. See also Jn 8:1-11.

On the basis of the eternal "unity of the two," *this dignity depends directly on woman herself, as a subject responsible for herself, and at the same time it is "given as a task" to man....* "Consequently, each man must look within himself to see whether she who was entrusted to him as a sister in humanity, as a spouse, has not become in his heart an object of adultery; to see whether she who, in different ways, is the co-subject of his existence in the world, has not become for him an "object": an object of pleasure, of exploitation.[22]

It is not difficult to imagine that Jesus's merciful response to the vulnerability of the woman caught in adultery was shaped by the example of his father Joseph's love for Mary. In Saint Joseph's actions, we see him unconditionally love, support, and protect his wife and child. Indeed, it is hard to imagine a more radical act of love than Joseph taking Mary as his wife after finding out that she was pregnant with a child who was not his biological child. In his fidelity to the will of God, and his loving and total acceptance of responsibility for Mary and her child, Joseph acts as the antithesis to the men who first abandon, then condemn the woman caught in adultery. Joseph accepted Mary and her child, assumed responsibility for them both, and guarded their reputations—to the point that Jesus is known as "the carpenter's son."[23] In Joseph's conduct we see how charity is lived in a thoroughly masculine way. We can glimpse how the suffering of the woman caught in adultery could have been alleviated if the men in her life had treated her with mercy.[24]

---

22   Pope John Paul II, *Mulieris Dignitatem,* 14.

23   Mt 13:55.

24   As the fruit of charity, mercy is governed by reason in such a way that it is exercised in accord with justice. Jesus acted with perfect mercy toward the adulterous woman, saving her from the condemnation of others while gently admonishing her to sin no more. In contrast, Joseph's acceptance of Mary and her child was based on love, not mercy, as her pregnancy was not the result of

Joseph as Father: Irreplaceable in the Life of Christ

Much of the scholarship on Joseph has focused on examining the legitimacy of his fatherly authority over Jesus in order to explore the nature and limits of Joseph's role as "foster father" of Jesus. In *Redemptoris Custos,* Pope Saint John Paul II is clear that Joseph acted as Jesus's father with full moral and legal authority. In other words, when the Church refers to Joseph as Jesus's foster father, it does not indicate any moral or legal limit to Joseph's role as father. He is fully responsible for Jesus's human development in virtue, just as every other father bears that responsibility. Pope Saint John Paul II points to Joseph's task of naming Jesus as an indication of his fatherly authority over Jesus:

> Joseph is the one whom God chose to be the "overseer of the Lord's birth," the one who has the responsibility to look after the Son of God's "ordained" entry into the world, in accordance with divine dispositions and human laws. All of the so-called "private" or "hidden" life of Jesus is entrusted to Joseph's guardianship.[25]
>
> At the circumcision Joseph names the child "Jesus." This is the only name in which there is salvation (cf. Acts 4:12). Its significance had been revealed to Joseph at the moment of his "annunciation": "You shall call the child Jesus, for he will save his people from their sins" (cf. Mt 1:21). In conferring the name, Joseph declares his own legal fatherhood over Jesus, and in speaking the name he proclaims the child's mission as Savior.[26]

---

a defect or sin that needed to be remedied. See Saint Thomas Aquinas, *Summa Theologica* IIaIIae, 30, 1-4.

25 Pope John Paul II, apostolic exhortation *Redemptoris Custos* (On the Person and Mission of Saint Joseph in the Life of Christ and of the Church) (August 15, 1989), 8, *http://www.vatican.va/holy_father/john_paul_ii/apost_exhortations/documents/hf_jp-ii_exh_15081989_redemptoris-custos_en.html.*

26 Ibid., 12.

Pope Saint John Paul II cites Joseph's role in registering Jesus for the census and in having Jesus circumcised and presented in the Temple as additional instances of Joseph exercising fatherly authority and officially assuming responsibility for his son in a legal and religious sense.[27]

Joseph's role as guardian of the redeemer, as *father*, consists of more than merely taking legal and religious responsibility for his child. Joseph acts as mediator between the outside world and his family, especially his son. First and foremost, as father, Joseph is responsible for his son's safety and welfare. From the moment of his birth, when Joseph was given the difficult task of finding a sheltered place where Mary could deliver her baby safely, to the flight to Egypt, we can imagine the concern and responsibility Joseph must have felt as he continually had to adapt his own plans to the divinely ordained circumstances of Jesus's birth. What father wants his child to be born among animals? Who would wish to have to leave job and home and go into exile to keep his child safe from harm?

In less dramatic but equally important circumstances, Joseph mediates between his family and the outside world when he teaches Jesus the Jewish Law and the trade of carpentry, and the accompanying virtues of obedience and industry. In Jesus's own ministry we see these virtues. For three years, obedient to his heavenly Father's will, Jesus tirelessly taught and healed while traveling from town to town. His agony and death on the cross were the work of one who had been schooled in the virtues of obedience to his Father's will and perseverance in difficult tasks for the sake of a greater good.

But Joseph's relationship with Jesus is even more profound than that of protector and mediator. In the relationship of Jesus and Joseph, we see a vivid reminder of the importance of a father's teaching and example for his child's growth in virtue and maturity. His lived example provided Jesus with a powerful illustration of the unity of the virtues of charity and

---

27 Ibid., 9, 11, 13.

justice. The compassionate way that Jesus treated the poor, the sick, and the sinful bears witness to Joseph's compassion. Jesus's forceful denunciation of the moneychangers in the temple indicates a deeply ingrained sense of how to live according to justice, honesty, and authentic piety.[28] Citing Pope Blessed Paul VI, Pope Saint John Paul II reminds us:

> Saint Joseph is the model of those humble ones that Christianity raises up to great destinies;...he is the proof that in order to be a good and genuine follower of Christ, there is no need of great things—it is enough to have the common, simple and human virtues, but they need to be true and authentic.[29]

Pope Francis notes that when Joseph discovered Mary was pregnant and resolved to send her away, he was seeking at that point to do the will of God and was acting out of justice. However, through his love of God and openness to God's will, Joseph realized what divine justice, justice radically purified and transformed by charity, was asking of him. Pope Francis declares: "This Gospel passage reveals to us the greatness of Saint Joseph's heart and soul. He was following a good plan for his life, but God was reserving another plan for him, a greater mission."[30]

In keeping with these virtues of justice and charity, Joseph's work was never an end in itself, but was a "daily expression of love."[31] In the Holy Family, work was at the service of the redemption of humanity, not through any dramatic undertaking, but through the constant loving subordination of work to the good of the family. In this way, work takes on profound

---

28   It is important not to mistake Jesus's righteous anger, the response of right reason to an objective evil, for a display of temper, which would not have been a measured, reasoned response to evil.

29   Pope John Paul II, *Redemptoris Custos*, 24.

30   Pope Francis, *Angelus,* December 22, 2013, *http://w2.vatican.va/content/ francesco/en/angelus/2013/documents/papa-francesco_angelus_20131222.html.*

31   Pope John Paul II, *Redemptoris Custos*, 22.

significance. In fact, every task, no matter how demeaning or humble in the eyes of others, carries immeasurable value if it is performed out of love. This is a message that resonates powerfully in Western societies where men are "falling behind"—increasingly relegated to menial labor and blue-collar jobs that elite society holds in disdain. It is equally important in societies where women are barred from public work and held in contempt for the menial work they do. Moreover, it reinforces the significance of work for one's family, whether inside or outside of the home.[32]

Finally, no discussion of Saint Joseph's fatherhood is complete without noting his silence, which indicates his profound interiority and Christ-centered spirituality of work.

> The same aura of silence that envelops everything else about Joseph also shrouds his work as a carpenter in the house of Nazareth. It is, however, a silence that reveals in a special way the inner portrait of the man. The Gospels speak exclusively of what Joseph "did." Still they allow us to discover in his "actions"—shrouded in silence as they are—an aura of deep contemplation....
>
> It was from this interior life that "very singular commands and consolations came, bringing him also the logic and strength that belong to simple and clear souls, and giving him the power of making great decisions—such as the decision to put his liberty immediately at the disposition of the divine designs, to make over to them also his legitimate human calling, his conjugal happiness, to accept the conditions, the responsibility and the burden of a family, but through an incomparable virginal love, to renounce the natural conjugal love that is the foundation and nourishment of the family.[33]

32 Ibid., 23, 24.
33 Ibid., 25, 26.

Pope Francis notes that, "in the silence of the daily routine, Saint Joseph, together with Mary, share a single common centre of attention: Jesus."[34] This profound contemplative spirituality, this close intentional embrace of divine will as his own, must have been an ideal example for the child Jesus of the virtue of justice perfected by charity, which has at its heart the ready desire to bring one's own will into conformity with divine will. Pope Emeritus Benedict XVI noted:

> It is no exaggeration to think that it was precisely from his "father" Joseph that Jesus learned—at the human level—that steadfast interiority which is a presupposition of authentic justice, the "superior justice" which he was one day to teach his disciples (cf. Mt 5:20).[35]

The Priority of Relationships

Pope Saint John Paul II points out that the love Joseph and Jesus had for each other must have profoundly influenced both men:

> Why should the "fatherly" love of Joseph not have had an influence upon the "filial" love of Jesus? And vice versa why should the "filial" love of Jesus not have had an influence upon the "fatherly" love of Joseph, thus leading to a further deepening of their unique relationship?[36]

These meditations on the relationship between Jesus and Joseph highlight an important aspect of the Holy Family that is not emphasized enough—their intimacy. The silence that surrounds the early years in Nazareth should not be mistaken for an empty silence, but rather indicates a rich and

---

34   Pope Francis, General Audience, May 1, 2013, *http://w2.vatican.va/content/francesco/en/audiences/2013/documents/papa-francesco_20130501_udienza-generale.html*.

35   Pope Benedict XVI, *Angelus*, December 18, 2005, *http://www.vatican.va/holy_father/benedict_xvi/angelus/2005/documents/hf_ben-xvi_ang_20051218_en.html*.

36   Pope John Paul II, *Redemptoris Custos*, 27.

shared interior life. In fact, Mary's awareness of Joseph's encounters with angels illustrates the privileged communication of husbands and wives that is the foundation for emotional intimacy.[37] Moreover, Jesus's rich teaching on God as father and the warm, vivid examples he gives of a father's unconditional love demonstrate an intimate understanding of human fatherhood that enables us to glimpse the depth of Joseph's love for Jesus.[38] Jesus's acceptance of suffering and death on the cross for the sake of those he loves also reveals that he knew, from the lived experience of his father Joseph's love, that love demands sacrifice from men.

Finally, an important aspect of relationships in the family is the virtue of gratitude. Pope Saint John Paul II indicates that gratitude plays an important part of the dynamic between men and women, especially during pregnancy:

> Parenthood—even though it belongs to both—is realized much more fully in the woman, especially in the prenatal period. It is the woman who "pays" directly for this shared generation, which literally absorbs the energies of her body and soul. It is therefore necessary that *the man* be fully aware that in their shared parenthood, he owes *a special debt to the woman*.[39]

Fatherhood not only prompts a man to accept the responsibility for another person freely and openly, but also awakens awareness of the role of a mother in sharing that responsibility and gives a man a sense of gratitude for her sacrifices. Women also are called to gratitude for the gifts men bring to family life and for the responsibilities that men shoul-

---

37 Father J. Anthony Giambrone, OP, suggests that the angel's admonition not to be afraid indicates that Mary already had revealed to Joseph the divine origin of her child—again illustrating the emotional intimacy of their relationship. See Giambrone, "Reigning as Steward," *The Magnificat Advent Companion*, December 22, 2013.

38 See, for example, Mt 6:9-15,26-33; 7:7-11; Lk 15:11-32.

39 Pope John Paul II, *Mulieris Dignitatem*, 18.

der in freely accepting their families. In each case, gratitude and appreciation of the gifts a man or woman brings to a marriage prevents that marriage from turning into a relationship of advantage or utility.

Similarly, gratitude for the unique gifts of each child is necessary to fathers and mothers, to encourage them to develop the talents and abilities each child possesses, and to prevent them from seeing their child as a mere extension of themselves. When Mary and Joseph found the child Jesus in the Temple, teaching and answering questions with astonishing insights, they must have marveled at their son's gifts. Aware of the circumstances of Jesus's birth, Joseph must have appreciated these gifts truly as gifts from God and thus was freed from the common prideful tendency of parents to appropriate their child's gifts as their own rather than God's. Certainly that awareness must have enabled Mary to accept and support Jesus's public life and ministry, which was so different from the humble and private life that she and Joseph had shared.

Conclusion

The example of the Holy Family and, in particular, Jesus's relationship with his father Joseph illustrates that fatherhood matters for children as well as for women. Through their relationship with their children's mother and their loving interaction with their sons and daughters, fathers enable their children to discover and confirm what it is to be a man or a woman. Fathers are called to teach their sons what it means to be a man, just as Joseph taught Jesus. Moreover, fathers teach their sons how to treat women and convey to their daughters how they should be treated. New societal norms that view fathers as optional and belittle fathers who are present not only harm mothers and their children, but also warp men's understanding of their own masculinity and women's understanding of their femininity. Equally destructive are different cultural norms that encourage men to devalue women and children, as well as cultural norms that see children, both male and female, as possessions or property of their fathers, rather than possessing an inherent dignity and value. In fact, any cultural or social norm that distorts fatherhood weakens that culture's or society's understanding of the dignity of the person.

This reflection on fatherhood as exemplified by Saint Joseph's fatherly care of his family is by no means exhaustive. It is intended to highlight the importance of Saint Joseph to the Holy Family as an example of the important role that fathers play in their families. Through the act of cherishing their wives and children, fathers bear witness to divine fatherhood. This requires them to cultivate a deeply contemplative inner life, formed by communion with Jesus and attentive to the needs of the most vulnerable.

As a lived expression of love ordered to the protection and care of others, fatherhood can transform not only the lives of women and children, but our culture as well.

Pope Francis's call for a more profound theology of women inevitably leads us from considerations of complementarity to the realization that the dignity and vocation of women requires men to live up to their own dignity and vocation. Currently much attention has been focused on the "problem" of women in the Church. Certainly as an institution the Church should be mindful of avoiding cultural or social norms that devalue different groups of people. However, as *teacher*, the Church must stay faithful to proclaiming the truth about the person—female and male—in its entirety. The anthropological vision of the person that the Catholic Church offers—intrinsically relational, created as man and woman in the image and likeness of God, possessing an intimate unity of body and soul, created to live and love in a family—is desperately needed to solve the larger problems of injustice, violence, and loneliness facing the family and society. A more profound theology of women must be supported by an equally profound theology of men and placed in the context of Christian anthropology's rich vision of the person in order to effectively proclaim the truths about the person and offer the hope of healing to a world wounded by sin.

Theresa Farnan, PhD (medieval studies), is a consultant to the United States Conference of Catholic Bishops, Committee on Laity, Marriage, Family Life, and Youth. Dr. Farnan is also an adjunct member of the philosophy department at Franciscan University of Steubenville, where she focuses on the philosophy of Saint Thomas Aquinas, the personalism of Pope Saint John Paul II, and Catholic teaching on women and the family. She co-hosted a series on EWTN entitled St. Thomas Aquinas in Today's World *and, with Charles and Ellen Rice, co-authored the book* Where Did I Come From? Where Am I Going? How Do I Get There?: Straight Answers for Young Catholics *(South Bend, IN: Saint Augustine's Press, 2006). Dr. Farnan and her husband are the parents of ten children.*

Part Three

PRACTICAL CONSIDERATIONS

Toward a "More Incisive Female
Presence in the Church"

CHAPTER EIGHT

With Motherly Care

Addressing the Crisis of Human Flourishing in Our Time

Catherine Ruth Pakaluk, PhD

In light of Pope Francis's call for a more "incisive presence" of women in the Church and society, this chapter focuses on the important role women play in implementing Catholic social teaching. I offer proposals for strengthening the collaboration between women and the Church in three specific areas: the social sciences, education, and care-oriented work. Taken together, these ideas highlight the need for a better understanding of women's vocations and an increased awareness of the pivotal role women play in revitalizing families, communities, and the mission of the Church. My hope is that these proposals will be seeds for fruitful discussion and dialogue.

The Social Question of Our Time

In 2009, economists Betsey Stevenson and Justin Wolfers stunned the world of social research with a surprising finding published in the prestigious *American Economic Journal*.[1] Their exhaustive survey of United States and European data sets showed conclusively that, since 1970, women's self-reported happiness had declined both absolutely and relative to men's happiness. But how could this be? After all, as the

---

1 Betsey Stevenson and Justin Wolfers, "The Paradox of Declining Female Happiness," *American Economic Journal: Economic Policy* 1, no. 2 (2009): 190-225.

authors pointed out, "Social changes that have occurred over the past four decades have increased the opportunities available to women, and a standard economic framework would suggest that these expanded opportunities for women would have increased their welfare."[2] The authors could make no sense of the effect, so they dubbed it "The Paradox of Declining Female Happiness."

Stevenson and Wolfers pointed out that in principle one of three things was responsible for the effect: (1) some unidentified, aggregate change that affected women more than men; (2) a change in the reference point that women held up for themselves; or (3) a change in the way women understood the question of happiness. They were able to rule out the second and third alternatives, leaving the first. But what was this aggregate change, affecting women more than men, that was responsible for such an effect? Stevenson and Wolfers could offer no plausible explanation.

Perhaps some earlier research provides the key. In 2005, sociologists Kathryn Edin and Maria Kefalas published a book called *Promises I Can Keep* that described the results of a remarkable study[3] they undertook by living for more than two years in some of the poorest neighborhoods in Philadelphia and in Camden, New Jersey. The goal of their study was to determine "what poor mothers think marriage and motherhood mean, and...why they nearly always put motherhood first."[4] Single motherhood is usually attributed to poverty, lack of contraceptives, and poor education. However, these researchers found that poor women were single moms mainly because they "judged children to be a necessity, an absolutely essential part of a young woman's life, the chief source of identity and meaning."[5]

---

2 Ibid., 191.

3 Kathryn Edin and Maria Kefalas, *Promises I Can Keep: Why Poor Women Put Motherhood before Marriage* (Oakland, CA: University of California Press, 2005).

4 Ibid., 5.

5 Ibid., 6.

Consider now that the epidemic of nonmarital births is a highly salient statistic for social theorists. Nonmarital births march steadily higher, with no real sign of retreat. In 1960, fewer than 5 percent of births were to single women. In 2011, that number stood around 41 percent. For certain minority groups, such as those in the neighborhoods studied by Edin and Kefalas, the number was nearly double even that: 72 percent and 53 percent for blacks and Hispanics, respectively.[6] In spite of our society's undertaking grand efforts and investing vast resources in a quest to reduce the cycles of destitution and poverty, *especially those linked with illegitimacy and broken families*, we have consistently been "losing ground" in dealing with this problem, as was pointed out as early as the mid-1980s in a book of the same title by Charles Murray.[7] Anyone who cares about human flourishing cannot but be disturbed by this trend, because single mothers and their dependent children are highly likely to be in poverty.[8] Note that the contraceptive revolution, culminating in *Griswold v. Connecticut*[9] and *Roe v. Wade*,[10] far from reducing the most vulnerable pregnancies, actually ushered in the largest increase in nonmarital births ever recorded in Western society.

So, even though nonmarital births have been increasing for forty years, it is interesting that until Edin and Kefalas nobody thought about living with the poor women who are actually having these nonmarital births. When these researchers did that, they discovered that the standard stories are wrong.

---

6   Child Trends Databank, "Births to Unmarried Women," 2014, *http://www .childtrends.org/?indicators=births-to-unmarried-women#_edn1*.

7   Charles Murray, *Losing Ground: American Social Policy, 1950-1980* (New York: Basic Books, 1984).

8   Lawrence L. Wu and Miodrag Stojnic, "Poverty among the Poorest-Poor in the United States: Trends for Never-Married Women and Their Children," paper presented at the Inaugural Conference, Center for Research on Inequalities and the Life Course (Yale University, 2007).

9   Griswold v. Connecticut, 381 US 479 (1965).

10   Roe v. Wade, 410 US 113 (1973).

Single motherhood among poor women, they found, springs not from a lack of resources or reproductive control. Rather, the women they lived with desperately wanted children. These women also wanted to get married, but, as Edin and Kefalas characterize it, "marriage was a dream that most still longed for, a luxury they hoped to indulge in someday when the time was right, but generally not something they saw happening in the near or foreseeable future."[11] In short, these women reasoned that, "If I can't have marriage, then I'll have a baby—because that places me in a relationship which can have the character of unconditional love, reciprocation, and permanence." The women were not seeking single motherhood as their ideal, and certainly not as a life-fulfilling free choice; rather, poor women were settling for single motherhood as a second-best in the face of heartbreaking constraints and grim realities.

Now suppose the world changes from one in which most babies are born to mothers in what the moms themselves regard as a best situation, to one in which babies are increasingly born to mothers in what they regard as a worse arrangement: In that case, one would precisely expect female happiness to trend downward. Could single motherhood, then, be that "aggregate change affecting women more than men" that accounts for the "Paradox of Declining Women's Happiness"? Yes, but only in part, because a similar story can be told about the other areas of women's lives: age at marriage, cohabitation and family formation, divorce, sub-replacement fertility, and complex work-family arrangements. In each case, women have moved into circumstances that their earlier counterparts would have regarded as second-best, preferable only out of necessity.

Later marriage, cohabitation, and divorce characterize American relationship patterns. The median age at first mar-

---

11   Kathryn Edin and Maria Kefalas, *Promises I Can Keep*, 6.

riage is 29 for men and 26.5 for women.[12] In 2003, 4.7 percent of the U.S. adult population lived in nonmarital cohabiting relationships and 10.2 percent of the U.S. adult population was divorced at the time.[13] For women in their twenties, nearly 40 percent of those who had a baby between 2000 and 2005 within a cohabiting relationship were separated from their partner by the time the child was five—triple the separation rate for women who were married when they had a child.[14] Fertility has declined to sub-replacement levels across the West, and increasingly this pattern is emerging in the rest of the world. In 2012, the total fertility rate in the United States was 1.88; in the European Union it was 1.58.[15] The past century has witnessed steadily increasing numbers of women in the workforce who have young children. In 1975, the labor force participation rate for women with children under six years of age was 39 percent; in 2012, the rate was 64.8 percent.[16]

So the "Paradox of Declining Female Happiness" turns out to be not much of a paradox. Instead, it is a tragic story about women, and men too, failing to flourish while living in one of the most prosperous nations on earth. Sadly, these

---

12   Kay Hymowitz, Jason S. Carroll, W. Bradford Wilcox, and Kelleen Kaye, *Knot Yet: The Benefits and Costs of Delayed Marriage in America* (The National Marriage Project at the University of Virginia, The National Campaign to Prevent Teen and Unplanned Pregnancy, and The Relate Institute, 2013).

13   Betsey Stevenson and Justin Wolfers, "Declining Female Happiness."

14   Kay Hymowitz et al., *Knot Yet*.

15   Joyce A. Martin, Brady E. Hamilton, Michelle J.K. Osterman, Sally C. Curtin, and T.J. Matthews, "Births: Final Data for 2012," *National Vital Statistics Reports* 62, no. 9 (Hyattsville, MD: National Center for Health Statistics, 2013), *http://www.cdc.gov/nchs/data/nvsr/nvsr62/nvsr62_09.pdf*; and European Commission, Fertility Statistics, "Total Fertility Rate," Eurostat, *http://ec.europa.eu/eurostat/statistics-explained/index.php/Fertility_statistics*.

16   U.S. Bureau of Labor Statistics, U.S. Department of Labor, *Women in the Labor Force: A Databook*, Report 1034, December 2011, *http://www.bls.gov/cps/wlf-databook-2011.pdf*; and Bureau of Labor Statistics, U.S. Department of Labor, "Happy Mother's Day from BLS: Working Mothers in 2012," *TED: The Economics Daily*, May 10, 2013, *http://www.bls.gov/opub/ted/2013/ted_20130510.htm*.

trends are even more pronounced in European nations and are spreading elsewhere in the world with astonishing speed. When, in 1931, Pope Pius XI first introduced the notion of the "social question," he did so in response to the increasing division of society "more and more into two classes," a smaller group enjoying the benefits of economic development and a larger group marked by "wretched poverty."[17] Today we can say that the social question presents itself anew, characterized by the stark divide between a small group who enjoy the blessings of marriage and family stability, and a much larger group experiencing unprecedented familial breakdown, massive retreat from institutional marriage, and cycles of poverty that are interconnected with family structure. A growing body of demographic and sociological evidence points to the fact that the real fault lines in Western society are familial fault lines—with differences in family formation and stability informing both economic realities and political ideologies.

How should we respond? What should we do? In what follows, I outline three proposals for consideration in the present context, which I offer not so much as policy solutions but rather as ideas and principles that, I hope, can serve as seeds for fruitful discussion and dialogue.

Close Collaboration between the Church and Competent Social Scientists

It has been quipped that, "while the individual man is an insoluble puzzle, in the aggregate he becomes a mathematical certainty."[18] This sober truth puts a social scientist in a privileged position, as sound social research uncovers common patterns that point the way to seeming *laws* of human

---

17   Pope Pius XI, encyclical *Quadragesimo Anno* (On Reconstruction of the Social Order) (1931), 2, 3, *http://www.vatican.va/holy_father/pius_xi/encyclicals/documents/hf_p-xi_enc_19310515_quadragesimo-anno_en.html*.

18   As Sherlock Holmes says, citing nineteenth-century British philosopher Winwood Reade.

flourishing. Despite all the limits of quantitative study, these laws can help to describe a pattern of human flourishing that proves to be highly consistent with the Christian vision of the family and society. We can interpret these patterns or laws as clarifying aspects of the natural law of persons in just the same way that natural science identifies patterns that characterize the natural laws of the created universe.

By classical definition, "the natural law is nothing else than the rational creature's participation of the eternal law," which is "the very Idea of the government of things in God."[19] That is to say, most basically the natural law is the ordering of things. It is *the way things are*, including what they are meant to be, and, accordingly, we can think of the natural law of persons as *the way people are*, which includes how they are meant to be. But how can we learn about the way people are in this sense? Obviously, philosophical and theological disciplines contribute to the metaphysical understanding of persons. Novels, plays, and great literature generally constitute a vast stock of informal understanding of who we are, and what the human condition is like. But social research also has its own contribution, albeit a modest one. The social sciences, since they are empirical, inform us about human nature in the manner of providing a certain confirmation of the order that we discern intuitively and from those other sources mentioned. After all, methods of statistical inference tell us what *tends to be true* about a population, and a tendency admits of being interpreted as the manifestation of a *telos*. For example, if we find that certain feelings, desires, or behaviors are statistically associated with positive or negative outcomes, we can take this finding to reflect certain truths about us as creatures. These interpretations are of course delicate, and they must be un-

---

19   Saint Thomas Aquinas, *Summa Theologica*: 2nd and rev. ed., trans. Fathers of the English Dominican Province (online edition, 2008), Q. 91, Art. 2, Art. 1, *http://www.newadvent.org/summa/1020.htm*.

dertaken with great care by persons who have a secure and thorough understanding of statistical models, as well as a sound formation in philosophical and theological premises about man.

Confident as we are that the truth is united, we can expect the proper exercise of social research to provide valuable insights into the nature of man. The philosophical and theological disciplines tell us that the final end of man is God: Social science has no role to play there. Yet there are *intermediate ends* involving what man should do and be in this life. An example of these would be what people refer to as vocations—for example, the vocation to be a man or to be a woman, to be a father or a mother. While we progress toward richer notions of these vocations, especially the vocations of male and female persons, we can be aided especially by the insights of natural and social science. This "listening" to the natural law of persons can assist in the development of the greater theological project: What is the masculine genius? What is the feminine genius? Are men and women flourishing today? To which aspects of social reality should the Church be most attentive in her pastoral care? Social science plays a necessary role here.

This leads immediately to my first proposal for consideration: that competent social scientists and theologians collaborate more closely with one another in this project of discerning the nature of persons and developing a keen sense of *what people are*. Despite popular myths to the contrary, the Church has been a great friend of science for many centuries. Popes of the modern era, too, have collaborated closely with scientists—notably Pope Pius XI, who founded the Pontifical Academy of Sciences; Pope John XXIII; and Pope Saint John Paul II, whose study of psychology had a tremendous influence on his philosophy of love and Christian marriage. What holds of science generally should hold of the social sciences too: The findings of modern social scientists can enrich and expand the sense in which the Church is an "expert in humanity."[20]

Observe that the genius of woman is especially well-suited to this work of integration between the human sciences and the mind of the Church. While males are more commonly suited for specialization, women, particularly by virtue of their vocation to be all things for a young child, are often especially gifted at this unifying task. Women trained in social science, philosophy, and theology might consider the value of this type of service to the Church, and, at the same time, the Church stands to gain much by seeking such counsel from those who possess such sound judgment.

Educational Guidelines Suitable for Vocations in Nature and Grace

Here I want to emphasize that the Church's teaching on education is an indispensable though neglected basis of its social doctrine, which needs particular attention today.

In his 1929 letter *Divini Illius Magistri,* Pope Pius XI writes, "Education consists essentially in preparing man for what he must be and for what he must do here below, in order to attain the sublime end for which he was created."[21] Pope Blessed Paul VI speaks to this point even more explicitly in *Gravissimum Educationis,* the Declaration on Christian Education, which came out of the Second Vatican Council, "Let them [teachers] work as partners with parents and together with them in every phase of education give due consideration

---

20 Congregation for the Doctrine of the Faith, *Letter to the Bishops of the Catholic Church on the Collaboration of Men and Women in the Church and in the World* (2004) 1, *http://www.vatican.va/roman_curia/congregations/cfaith/documents/rc_con_cfaith_doc_20040731_collaboration_en.html.*

21 Pope Pius XI, Encyclical *Divini Illius Magistri* (On Christian Education) (1929), 7, *http://w2.vatican.va/content/pius-xi/en/encyclicals/documents/hf_p-xi_enc_31121929_divini-illius-magistri.html.*

to the difference of sex and the proper ends Divine Providence assigns to each sex in the family and in society."[22]

We have observed above that society is experiencing widespread gender confusion, unprecedented familial break-down, a massive retreat from institutional marriage, and cycles of poverty that are radically linked to family structure. In light of these realities, the Church's social doctrine on education, I maintain, deserves to be revisited. The reason is that state-sponsored educational programs in the West simply *do not aim* to educate men and women for their proper vocations in this life; actually, they do not aim to educate children for their ultimate end in any sense.

The vast majority of schoolchildren are educated by the state: about 90 percent in the United States and 82 percent across the countries represented in the Organization for Economic Co-operation and Development.[23] Coeducational schools are the norm, and 60 percent of very young children experience some form of nonparental care before age five.[24] We are complacent about this and usually fail to see it as a difficulty. But we should be worried that such a state of affairs is exactly what has historically been aimed at by enemies of the Church—understandably so, since the swiftest and surest way to remake society is through education. For example, Karl Marx and Frederick Engels wanted to eradicate gender difference, and they understood that education would be the

---

22 Second Vatican Council, *Gravissimum Educationis* (Declaration on Christian Education) (1965), 8, *http://www.vatican.va/archive/hist_councils/ ii_vatican_council/documents/vat-ii_decl_19651028_gravissimum-educationis_ en.html.*

23 OECD, *Public and Private Schools: How Management and Funding Relate to their Socio-economic Profile* (OECD Publishing, 2012), *http://dx.doi. org/10.1787/9789264175006-en.*

24 Gail M. Mulligan, DeeAnn Brimhall, Jerry West, and Christopher Chapman, *Child Care and Early Education Arrangements of Infants, Toddlers, and Preschoolers: 2001,* U.S. Department of Education, National Center for Education Statistics 2006-039 (Washington, DC: U.S. Government Printing Office, 2001), *http://nces.ed.gov/pubs2006/2006039.pdf.*

key to achieving this. The 1847 Communist Confession of Faith states this clearly: Q: *"How will you [guarantee the subsistence of the proletariat]?"* A: "By educating all children at the expense of the state." Q: *"How will you arrange this kind of education during the period of transition?"* A: "All children will be educated in state establishments from the time when they can do without the first maternal care."[25] When in a later document the question is raised as to how communism will revolutionize the family, the answer given is nothing short of astounding:

> A: It will transform the relations between the sexes into a purely private matter which concerns only the persons involved and into which society has no occasion to intervene. It can do this since it does away with private property and educates children on a communal basis, and in this way it removes the two bases of traditional marriage—the dependence rooted in private property, of the woman on the man, and of the children on the parents.[26]

Thus, for the early communists, state education was a key to eliminating gender difference, as well as a strategic tool for the destruction of the family.

Despite the decline of communism as an intellectual and political force, is it perhaps the case that practices in government-sponsored schools have a similar direction and tendency? Recall that all right ordering of society rests upon what happens with the family, which in turn depends upon the relation between the sexes. One might view education just as that mission field in which we prepare young people for their

---

25 Karl Marx and Frederick Engels, "A Communist Confession of Faith" (1847), *Marx/Engels Selected Works* 1 (Moscow: Progress Publishers, 1969), 98-137.

26 Karl Marx and Frederick Engels, "The Principles of Communism" (1914), *Marx/Engels Selected Works* 1 (Moscow: Progress Publishers, 1969), 81-97. Marriage and family law, both in the United States and abroad, has uncannily arrived at a similar conception of the family by a different route.

various natural and supernatural vocations, and, most fundamentally, for marriage and the procreation and education of offspring. Arguably, technical education and even a classical, liberal education are of little worth if a young person is unable to be a good husband or wife, father or mother. Therefore, getting education right with respect to the ends of man in nature and grace is the first task of any society.

These considerations lead to an interesting possibility. It has long been thought that *Rerum Novarum*,[27] written in 1891, marked the beginning of the formal tradition of Catholic social doctrine, as well as the most devastating response to Marx and Engels. Yet a better and more fundamental starting point for Catholic social doctrine is arguably Pope Leo XIII's earlier work on the family and education.

In *Quod Apostolici Muneris*,[28] written in 1878, Pope Leo XIII criticizes socialism precisely for its destructive impact on the family. He begins, "[The socialists] debase the natural union of man and woman, which is held sacred even among barbarous peoples; and its bond, by which the family is chiefly held together, they weaken, or even deliver up to lust."[29] And he continues:

> For you know, venerable brethren, that the foundation of this society rests first of all in the indissoluble union of man and wife according to the necessity of natural law, and is completed in the mutual rights and duties of parents and children, masters and servants. You know also that the doctrines of socialism strive almost completely to dissolve this union; since, that stability which

---

27 Pope Leo XIII, encyclical *Rerum Novarum* (On Capital and Labor) (1891), *http://w2.vatican.va/content/leo-xiii/en/encyclicals/documents/hf_l-xiii_enc_15051891_rerum-novarum.html.*

28 Pope Leo XIII, encyclical *Quod Apostolici Muneris* (On Socialism) (1878), *http://www.vatican.va/holy_father/leo_xiii/encyclicals/documents/hf_l- x i i i _ enc_28121878_quod-apostolici-muneris_en.html.*

29 Ibid., 1.

is imparted to it by religious wedlock being lost, it follows that the power of the father over his own children, and the duties of the children toward their parents, must be greatly weakened. But the Church, on the contrary, teaches that "marriage, honorable in all"...which God himself instituted in the very beginning of the world, and made indissoluble for the propagation and preservation of the human species, has become still more binding and more holy through Christ, who raised it to the dignity of a sacrament, and chose to use it as the figure of His own union with the Church.[30]

Two years later in *Arcanum Divinae Sapientiae* (1880),[31] Pope Leo XIII taught with even greater insistence:

Can anyone, therefore, doubt that laws in favor of divorce would have a result equally baneful and calamitous were they to be passed in these our days? There exists not, indeed, in the projects and enactments of men any power to change the character and tendency [which] things have received from nature. Those men, therefore, show but little wisdom in the idea they have formed of the well-being of the commonwealth who think that the inherent character of marriage can be perverted with impunity; and who, disregarding the sanctity of religion and of the sacrament, seem to wish to degrade and dishonor marriage more basely than was done even by heathen laws. Indeed, if they do not change their views, not only private families, but all public society, will have unceasing cause to fear lest they should be miserably driven into that general confusion and overthrow of order which is even now the

---

30   Ibid., 8 (citation omitted).

31   Pope Leo XIII, encyclical *Arcanum Divinae Sapientiae* (On Christian Marriage) (1880), http://www.vatican.va/holy_father/leo_xiii/encyclicals/documents/hf_l-xiii_enc_10021880_arcanum_en.html.

wicked aim of socialists and communists. Thus we see most clearly how foolish and senseless it is to expect any public good from divorce, when, on the contrary, it tends to the certain destruction of society.[32]

And again in 1885, as if to provide the binding tie between *Arcanum* and *Rerum*, Pope Leo XIII produced *Spectata Fides*,[33] an encyclical letter devoted to Christian education, stating:

> For it is in and by these schools that the Catholic faith, our greatest and best inheritance, is preserved whole and entire. In these schools the liberty of parents is respected; and, what is most needed, especially in the prevailing license of opinion and of action, it is by these schools that good citizens are brought up for the State; for there is no better citizen than the man who has believed and practiced the Christian faith from his childhood. The beginning and, as it were, the seed of that human perfection which Jesus Christ gave to mankind, are to be found in the Christian education of the young; for the future condition of the State depends upon the early training of its children. The wisdom of our forefathers, and *the very foundations of the State, are ruined by the destructive error of those who would have children brought up without religious education.* You see, therefore Venerable Brethren, with what earnest forethought parents must beware of intrusting their children to schools in which they cannot receive religious teaching.[34]

---

32   Pope Leo XIII, *Arcanum Divinae Sapientiae*, 32.

33   Pope Leo XIII, encyclical *Spectata Fides* (On Christian Education) (1885), *http://www.vatican.va/holy_father/leo_xiii/encyclicals/documents/hf_l-xiii_enc_27111885_spectata-fides_en.html.*

34   Ibid., 4 (emphasis added).

And finally, to complete the arc, in *Rerum Novarum* Pope Leo XIII invokes the family as the very justification for the right to private property: There is a right to private property because property is necessary for family life, and family life is necessary for the state and civil society.

Thus, for Pope Leo XIII, the complete response to the errors of socialism and to the social question more generally was captured in the triad consisting of *Arcanum, Spectata*, and *Rerum*: family, religious education, and sociopolitical justice and charity. Taken together, these documents, along with many others like them, build an argument about the reform of society based upon the following insights: that the family and right relations between the sexes must form the foundation of any good society; that religious education is the indispensable aid to forming children who will be good citizens in this life and the next; and that the structures of political and economic life exist to serve the family and the common good, rightly understood.[35]

We see an insistence on the same triad of insights in the encyclical letters of Pope Pius XI. In fact, a similar arc can be observed in *Casti Connubii* (1930),[36] *Divini Illius Magistri* (1929),[37] and *Quadragesimo Anno* (1931).[38] Because Catholic social doctrine always supplies an integral response to the various social questions, the Church's teachings on the fam-

---

35 The second point, that good Christians make good citizens, is a point that Pope Leo XIII frequently made, and Pope Pius XI after him. See, for example, Pope Leo XIII, encyclical *Quod Multum* (On the Liberty of the Church) (1886), 4: "Nevertheless to restrain the danger of socialism there is only one genuinely effective means, in the absence of which the fear of punishment has little weight to discourage offenders. It is that citizens should be thoroughly educated in religion, and restrained by respect for and love of the Church." See *http://www. vatican.va/holy_father/leo_xiii/encyclicals/documents/hf_l-xiii_enc_22081886_ quod-multum_en.html*.

36 Pope Pius XI, encyclical *Casti Connubii* (On Christian Marriage) (1930), *http://www.vatican.va/holy_father/pius_xi/encyclicals/documents/hf_p-xi_ enc_31121930_casti-connubii_en.html*.

37 Pope Pius XI, *Divini Illius Magistri*.

38 Pope Pius XI, *Quadragesimo Anno*.

ily and education are no less social in this sense than are its teachings on civil society, politics, and economics. Thus, from this vantage point, although *Rerum Novarum* has called forth many important encyclicals on its major anniversaries, and the teachings of *Arcanum Divinae Sapientiae* and *Casti Connubii* have been affirmed and reaffirmed (as, for example, in *Familiaris Consortio*[39] and *Humanae Vitae*),[40] it would seem that the Church's teaching on education—*Spectata Fides, Divini Illius Magistri,* and *Gravissimum Educationis*—cries out for renewed pastoral attention, given the real and painful afflictions of contemporary human life. Even in Christian nations—perhaps especially in Christian nations—people have not been prepared well "for what [they] must be and for what [they] must do here below."[41] The social crisis is a crisis of education.

A close reading of these documents reveals, among other things, two fundamental points that should be stressed anew and reevaluated in light of present circumstances. The first is the clear and consistent teaching that true education is religious education. This includes the related insights that all the teachers, not simply teachers of religious subjects, should be imbued with Christian spirit; that Christian children should be educated in Christian schools, not just offered supplemental religious education outside of school time; and that so-called neutral schools are not neutral.

Looking to the American public school system, at least, in which the vast majority of American Catholics are currently educated, we must conclude that there is very little correspon-

---

39 Pope John Paul II, apostolic exhortation *Familiaris Consortio* (On the Role of the Christian Family in the Modern World) (1981), *http://www. vatican.va/holy_father/john_paul_ii/apost_exhortations/documents/hf_jp-ii_ exh_19811122_familiaris-consortio_en.html.*

40 Pope Paul VI, encyclical *Humanae Vitae* (On the Regulation of Birth) (1968), *http://www.vatican.va/holy_father/paul_vi/encyclicals/documents/hf_p-vi_enc_25071968_humanae-vitae_en.html.*

41 Pope Pius XI, *Divini Illius Magistri,* 7.

dence between these ideals and practiced reality. Can it be surprising, then, that the social trends are so discouraging? One is reminded of Pope Pius XI's prophetic warning in *Mit Brennender Sorge* (1937): "The Church cannot wait to deplore the devastation of its altars, the destruction of its temples, if an education, hostile to Christ, is to profane the temple of the child's soul consecrated by baptism, and extinguish the eternal light of the faith in Christ for the sake of counterfeit light alien to the Cross."[42]

A second point that emerges from these earlier teachings is a stress on education suitable for separate vocations. Historically this took the form of so-called single-sex education. I quote Pope Pius XI here from *Divini Illius Magistri*:

> False also and harmful to Christian education is the so-called method of "coeducation." This too, by many of its supporters, is founded upon naturalism and the denial of original sin; but by all, upon a deplorable confusion of ideas that mistakes a leveling promiscuity and equality, for the legitimate association of the sexes. The Creator has ordained and disposed perfect union of the sexes only in matrimony, and, with varying degrees of contact, in the family and in society. Besides there is not in nature itself, which fashions the two quite different in organism, in temperament, in abilities, anything to suggest that there can be or ought to be promiscuity, and much less equality, in the training of the two sexes. These, in keeping with the wonderful designs of the Creator, are destined to complement each other in the family and in society, precisely because of their differences, which therefore ought to be maintained and encouraged during their years of formation, with the necessary distinction and corresponding separation,

42   Pope Pius XI, encyclical *Mit Brennender Sorge* (On the Church and the German Reich) (1937), 39, *http://www.vatican.va/holy_father/pius_xi/encyclicals/documents/hf_p-xi_enc_14031937_mit-brennender-sorge_en.html.*

according to age and circumstances. These principles, with due regard to time and place, must, in accordance with Christian prudence, be applied to all schools, particularly in the most delicate and decisive period of formation, that, namely, of adolescence. (68)

Of course, in the past the strong commitment of the Church to single-sex education was complemented by the heavy involvement of religious orders in the instruction of youth. Whether the Church should still uphold single-sex education as the ideal and norm is perhaps debatable. But at minimum, schools and parents should pursue all legitimate avenues for creating and sustaining formative programs specific to each sex, such as single-sex classrooms within a coeducational school; after-school clubs and recreational activities aimed at single sexes; and renewed support for the teaching orders—for example, Dominicans, Sisters of Charity, Jesuits.

Women, with their special responsibility to nurture, should play a pivotal role in helping to shape these new guidelines—not only women religious, with their long history of educating women, but also laywomen who are involved in educational initiatives at all levels of education from early childhood to higher education.

Social Work Carried Out in Radical Relationships of Love and Dependency (or Rejecting the Bureaucratic Model in Favor of the Motherly Model)

My third proposal builds on the groundbreaking new findings by leading American economist Raj Chetty.[43] In a massive project utilizing decades of data, Chetty and his team uncovered the strongest evidence to date that the family is critical to economic mobility. They report, notably:

---

43   Raj Chetty, Nathaniel Hendren, Patrick Kline, and Emmanuel Saez, "Where Is the Land of Opportunity? The Geography of Intergenerational Mobility in the United States," *National Bureau of Economic Research Working Paper No. 19843* (January 2014), *http://www.nber.org/papers/w19843.*

The strongest predictors of upward mobility are measures of family structure such as the fraction of single parents in the area. As with race, parents' marital status does not matter purely through its effects at the individual level. Children of married parents also have higher rates of upward mobility if they live in communities with fewer single parents.[44]

Chetty's findings confirm my claim in the last section that the Church's teaching on family and education is just as much a part of its "social" doctrine as are the economic encyclicals. But the findings also suggest that policy and welfare programs are not the *primary* way to address the social problem. Rather, we can generalize from Chetty's findings and say that cycles of poverty are broken mainly through relationships of love and constructive dependency. What is most needed in response to the human desolation and suffering described in the first section is achieved mainly through old-fashioned pastoral work—*heal families, teach the young, and convert all people.*

Women have an essential role to play in such pastoral work, because the necessary task of nurturing depends on a maternal model of care, as Pope Saint John Paul II taught in his apostolic letter *Mulieris Dignitatem*:

> The moral and spiritual strength of a woman is joined to her awareness that *God entrusts the human being to her in a special way.* Of course, God entrusts every human being to each and every other human being. But this entrusting concerns women in a special way—precisely by reason of their femininity—and this in a particular way determines their vocation....
>
> A *woman is strong because of her awareness of this entrusting,* strong because of the fact that God "entrusts the human being to her," always and in every way, even

---

44 Ibid., 4.

in the situations of social discrimination in which she may find herself. This awareness and this fundamental vocation speak to women of the dignity which they receive from God himself, and this makes them "strong" and strengthens their vocation.[45]

While this reflection may be taken to mean that women in particular are called to a special posture with respect to all other persons, it should also be taken to mean that the Church *as mother* has a vocation to seek the good of persons in a maternal way—in reciprocal relationships of *love and dependency*. This implies essentially rethinking the professional model of care that has become dominant in the era of the decline in religious orders. The professional model involves caring for the poor and vulnerable through bureaus and agencies, with paid employees, contractual arrangements, and arms-length transactions where the essential goal is to provide a good, a service, or other consumables. But such arrangements on their own often aid without healing and feed without nourishing.

In short, my third proposal calls for a careful examination of how the care work of the Church can become more fully "feminine." In reality, the model provided by religious communities—for example, the Missionaries of Charity—is the model *par excellence* of healing and forming through relationship and solidarity. Various steps to the Church's becoming more feminine in this way might include: the revival and renewal of third orders, which at their origin were predominantly female and oriented toward works of charity; the revival, which I have already mentioned, and which is already occurring, of teaching orders; the reestablishment and

---

45   Pope John Paul II, apostolic letter *Mulieris Dignitatem* (On the Dignity and Vocation of Women) (1988), 30, *http://www.vatican.va/holy_father/john_paul_ii/apost_letters/documents/hf_jp-ii_apl_15081988_mulieris-dignitatem_en.html*.

renewal of nursing sisters; and the renewed practice of widows entering religious communities. There are many other possibilities here that should be eagerly explored.

This "feminine" approach has been close to the heart of recent pontiffs. One might say that the main task of the second (and ignored) part of *Deus Caritas Est*,[46] a joint effort of Pope Saint John Paul II and Pope Benedict XVI, was to put forward precisely this kind of vision of social charity. And, of course, it is close to the heart of *Evangelii Gaudium*.[47]

Conclusion

My proposals have concerned the role of women in the implementation of Catholic social doctrine in order to address "the social question" in the distinctive form it takes today. I have argued that social scientists who are women are especially suited to play the needed integrative role of illuminating Catholic social doctrine by reference to social science research, and illuminating that research by reference to social doctrine. I have argued that women, in view of their concern for the vocation of the person to marriage and procreation, have a special role in restoring a correct understanding of education and a sound appreciation for the vital importance of Catholic education. And I have argued that, in adopting the "feminine" posture to social relief necessary in present circumstances, the Church can be aided by both the historic and contemporary insights of women, who have a special vocation to nurturing and healing.

---

46   Pope Benedict XVI, encyclical *Deus Caritas Est* (On Christian Love) (2005), *http://www.vatican.va/holy_father/benedict_xvi/encyclicals/documents/ hf_ben-xvi_enc_20051225_deus-caritas-est_en.html*.

47   Pope Francis, apostolic exhortation *Evangelii Gaudium* (On the Proclamation of the Gospel in Today's World) (2013), *http://w2.vatican.va/content/ francesco/en/apost_exhortations/documents/papa-francesco_esortazione-ap_20131124_evangelii-gaudium.html*.

Catherine Ruth Pakaluk, PhD (economics), is an assistant professor of economics at Ave Maria University in Florida. She is also a faculty research fellow at the Stein Center for Social Research at Ave Maria, where her research interests focus on applied microeconomics, gender, family, and reproductive dynamics, as well as the economics of education and religion. She speaks and writes frequently on topics related to women, feminism, education, and families. Dr. Pakaluk and her husband live in Florida with seven children.

CHAPTER NINE

Engaging Women

Finding a New Translation for Catholic Sexual Teaching

Erika Bachiochi, JD

In order to speak to the Church about women, or to women about the Church, we have to start with the Church's beleaguered sexual teachings.[1] To the world, it is these teachings, alongside the reservation of the priesthood for men, that bespeak a deep-seated misogyny, that tell the world the Church is not a home for self-respecting women or women-loving men.

Faithful Catholic women (and men) see these teachings quite differently.[2] It is *these teachings* that attest to the Church's love and deep respect for women, for our relationships, our children, and, yes, for sex. It is *these teachings* that offer both healing succor to those women and men broken by the ways of the world and an integrated view of human flourishing, of authentic happiness. And it is *these teachings*—on monogamy, divorce, birth control, abortion, and infanticide—that, in the Church's infancy, first drew pagan women into the

---

1   References to "we" in this paper refer most especially to lay Catholic scholars, apologists, and advocates, but also, as appropriate, to the magisterium—that is, the "we" is the Church in its fullness, in its hierarchical and lay dimensions.

2   See, for instance, Erika Bachiochi, ed., *Women, Sex, and the Church: A Case for Catholic Teaching* (Boston: Pauline Books & Media, 2010), and Helen M. Alvaré, ed., *Breaking Through: Catholic Women Speak for Themselves* (Huntington, IN: Our Sunday Visitor, 2012).

Christian fold.[3] It is no wonder then that it is on these sensitive matters, these "women's issues," that the daughters of the Church and the women of the world spar most passionately.

Part of our current trouble in making inroads into the culture with the Church's extraordinarily liberating pro-woman message is our inability to *translate* it adequately for the modern world. [4] (And Pope Francis does seem to think the trouble is primarily with us, Christ's disciples, and not with the lost sheep who no longer heed the Christian message.[5]) Pope Saint John Paul II single-handedly made such a strong theological case for the sexual teachings in his writings that those Catholics listening, studying, and conforming their lives to Jesus Christ's, illuminated by that great pope's lights, have been deeply formed in, and persuaded by, the teachings of the faith. To the "JPII Catholic," guided by the light of faith and strengthened by sacramental grace, the Church's sexual teachings seem so right and lifesaving, and so good for marriage, children, men, and women, that there could be no other way.[6]

---

3   Rodney Stark, *The Rise of Christianity: How the Obscure, Marginal Jesus Movement Became the Dominant Religious Force in the Western World in a Few Centuries* (New York: HarperOne, 1997), 95ff.

4   Until recently, lay efforts to articulate a "new feminism" have been largely theoretical, speaking with the theologically rich language of the Church to an audience within the Church whose hearts, minds, and feet are firmly planted herein. This was surely necessary in the days of the movement's infancy, when Catholic thinkers, with Edith Stein, Pope Saint John Paul II, and Prudence Allen as their guides, looked to Scripture, philosophy, and theology to lay the proper foundations for this new feminism. The important and wide-ranging book *Women in Christ* comes to mind: "[O]ur aim is primarily theoretical: the laying of a solid foundation from which there may proceed an intelligent and faith-filled praxis." See Michele M. Schumacher, ed., *Women in Christ: Toward a New Feminism* (Grand Rapids, MI: Wm. B. Eerdmans Publishing Co., 2004), xvi.

5   See Pope Francis, apostolic exhortation *Evangelii Gaudium* (On the Proclamation of the Gospel in Today's World) (2013), *http://w2.vatican.va/content/francesco/en/apost_exhortations/documents/papa-francesco_esortazione-ap_20131124_evangelii-gaudium.html.*

6   Pope Saint John Paul II began the difficult task of re-articulating the Church's sexual teachings for the modern world in his vast and exquisite *Theology of the Body.* The *Theology of the Body,* as well as Pope John Paul II's writings on the

As a result, a vast gulf exists between the well-formed Catholic and the world's sojourner, a sojourner who has been deeply formed, on the other hand, by the secular feminist worldview, whether or not she knows it or would even describe herself as a feminist. Key phrases used by Pope Saint John Paul II, such as "sexual complementarity," "feminine, or nurturing, nature," or "the nuptial meaning of the body" may mean gift and purpose to the well-formed Catholic but represent oppression and confinement to the feminist-minded. Just as in the days of the early Church, members of the same family speak as though foreigners, lacking not only a common moral framework, but also a common language. If we do not find a new translation, a mediating bridge that better articulates Church teaching in a world shaped by feminist views, we will remain forever a booming gong and clashing cymbal, a self-referential Church, the pope says, that thinks itself better than the world, but meanwhile shrivels in its pride, in its inability to love the other enough to go out and find her.[7]

---

person and on women, have provided a rich Catholic and thoroughly modern philosophical critique of widely held secular humanist and feminist ideals, providing a springboard for many other deeply profound works, like those of Sister Prudence Allen, most notably. See Prudence Allen, *The Concept of Woman, Volume I: The Aristotelian Revolution, 750 BC-AD 1250* (Grand Rapids, MI: Wm. B. Eerdmans Publishing Co., 1985), and Prudence Allen, *The Concept of Woman, Volume II: The Early Humanist Reformation, 1250-1500* (Grand Rapids, MI: Wm. B. Eerdmans Publishing Co., 2002). Still, these learned and inspired works do not seem to speak to most of the men and women in the pews each Sunday (if they have even heard of them), and certainly not to the baptized Catholic who has long abandoned the Church because of, for instance, Catholic teaching on birth control. The *Theology of the Body* in its pure form is fit for intellectuals, and in its more accessible form—for example, as taught by American Christopher West—for those who have already assented to the truths of the faith or are on a journey toward deeper conversion to Christ and a life lived as a sign of contradiction in the world.

7   Intervention of then-Cardinal Jorge Bergoglio during pre-conclave General Congregation meetings of the cardinals: "When the Church does not come out of herself to evangelize, she becomes self-referential and then gets sick (cf. the deformed woman of the Gospel). The evils that, over time, happen in ecclesial institutions have their root in self-referentiality and a kind of theological narcissism." See "Bergoglio's Intervention: A Diagnosis of the Problems in

Those of us who are converts or reverts had translators, mediators between the Church and us, who made the Gospel accessible to us, in our own language, seeking to understand and resolve our biases and misconceptions, and making the Gospel attractive all the while. Such a translation happened for me quite literally. I was a pro-choice feminist activist and women's studies student at Middlebury College in Vermont in the 1990s. I had been raised by a mother who would marry and divorce three times, a course of events that sent me quite far from the Church and her sexual teachings during my teenage years. Textbook acting out led to textbook anxiety and depression and then, at sixteen years old, into "new age spirituality" and eventually twelve-step recovery programs. By the time I arrived at college, I was fervently prayerful and, at the same time, fervently anti-religious. A graced series of events led me into a friendship with a Catholic student who had the wisdom to translate Christian language—words such as *sin, grace, redemption, conversion*—into a conceptual framework that was accessible to me, a "socialist feminist" whose life had been saved and whose heart had been captured by a God who was utterly mysterious to me. Since my reversion to Catholicism in 1997 and the intense study that both preceded and followed, I've found myself eager to give satisfactory responses to the questions I first had as an anti-Catholic feminist looking in on Catholicism.

This need for translation is nothing new in the life of the missionary Church. While Peter courted the Jews, Jesus sent Paul to the Gentiles, to become all things to all people (see 1 Cor 9:19-22). Upon confrontation with new cultures, missionaries have always fashioned new ways of speaking to those cultures, prudently and humbly retaining that which advances or does no damage to Gospel teachings, while inspiring conversion of heart away from practices contrary to Gospel truth.

---

the Church," *Vatican Radio*, March 27, 2013, *http://en.radiovaticana.va/storico/2013/03/27/bergoglios_intervention_a_diagnosis_of_the_problems_in_the_church/en1-677269.*

From confrontations of the Gospel with these divergent cultures, questions arise that challenge settled or implicit Church teaching, inspiring the Holy Spirit to guide reformulations that, though entirely consistent with the tradition, give way to new, more accessible and substantive explanations. Indeed, authentic development of doctrine springs forth from Gospel engagement of different or erroneous ideas, diverse practices, and new discoveries. Thanks be to the Nestorians who were the catalyst for the Council of Chalcedon's explication of the God-man; the Manicheans, among others, who inspired Augustine's *City of God*; and the communist materialists whose errors gave us the personalist reformulations of Pope Saint John Paul II.

And so for the last half century, the Church has been inundated with feminist critiques of her sexual teachings. Teachings whose merits heretofore had been assumed were suddenly thrown into question—and with inadequate recourse to traditional formulations.

Surely today we are confronted by a different challenge than the early councils, than the pre-modern saints and Doctors of the Church: We must speak of the most intimate of matters with a world that thinks it has already heard—and rejected—the Church's message, when in truth it has heard and rejected nothing of the sort. Still, that same Holy Spirit wants to work in us today to bring souls to Christ, home to the Church. It is up to well-formed Catholics, and scholars especially, to separate—carefully, charitably, and prayerfully—the wheat from the chaff in feminist thinking in order to better articulate Church teaching to a feminist-minded culture.[8]

In the balance of this chapter, I will offer three guides to this work. I think our success in winning women over

---

8 Those who would want to reject feminism root and branch have a problem not just with feminism and its ill-conceived political and social prescriptions, but with the modern project itself, with modernity's notable elevation of freedom and equality as political and social aspirations.

depends upon our willingness to, first, really listen to those with whom we disagree, to seek to understand their arguments, and to take a real interest in their questions, and in them as persons.[9] Second, we need to speak in a language that is accessible to feminist-minded interlocutors with a narrative that seeks to answer the questions feminism poses. Here I'll discuss four points of entry: the body, the poor, men, and work. Third, we need to confront our own poverty and recognize that this task is much too big for us but is conquerable by Christ.

In sum, to borrow from Pope Francis, we must *accompany* and *inculturate*: accompany those in a culture that has been deeply informed by secular feminist ideals, even as we inculturate that culture with an understanding of how Catholic principles better effectuate it. *We must go into the streets of feminist discourse, unafraid to get dirty, but without getting lost.*

Three Guides to Engaging Women

Guide One: Seek to Understand

In order to advance successfully a new feminist worldview in public life or in scholarship, we have to take the time to listen to our feminist-minded interlocutors, read them, and get to know them. If we are convinced, with Saint Thomas, that human beings seek the good and the true, we can turn to feminist theory and argument and make an effort to identify the good intentions, insights, and authentic advances. In order to love them, we must take them seriously and sympathize with their position the best we can. We must have the confidence to ask humbly what we can learn from our interlocutors. What is it that makes their viewpoint, their writings, so compelling to others? Listening to them can teach

---

9   President Abraham Lincoln: "Do I not destroy my enemies when I make them my friends?" Robert Greene and Jost Elfers, *The 48 Laws of Power* (London: Penguin Books, 2000), 12.

us much—about their presuppositions first and foremost, and about potential areas of agreement. In general, though, of course, there are myriad exceptions, feminist-minded scholars and laypersons tend to care deeply about the sorts of things Catholic women care about: women and children, relationships, and the vulnerable. We just have starkly different ways of addressing these shared concerns.

It's also important to understand and have some sympathy for their view of what the Church teaches. Catholic teachings on sex and marriage are often difficult to swallow because they are difficult to live. Though we may not want to lead with this insight, it's best to be frank, to be honest. Like much that is good in life, the sexual teachings require a practiced self-mastery that takes work, and often much grace.

At first glance, Church teaching also seems to cut sharply against our natural human desires for intimacy, union, and sexual pleasure. If abortion, for instance, really ends the life of a vulnerable and dependent child to whom I owe parental duties—that is, if abortion really ends the life of *my* child—then my ability to show love and affection for my beloved, in the most natural and powerful way through full bodily union in sexual intercourse, is compromised. If abortion is off-limits, I have to change my behavior, my mode of dress, my self-concept, my very life. I can no longer love the other the way my body urges me to love. I must change. We need to really grasp how very radical this is; it's not like switching political parties because I like the other's tax policy better. Sex goes to the very fabric of existence in a profound way.

Finally, it is important for us not to fear acknowledging that the Church has developed in her thinking about women. In point of fact, notable Doctors of the Church wrote about women and sexual matters in a way that sounds, to modern ears, disparaging to women, because they were based, in greater or lesser degrees, on a flawed Aristotelian theory of the sexes that rejected the equality of man and woman.[10] If we are sympathizing with our interlocutors, we can see that it really is not all that unreasonable for them to think that once that old Aristotelian view of women's inferiority was discarded, the sexual teachings (and the restriction on the priesthood) would be too. But we must then be able to articulate for them the insight inspired by noted theologian Sister Sara Butler: Just because dominant strains of the tradition viewed the sexual teachings and women's role in Church and society through the lens of women's presumed inferiority, it does not follow that the sexual teachings were *themselves actually grounded in women's inferiority.*[11] But if the Church does not offer an accessible, pro-woman explanation of her teachings, the Church's consistent reaffirmation of them seems only to belie her claim that she now holds fast to the equal dignity of the sexes. The Church's talk of sexual equality sounds much like empty rhetoric. With all due respect, the Church and the Catholic lay faithful have to do better.

Guide Two: Work toward a New Translation

So what might an accessible, pro-woman explanation look like? Here I will suggest four points of entry: the body, the poor, men, and work.

First Point of Entry: The Body and Sexual Asymmetry

Following the great insight of Pope Saint John Paul II, we must speak to the world about the body, but we have to be careful

---

10   Aristotle based his views on women on an ill-conceived theory of generation that held that the female was a misbegotten or ill-formed male. For an extensive study of the profound influence of Aristotelian views of the sexes in the history of philosophy, see Prudence Allen, *Concept of Woman, Vols. I and II, supra* note 6.

11   See Sister Sara Butler, *The Catholic Priesthood and Women: A Guide to the Teaching of the Church* (Chicago: Hillenbrand Books, 2007). [Editor's note: See also Chapter Two of this book, "Some Thoughts on the Theology of Woman in the Church," in which Sister Sara encourages the Church to address squarely feminist critiques of Church teaching.]

about how we do so if we are to translate successfully *Theology of the Body*–type insights for a feminist-minded audience. Indeed, it is precisely because Catholics take the body so seriously (our embodiedness) that we have an enormous contribution to make to feminist theory and discourse. We have an ability to hold fast to equal sexual dignity very much in the presence of bodily difference—something no other strain of modern feminist thought can do very well.[12]

Developing a full-blown "theology of woman" is a noble aspiration, but it is one that is ultimately unnecessary to translating successfully the sexual teachings for a feminist-minded audience.[13] Indeed, in order to translate effectively, it is best to prescind from questions of *sexual identity* (now usually referred to as "gender") and to speak about the male and female *sex*, about the body.[14] Though *sex* and *gender* can-

---

12 "The crucial factor in [the modern Catholic theory of sexual equality in difference, termed 'complementarity'] is that a woman and man are considered as two separate and complete human individuals who are equal in dignity and worth and who have philosophically significant differences.... [D]ifferences [that] arise from the respective data they appropriate and reject as self-defining individuals...different genetic, hormonal, and anatomical structures, their different experiences of the body, their different cultural or gendered experiences within a particular society. [T]heir similar human capacities for judgment, reflection, choice, and action all form the basis for their equality." Prudence Allen, *The Concept of Woman: Vol. I, supra* note 7.

13 Pope Francis refers to the need to develop a "theology of women" in his *America* interview. See Antonio Spadaro, SJ, "A Big Heart Open to God: The Exclusive Interview with Pope Francis," *America,* September 30, 2013, http:// americamagazine.org/pope-interview. As others have noted throughout this book, a "theology of women" ought to be accompanied by a "theology of men" in order to avoid the historical error of analyzing or contextualizing "woman" only *in relation* to "man." See my further comment, *infra* note 32.

14 The term "gender" was coined in the 1970s and 1980s to distinguish masculine and feminine psychological or social characteristics from simple biological difference ("sex"). The question, for instance, of whether man and woman have masculine and feminine souls, respectively, is far more complex philosophically (and controversial) than the basic biological fact that woman has a female body and man a male body. The ontological, psychological, and/or social *gender* question is complicated further, for the Catholic, by the reality of sin and grace, and of nature and nurture; simple biology prescinds from such complex questions and warrants attention in and of itself. This is not to say that

not be divorced from each other since the body can never, in this life, be divorced from the soul, it is essential that we be free to speak conceptually of the body and the consequences of biological difference, without the complicated overlay of gender theory. That is, we need to sit and appreciate the significance of "sexual difference"—the basic *biological* realities—before we can move on to more theoretical discussions about the "meaning of the body" vis-à-vis God or vis-à-vis societal arrangements.[15] To forge successfully a new feminist translation of our sexual teachings, we need to first disaggregate sex from gender (to use feminist categories), get down to the bare bones, the basic, foundational starting points, and then make careful distinctions that reveal that the Church's teachings are not only more reasonable, based on reality as it is, but also superior for women's flourishing. As Pope Benedict taught us, the Church's defense of reason (of reality) is as important in the postmodern world as her defense of the truths of the faith.

So here is a bare-bones starting point, wholly accessible and agreeable to the feminist-minded and unaffected by personal sin: *biological difference between men and women leads inextricably and necessarily not to rigid social roles or even to distinctive masculine or feminine traits but, more basically, to sexual asymmetry.* This is the phrase evolutionary psychologists use to describe the *fundamental reality that the potential consequences of sexual intercourse are far more immediate and serious for women than they are for men.* Simply put: Women get pregnant, men do not. This basic fact of life is that which

---

the ontological and psychosocial questions of "gender" ought not be studied at all; indeed, they should. But, for the reasons set forth in this section of the paper, it is to say that attention needs to be directed, in an independent way, to the reality of biological difference. The recent movement in the United States and Europe to replace entirely "sex" with "gender" illustrates the trend to devalue basic biological difference, with consequences that are especially troublesome for women.

15   For example, Pope John Paul II liked to analogize the total self-emptying of the nuptial relationship between man and woman to the self-emptying love of the persons of the Trinity, and vice versa.

animates feminism—its raison d'être—though, in the post-modern world, that has largely been forgotten. It is time to do some reminding. As the American feminist Camille Paglia put it, "It's not male society but mother nature who lays the heaviest burden on women."[16]

So how do we talk effectively to the feminist-minded about sexual difference or, better, sexual asymmetry, without walking straight into a minefield? To start, we need to speak about our reproductive differences in a way that does not make an *ought* out of an *is*, that does not make normative—all women should have babies—out of the fact that women's bodies can have babies. For example, making a strong legal or moral argument that a pregnant woman has an affirmative duty of care to bear her unborn child in her womb—because the vulnerable child is biologically dependent upon her (even more so than an infant would be)—is quite different from saying or intimating that women have a *general* duty to bear children, or that because women can bear children they have a nurturing nature, or that a woman's social role must be exclusively determined by the fact that she has children.[17] The language of sexual asymmetry allows us to talk about sexual difference and the disproportionate burden women have in reproduction without drawing ultimate conclusions about women's roles in their families or in society, and without confusing the matter by alluding to the content of women's souls (which "sexual difference" tends to represent in current gender-heavy parlance).

The trouble with much feminist argument is not that it takes issue with biological determinism, or the traditional idea that women's reproductive capacities ought to circumscribe definitively women's roles into those of wife and mother. In fact, it is completely compatible with Catholicism to agree that

16 Camille Paglia, *Sex, Art, and American Culture: Essays* (New York: Vintage, 2011), 89.

17 See Erika Bachiochi, "Embodied Equality: Debunking Equal Protection Arguments for Abortion Rights," *Harvard Journal of Law and Public Policy* 34, no. 3 (Summer 2011).

the view of childrearing that made it exclusively or predominantly "women's work" kept fathers at bay for far too long. Christian fathers are, after all, the most active and engaged of fathers, even more than feminist-minded men.[18]

Rather, the real trouble with the feminist argument is that in rightfully rejecting biological determinism, it too often jettisons the significance of the body altogether, to the great detriment of women. We need to make clear that, by ignoring or denying asymmetrical biological realities, we make it far more likely that social arrangements will end up exacerbating asymmetry. In a word, we ignore sexual asymmetry at women's peril.[19]

Once the fact of sexual asymmetry is acknowledged *simpliciter*, again, without the complicating overlay of gender theories (ours or theirs), it becomes obvious that our great discord about women's issues today has to do precisely with how we respond to this basic fact of human existence.

For second-wave feminists, the response to sexual asymmetry was and continues to be contraception and abortion.[20] These technological incursions into women's bodies have become so "natural" in our society that most fail to discern their underlying purpose: to "equalize" the sexual asymmetry of men and women, such that women, like men, could enjoy sex without having necessarily to succumb to its reproductive consequences. Men's bodies, after all, do not carry the consequences of their fertility within them; contraception and abortion afford women a means to imitate masculine reproductive detachment from childbearing. Sexual asymmetry—

---

18   See W. Bradford Wilcox, *Soft Patriarchs, New Men: How Christianity Shapes Fathers and Husbands* (Chicago: University of Chicago Press, 2004).

19   "If equality depends on 'sameness,' then the recurrence of difference undermines the chances for equality." See Martha Minow, *Making All the Difference: Inclusion, Exclusion, and American Law* (Ithaca, NY: Cornell University Press, 1990), 74.

20   Second-wave feminists departed from the pro-life position of the early American feminist suffragists.

and the feminine vulnerability that accompanies it—would be cured, it was thought, by decoupling sex from procreation, relieving women of the consequences of sex and thus equalizing the sexual experiences of men and women. This is, of course, why equality arguments for abortion rights are so popular: They speak most intuitively to the leading feminist rationale for abortion—equality through imitation. Imitation of whom? Of men, whose bodies are reproductively autonomous.[21]

There is a very different response to sexual asymmetry, one held by pro-life feminists from the nineteenth century on, that puts the onus not on women and women's "different" bodies, but more squarely on men and societal attitudes. And that really is the Catholic or "new feminist" response too.[22] Authentic reproductive justice and sexual equality would require that men (and society at large) respect, protect, and support both women's unique childbearing capacity and the procreative potential of sex that disproportionately impacts women, and is not going away. Women ought not to ape men's bodies; men (and society) ought to respect women's.

How does the feminist response to sexual asymmetry actually exacerbate sexual asymmetry? First, in the really obvious way. Camille Paglia again: "It is absurd to avoid the harsh reality that boys have less to lose from casual sex than do girls, who risk pregnancy and whose future fertility can be compromised by disease."[23] Women are also impacted hormonally and psychologically far more by casual sex—and abortion and

---

21 For more of this sort of argument, see Erika Bachiochi, "Embodied Equality," *supra* note 17. As pro-choice Harvard law professor Laurence Tribe has written, "While men retain the right to sexual and reproductive autonomy, restrictions on abortion deny that autonomy to women." Laurence H. Tribe, *Abortion: The Clash of Absolutes* (New York: W.W. Norton & Co., 1992), 105.

22 While the early American feminists were universally pro-life, and some criticized newly minted contraceptive methods (judging both abortion and contraception to encourage infidelity in husbands), skepticism of Catholicism, and religion in general, abounded.

23 Camille Paglia, "Put the Sex Back in Sex Ed," *Time*, March 13, 2014, *http://time.com/23054/camille-paglia-put-the-sex-back-in-sex-ed/*.

contraception have their own ill effects on women's health as well.[24] Compiling the impact on women of the sexual revolution and revealing the pro-woman Catholic alternative was the very purpose of our book *Women, Sex, and the Church: A Case for Catholic Teaching* (2010).[25]

Sexual economics also shows us that liberal abortion laws and widespread contraception, especially when acting together, first, have weakened women's ability to find men willing to commit to more than limited sexual encounters, and second, have led to increased sexual risk-taking among sexual partners.[26] The important insight sexual economics offers is that the use of contraception, with abortion available as secondary insurance, is not properly viewed as an autonomous choice made by an individual couple, with no effect on others. When promoted and used societywide, these "technological shocks" have altered the so-called mating market, and each male-female sexual relationship within it, by changing the behaviors of the actors.

Poignantly, this change in behavior toward male-oriented, low-commitment sex has had a disproportionately negative effect on women, especially more traditionally minded women who seek childbearing within marriage, but even more profoundly on poor women.[27] For poor women, a reasonably direct line can be drawn from contraceptive sex, with abortion as a backup, to the sharp decline in marriage and the precipitous rise in single motherhood, both associated with the rapid feminiza-

---

24   See Erika Bachiochi, *Women, Sex, and the Church, supra* note 2.

25   Ibid.

26   George A. Akerlof and Janet L. Yellen, "An Analysis of Out-of-Wedlock Births in the United States," *Quarterly Journal of Economics* 111 (1996); Peter Arcidiacono, Ahmed Khwaja, and Lijing Ouyang, "Habit Persistence and Teen Sex: Could Increased Access to Contraception Have Unintended Consequences for Teen Pregnancies?" *Journal of Business and Economic Statistics* 30, no. 2 (2012), 312-325; Phillip B. Levine, *Sex and Consequences: Abortion, Public Policy, and the Economics of Fertility* (Princeton: Princeton University Press, 2004).

27   Erika Bachiochi, *Women, Sexual Asymmetry, and Catholic Teaching.* The Journal of Christian Bioethics (Oxford University Press), *http://cb.oxfordjournals.org/content/19/2/150.abstract.*

tion of poverty.[28] Though social science data is never foolproof, the economics of sex offers a compelling, alternative narrative to a set of data that is not otherwise well explained within the popular libertine view of sex and relationships. And religion has nothing to do with it. (A personal note: This economic narrative made good sense to my nonreligious father, a now-retired inner-city football coach, teacher, and administrator at an alternative school for at-risk teenagers. This narrative—that contraception and abortion have made women more available to noncommitted men, and thus more vulnerable to abandonment by men—was perfectly true to his forty years of experience working with disadvantaged populations.)

Second Point of Entry: The Concern for the Poor and Vulnerable

The second point of entry—the poor—thus follows quite readily from the first. The Western world is enamored with the Church's teachings on the poor, even as it despises her teachings on sex. We must make it clear—and sexual economics may contribute something important to this effort—that the heralded teachings on the poor are bound up tightly with the Church's sexual teachings. Straying from Church teaching on contraception, abortion, sex, and marriage has harmed all women, but it has harmed poor women the most. The kinship between these two sets of teachings, often thought to be at odds, must be better articulated from the very highest levels of the Church, down to our individual scholarship and apostolates.

Critics have claimed that the social teachings of the Church are more philosophically nuanced, complex, and compassionate than the Church's more "rigid" sexual teachings, implying that the Church should not dictate sexual norms to the extent that she does.[29] But absolute principles

---

28 Ibid.

29 See, for instance, Thomas C. Fox, *Sexuality and Catholicism* (New York: George Braziller Inc., 1995), 126.

guide particular judgments in both areas of Church teaching.[30] The Church's social and sexual teachings differ in specificity because each has a different object: The object of social doctrine is the wildly complex political, social, and economic order, and particular judgments in the social order are not the province of the Church; the object of the sexual teachings is, more directly, the human person, about which the Church enjoys special expertise.

Both sets of teachings are built upon the foundation of the dignity of the human person as created by God, practiced through a persistent dying to self and growth in virtue, and necessary to the development and success of civilizations. Catholics are called to care for the materially and spiritually poor by meeting them face-to-face, by recognizing each as a human person, a beloved child of God. By respecting their inherent human dignity and treating them with the justice they deserve, we advance our own moral and spiritual development as well. Such attention to the human person, and to the growth in virtue that it entails, is quite similar to how we are to live out the Catholic sexual ethic. Like the call to authentic charity and justice in the social order, the sexual ethic demands our growth in virtue, because it requires selflessly placing the other ahead of ourselves.

Ultimately, at the center of each set of teachings is concern for the most vulnerable. This is quite explicit in the

---

30   Slavery is the type of act, governed by social teaching, that is always and everywhere wrong (an absolute judgment); whether or not to utilize natural family planning to avoid pregnancy is an act, governed by sexual teaching, that is left to the actors' particular judgment. According to Father Joseph Fessio, SJ: "[Moral] norms themselves are unchanging. However, our approach to obeying them is gradual and our efforts are a mixture of success and failure. This means that while certain moral norms are absolute, that is, they hold in all circumstances without exception, our approach to obeying them may be halting and imperfect. This is commonly referred to as 'the law of gradualism' and is opposed to 'the gradualism of the law,' as if the law itself were somehow variable." See "Guestview: No Good Deed Goes Unpunished," Reuters, May 11, 2010, http://blogs.reuters.com/faithworld/2010/05/11/guestview-no-good-deed-goes-unpunished/.

Church's social teachings. But concern for the vulnerable is properly the starting point for her sexual teachings as well: *The Church must concern herself with sexual morality, because the act of sexual intercourse has the potential to bring into existence a vulnerable, dependent human life who has an eternal destiny.* Women, by design, are the custodians of vulnerable life.[31] When women are abandoned by the men who have assisted in this co-creation of new, vulnerable human life, or by society, which properly protects the lives of the vulnerable above all, women and their children are far more apt to be poor, dependent, and outcast. *The Church must strongly proclaim, then, with humility, mercy, and love, that when she advocates her sexual teachings, she is advocating for the poor and the vulnerable above all.*

Third Point of Entry: Sexual Asymmetry as Gift to Women and Obligation for Men

Though Sister Prudence Allen's theory of integral complementarity provides a rich philosophical foundation for us to think properly about the complementarity of men and women, *sexual asymmetry* may again begin to pave a way to *translate* this reality for the feminist-minded who are repelled by the term *complementarity*.[32]

So once we have acknowledged the disproportionate *burden* that befalls women due to sexual asymmetry—and

---

31 Throughout history, woman has been defined *in relation* to man. Perhaps a more Catholic view (one that takes seriously the dignity of the human person as the centerpiece of Catholic social and sexual teachings) would be to place the vulnerable child at the center of concern and work in concentric circles outward, with woman the more immediate custodian of the child, and man seeking to provide the necessary supports in this key human work. Putting the dependent, vulnerable child at the center would impact how we think about marriage, the family, work, government, and potentially even the Church. Similarly, in his acclaimed work on human virtue, Scottish philosopher Alasdair MacIntyre makes the case for acknowledging embodied vulnerability and dependence as a centerpiece of human existence. Alasdair MacIntyre, *Dependent Rational Animals: Why Human Beings Need the Virtues* (Chicago: Open Court, 1999).

32 See *supra* note 12.

have shown how contraception and abortion have only exacerbated the same—we can then point to the disproportionate *gift* of women's reproductive capacity, that gift of intimate closeness with a new human being. Pope Saint John Paul II taught that this gift, when accepted as such, endows women with the ability to see "the person" more clearly, in all their endeavors, whether working at home or on Wall Street. This feminine genius, borne of self-giving love for the other, has the power, if unleashed, to raise the tenor of a family, a business, and a culture.

But acknowledgment of both the burden and the gift of sexual asymmetry—that is, acknowledging the special relationship and responsibility women have as custodians of the next generation—places very real and corresponding duties upon men, who play their own essential part in reproduction. *Because men's duties are not as deeply inscribed in their bodies, men need cultural (and legal) norms and pressures to call them to their duties, marriage being the most obvious.* In sum, just as nature has both gifted and burdened women with the capacity to bear children, culture ought both to gift and burden men with the duties that come with begetting them.

In the quest to get women out of the home, the feminism of old called upon women to imitate the reproductive autonomy of men's bodies and in so doing sought to push women away from the care of the person; by contrast, the new feminist ethic calls upon men to acknowledge the gift of women's bodies and join women, as partners, in prioritizing the person, first in our families, but also in politics, business, economics, and law. *The complementarity of men and women, then, is less about the interplay of static roles and traits than it is about a respectful regard for the other's gifts and talents, a courageous affirmation of corresponding duties that arise out of sexual asymmetry, and a discernment of how each is called to love and serve amidst his or her particular circumstances in the enterprises of the family and of society.*

Fourth Point of Entry: Pope Saint John Paul II's Teachings on Women and Work

If secular feminists and the Church are furthest from one another on sexual ethics, we may be closest on the issue of work. Indeed, work is an issue on which thinkers from across the spectrum could really join together—especially for the benefit of disadvantaged women. As Elizabeth Schiltz's leading scholarship in this area has shown, both Catholic social teaching, especially as articulated by Pope Saint John Paul II, and relational feminism have come to some similar conclusions about women and work.[33] Thus, in courting women, it would behoove the Church to emphasize Pope Saint John Paul II's revolutionary teachings on work.[34]

First, Pope Saint John Paul II taught that societies ought to find ways to more appropriately value the care work in the family that is disproportionately performed by women. As some relational feminists have argued, children are an essential "public good" (far more essential than many other resources); women's disproportionate care of them creates a "collective or societal debt" toward women: Women take on the costs, but all of society benefits. From an economic perspective, if we do not publicly support the caretaking work of women and the sacrifices of present and future earnings they make to do so, then ours is a system of "free-riders."[35]

For nearly one hundred years, the Church argued for a family wage to justly remunerate both breadwinning hus-

---

33 See "Dueling Vocations: Managing the Tensions Between Our Private and Public Callings," in *Women, Sex, and the Church*, *supra* note 2.

34 See Pope Saint John Paul II, *Laborem Exercens* (1981), 19.

35 See Chapter Six in Erika Bachiochi's *Teaching Guide for Women, Sex, and the Church: Designed for Professors and Students of Law, Feminist Theory, and Sexual and Social Ethics* (Minneapolis: Terrence J. Murphy Institute for Catholic Thought, Law, and Public Policy, 2012), *http://www.stthomas.edu/media/terrencejmurphyinstitute/Teaching_Guide_for_W1.pdf*.

band and caretaking wife.[36] In Western democratic capital-
ist regimes, it's probably more feasible to think about remu-
nerating care work through tax policy, offering a means-
tested tax deduction or credit to those who have children,
regardless of who is doing the caretaking—usually the
mother, but also the father, grandparents, other family
members or friends, or an institutional day-care provider.
Currently, the U.S. tax code, for instance, rewards only the
last option. For many, taking care of their children in their
own home is its own reward, but for working and middle-
class families, the financial stress of one parent at home or
the myriad stresses of two working parents juggling child-
care can often be all-consuming. Society owes much to its
mothers and fathers. In business terms, we need to make
an upfront investment in the physically, emotionally, and
financially demanding work parents do in raising the next
generation.

The second and more daunting piece is the institutional
restructuring of the workplace such that women (and men)
are not penalized professionally for dedicating some portion
of their energies to the care of children and, increasingly, elderly parents. This is important not only for women who continue to take on a disproportionate share of the caretaking,
but also for men, who, generationally speaking, are more and
more eager to be fully engaged fathers on the home front.
George Washington University Professor of Law Michael Selmi suggests that "increasing workplace equality will require
persuading men to behave more like women, rather than trying to induce women to behave more like men. Achieving
this objective would create a new workplace norm where all
employees would be expected to have and spend time with

------

36   From *Rerum Novarum* in 1891 to as recently as 1981 (*Laborem Exercens*),
the Church has sought to prescribe institutional protections for male workers
on whom the economic stability of the family depended through the delivery of
the family wage. See Pope Leo XIII, encyclical *Rerum Novarum* (On Capital and
Labor) (1891), and Pope John Paul II, *Laborem Exercens*.

their children, and employers would adapt to that reality."[37] This attention to the family would not only serve children and marriages well but would also benefit the workplace. It could potentially serve to rewire the world of work such that persons were attended to as a matter of priority, both as the subjects of their work and also, one hopes, in the broader decision-making of an enterprise such that the drive for efficiency and profits would not overtake the more human quest to serve the person above all. More practically, greater flexibility and respect for the demands of the family would undoubtedly translate into decreased rates of burnout, higher morale, and, studies have shown, greater profits over the long run.[38]

Former U.S. ambassador to the Vatican and Harvard Law Professor Mary Ann Glendon offers an important rationale:

> [T]hose who do not want to see any interference with market forces in the form of family policy or labor policy need to think again.... The market, like our democratic experiment, requires a certain kind of citizen, with certain skills and certain virtues...it depends on culture, which in turn depends on nurture and education, which in turn depends on families.
>
> Capitalism...long took...women's roles in nurture and education for granted.... Today we need to attend to social capital, to consider how to replenish it, and to reflect on how to keep from destroying it.... Promoting women's exercise of all their talents, rights, and responsibilities without undermining their roles within the family will require calling not only husbands and fathers to their family responsibilities but also governments and private employers to their social duties.

---

37 Michael Selmi, "Family Leave and the Gender Wage Gap," *North Carolina Law Review* 707 (2000), 775-76.

38 Joan C. Williams, *Reshaping the Work-Life Debate: Why Men and Class Matter* (Cambridge: Harvard University Press, 2010).

That will involve nothing less than a cultural transformation.[39]

Guide Three: Recognize Our Own Poverty

Ultimately, authentic cultural transformation is the fruit of prayer and sacrifice. Bringing the Gospel to women and men deeply informed by an anti-Catholic feminist worldview is surely an enormous task, and the path is only just being cleared. On our own, such travail is impossible. But God stands ready and willing to show us the way, if we but ask. What the Church teaches is good and true for women, men, children, and culture. But this is a knowledge borne of grace and faith. We must go out to the world, with the humility of a daughter of God, confident in the activity of the Holy Spirit, yet always remembering, as our beloved Holy Father has said, we do not possess the truth; the truth has possessed us.

Erika Bachiochi, JD, is an American legal scholar and theologian specializing in U.S. constitutional law and Catholic teaching on sex and women. She is the author of "Women, Sexual Asymmetry and Catholic Teaching," *Journal of Christian Bioethics (Oxford: Oxford University Press, 2013) and* "Embodied Equality: Debunking Equal Protection Arguments for Abortion Rights," *Harvard Journal of Law and Public Policy 34, no. 3 (Summer 2011), and the editor of* Women, Sex, and the Church: A Case for Catholic Teaching *(Boston: Pauline Books and Media, 2010) and* The Cost of "Choice": Women Evaluate the Impact of Abortion *(Jackson, TN: Encounter Books, 2004). Bachiochi and her husband are the parents of six children.*

---

39 Mary Ann Glendon, "Is the Economic Emancipation of Women Today Contrary to a Healthy, Functioning Family?" in *The Family, Civil Society, and the State*, ed. Christopher Wolfe (Lanham, MD: Rowman and Littlefield Publishers, 1998), 93.

CHAPTER TEN

Can Catholic Women *Lean In?*

Working Women in the Church

Mary Hallan FioRito, JD

Although she had been a rising star in the tech field for years, Facebook chief operating officer Sheryl Sandberg[1] became a household name when her book rose to number one on *The New York Times'* bestseller list last year. *Lean In: Women, Work and the Will to Lead* quickly became a must-read manifesto for any twenty- or thirtysomething woman who struggles—with or without husband and family—to be taken seriously, and succeed, in her chosen profession. Her book struck a chord with many women, because Sandberg clearly named and explained the various institutional and societal prejudices, structures, and expectations that—despite almost fifty years of struggle for women's equality in the United States—still prevent many women from fully using their talents in the workplace or from remaining in the workplace once they have families.

Sandberg is quick to point out that, while she worked hard in college and had a lot of help along the way, she was able to obtain the position she currently holds at Facebook because of the contributions of so many women who came

---

1   Sheryl Sandberg, ranked ninth on *Forbes'* list of the world's "power women," with a net worth of one billion dollars, is the chief operating officer of social media giant Facebook and the author of *Lean In: Women, Work, and the Will to Lead* (New York: Knopf Publishers, 2013) and *Lean In for Graduates* (New York: Knopf Publishers, 2014), *http://www.forbes.com/profile/sheryl-sandberg/*.

before her, breaking "glass ceilings" along the way. It's likely that any woman in a position of leadership today has benefited from the accomplishments of many other women who went before her, myself included.

I am grateful to both the religious and laywomen who strove to create a climate both inside and outside the Church where there is generally an attitude of respect for the gifts and talents that God has given to women. I was in the first class of young women ever admitted to my Jesuit high school in Chicago, Saint Ignatius College Prep. While my daughters are often horrified to learn that, during that first year, there was only one girls' bathroom for all ninety-three of us, what I most remember from those days were the strong expectations for me and my female classmates to succeed academically and to go on to a profession where we, as "women for others," would make a difference in the world.

Much to my surprise, especially given the amount of publicity the book received and its spawning of "Lean In" groups at workplaces around the globe, it seemed to me that *Lean In* actually had very few original ideas to add to the conversation about feminism and the challenges faced by women who work outside the home. What Sandberg did offer—for example, that women and men are, well, *different*, and that men were just as important to child-rearing and family harmony as women—was vaguely reminiscent to me of what the Catholic Church has been saying in documents and in encyclicals for years.

For example, Sandberg bemoans the fact that most women refuse to take the feminist label. She notes, "Currently, only 24% of women in the United States consider themselves feminists."[2] But even since the very beginnings of the feminist movement in the United States, women have been hesitant to identify themselves with it.

The premier issue of the American version of *Marie Claire*, a chic French woman's magazine, contained a story ti-

---

2   Sheryl Sandberg, *Lean In*, 158.

tled the "Feminist Mistake" (an obvious play on Betty Friedan's "Feminine Mystique"). According to a 1994 Gallup poll taken for the magazine, "51% of American women think that the woman's movement hurts relations between the sexes and 57% say feminist leaders do not reflect the views of a majority of American women." *Marie Claire* asked, "Could it be that women believe feminism—with its emphasis on victimization and gender wars—has abandoned them?"[3]

A few years later, a 1999 Gallup/*USA Today* poll showed that two-thirds of American women, and more than four out of five college-educated women, answered "no" when asked if they considered themselves feminists.[4]

Academics who specialize in gender studies have noted that the fact that so many women are uncomfortable with the idea of identifying themselves as feminists is rooted in a disagreement about what the word *feminist* means. If, however, you take what I would argue is a decidedly Catholic/Christian definition of feminism—that women have particular gifts that they bring to families and the greater society *as women*, and that these feminine gifts should be welcomed and celebrated—not only would you have a much greater acceptance of the word *feminism*, but the practical outcome would be the real, lasting changes in policy and in attitude articulated in Sandberg's book.

Catholic Women: Ahead of the Trend

As a woman who has spent almost three decades working for the institutional Church, I submit that it is Catholicism that can most definitively contribute to a conversation about where women "fit" in the workplace and how to best accommodate women's unique contributions to society—especially, but not exclusively, our ability to bear children. As evidenced

---

3   "The Feminist Mistake: The *Marie Claire* Gallup Poll," *Marie Claire*, September/October 1994, 126-29.

4   See Jennifer Robison, "Feminism—What's in a Name?" *Gallup*, September 3, 2002, *http://www.gallup.com/poll/6715/feminism-whats-name.aspx*.

by Sandberg's book and the public's reaction to it, this is a conversation that seems to be going full circle every decade or so—from "women should be fully present in the workplace" to "women should be at home more when their children are small" and back again. Perhaps—and surprisingly, no doubt, to many—what could *really* change the conversation about how women are viewed both at home and at work would be a truly Catholic influence. An authentic Catholic contribution to the public discourse on the dignity and value of women and their unique contributions would—far from undermining women's advancement—significantly help in bringing about the kind of change for which Sandberg hopes. As Pope Saint John Paul II notes in his *Letter to Women*: "Thank you, *women who work*! You are present and active in every area of life—social, economic, cultural, artistic and political. In this way you make an indispensable contribution to the growth of a culture which unites reason and feeling, to a model of life ever open to the sense of 'mystery,' to the establishment of economic and political structures ever more worthy of humanity."[5]

Perhaps the public conversation remains stagnant because it has not engaged a number of truths about the human person, truths grounded in the natural law and acknowledged and articulated by the Church: the truth about the dignity of each human life, the truth that, as Pope Francis has noted, "it is necessary to reaffirm the right of children to grow up in a family, with a father and a mother,"[6] the truth about people being more important than profit, the truth about service being more influential than power. By introducing natural-law arguments into the conversation, the Church can help to create workplaces where gender differences are not only respected, but also celebrated, where those with different vocations are

---

5   Pope John Paul II, *Letter to Women* (1995), 2, *http://www.vatican.va/holy_ father/john_paul_ii/letters/documents/hf_jp-ii_let_29061995_women_en.html.*

6   Zenit.org News Agency, "Francis Asks Forgiveness Because of Priests Who Have Harmed Children," EWTN, April 11, 2014, *http://www.ewtn.com/vnews/ getstory.asp?number=129225.*

accommodated, where marriage and family life (which sociologists have noted most often protect women from poverty) are supported, and where work—for both women and men—is a path to holiness, to wholeness, and to a place where one's gifts and talents are well used.

The Church's insistence that your work—whether at home or in a workplace—is not necessarily all about *you* and your personal fulfillment is not heard well in a culture that is increasingly narcissistic. But that message is a necessary component to creating successful companies, schools, hospitals, and public-service sectors. And the Church's proposal that one's work can actually be a path to holiness, a way or service, and a method of prayer would be seen as positively revolutionary! If every man and woman were confident that their daily activities held such potential, we would see dramatic changes that would cross all demographic, educational, and business sectors. A friend who is an elementary school mathematics teacher summed up this concept by saying: "When I am having a difficult day with my students, I can quickly become discouraged. But when I remind myself that if I offer my work as an act of love for God, who made these children and wants them to learn, suddenly it becomes much easier!"

Work as Vocation: We Are Called

Contrary to what is often portrayed about the Catholic Church, it has high expectations for women. At the same time that the women's liberation movement began in the United States, the Second Vatican Council gave women worldwide a rather daunting—some might say unrealistic—task: We were literally entrusted with the future of the human race. (I like to call it the "Wonder Woman!" passage of Vatican II.) It ends by telling women that "*it is for you to save the peace of the world.*"[7]

---

7   Pope Paul VI, *Address of Pope Paul VI to Women* (1965) (emphasis added), *http://www.vatican.va/holy_father/paul_vi/speeches/1965/documents/hf_p-vi_spe_19651208_epilogo-concilio-donne_en.html.*

And in his *Letter to Women* on June 29, 1995, Pope Saint John Paul II wrote: "As far as personal rights are concerned, there is an urgent need to achieve *real equality* in every area: equal pay for equal work, protection for working mothers, fairness in career advancements, equality of spouses with regard to family rights and the recognition of everything that is part of the rights and duties of citizens in a democratic State."[8] This is exactly what *Lean In* was encouraging corporations to do, but, tellingly, Sandberg never mentions what a Catholic pope (and saint!) said a full twenty years before she articulated it. And likely not because she knew it and simply wasn't citing it—but because she was totally unaware he had said it.

Why would a woman who took years to write a book on women in the workplace, doing countless hours of research on the contribution of different national and world leaders to the conversation, be unaware that the pope had made such a groundbreaking statement on the place of women in the workplace? Could it be because, generally speaking, the Church does not do a particularly good job of making certain that such statements are taught to the faithful? Perhaps it is also because the Church has not been a leader in promoting, in its own workplaces, the very same principles that it argues (theoretically at least) should guide it.

Adding to the puzzle, the Church has much to be proud of in terms of its prescience in accepting and advancing women in leadership roles—such as hospital CEO and university president—well before those positions were available to women in the secular world. At a time when society did not promote or accept women as leaders, the Church provided tremendous opportunities for the education and promotion of women through the institutions it sponsored.

---

8   Pope John Paul II, *Letter to Women*, 4.

That Was Then, This Is Now

But almost without exception, those leadership roles were held by women who were vowed religious and not by lay married women, whose primary vocations are oriented to their spouses and families. (Two exceptions were the professions of nursing and teaching, especially as the number of women religious decreased dramatically after the Second Vatican Council.) As vocations to the priesthood and the number of women entering religious life diminished, laywomen and men, both married and single, chose to serve the Church in many of the roles once held by priests and religious. This shift in demographics brought with it a host of other relevant issues—pastoral, practical, and economic.

In recent years an increasing number of laywomen, well-versed in the Church's teachings and energized and empowered by the spirit of Pope Saint John Paul II's *Mulieris Dignitatem*, have sought "careers"—to use Sandberg's term—within arch/diocesan structures, sharing with the Church their skills and talents as administrators, teachers, evangelizers, writers, editors, and attorneys, among other positions. Most of these women, answering what they have discerned as a call to serve, have made a conscious choice to seek employment with the Church, even when offered better-paying or more prestigious positions with for-profit companies. Many are married women with families.

Yet in addition to facing all of the same challenges that women who work in the secular world encounter (division of labor at home, child-care, and finding time for one's spouse and oneself), women who are called to share their gifts and talents with the Church in varying capacities face additional hurdles, such as misconceptions about or minimizations of their roles, along with practical structures that inhibit them from continuing their work long-term. If our secular culture retains an ambivalence about women in the workplace (and a quick glance at *The New York Times* nonfiction bestseller list for the past few years indicates there is quite a market for modern working mother how-to guides), women who labor in the Church's workplace encounter that same ambivalence, but perhaps more intensely. In addition, for Catholics and non-Catholics alike who equate the ordained priesthood with power or the top of the corporate ladder, the question inevitably arises as to what impact women could possibly have in a hierarchical structure like the Church.

The "Indispensable" Contribution of Women

The Church could not possibly image God's presence to the faithful without the complementary gifts of women being brought to bear on ministry, evangelization, and service. Women's influence, ideas, and input are necessary, not only for the practical purposes they serve, but also because an authentically Catholic environment demands it. Pope Francis has noted the benefits to all from the presence of women in Church structures: "I have rejoiced in seeing many women sharing some pastoral responsibility with priests in accompanying people, families and groups, as in theological reflection."

Yet Pope Francis also points out that a woman's contributions also remain "indispensable" within the domain of the family, thereby implying that whatever "pastoral responsibility" a woman undertakes for the Church, her role at home is essential and therefore should be accommodated as such:

> At this point it is natural to ask: how is it possible for women to increase their effective presence in many contexts within the public sphere, in the world of work and in places where the most important decisions are made, and at the same time maintaining their presence and preferential and entirely special attention in and for the family? Here it is the field of discernment that, aside

from reflection on the reality of women in society, presupposes assiduous and persistent prayer.[9]

The Holy Father's comments are music to the ears of any woman who works for the Church in any arch/diocesan, parish, or institutional setting, especially those who are familiar with the Church documents that call for equality in the workplace and for the rightly placed priority given to the dignity of each human life. Although he has made quite good use of social media, I am quite certain that Pope Francis has never read *Lean In*, yet he really asks the same questions that Sandberg does (though hers lack the "assiduous and persistent prayer" component): What can be done to make certain that women who feel called to work outside the home nonetheless also maintain "preferential" attention to their families?

It seems that the secular world, not the Church, has been more innovative in offering those benefits that provide women with what they need if they are to serve both the Church and their children. Janne Matlary, a Norwegian political scientist, Catholic convert, member of the Pontifical Council for Justice and Peace, and consultor to the Pontifical Council for the Family, has noted:

> The housewife of yesteryear cannot cease to exist. On the other hand, fewer and fewer families these days have the possibility to sustain two adults and children with one salary. The question becomes more complicated when children are introduced into the equation. What should be a natural process, and a happy one, becomes distorted and dramatic in our modern societies. The birth of a child becomes a drama, a destabilizing el-

9   Zenit.org News Agency, "Pope: Make More Room for Women in the Church," EWTN, January 28, 2014, *http://www.ewtn.com/vnews/getstory. asp?number=127829.*

ement in the modern family, rather than a fruit of love. If this is the norm, then something is wrong.[10]

Yes, something *is* wrong when the arrival of a child provokes crisis in a family, and it seems that, at least on paper, the secular working world in the United States has understood and responded to some degree, at least in white-collar jobs. For those women who work in the service industry, or are part-time employees, a pregnancy may mean that she must resign from her position, depriving her already-struggling family of much-needed financial resources. Moreover, across the board, companies seem to assume that maternity leave will be at most three to four months, leaving few opportunities for women to temporarily exit the workforce for, say, a year or two and then return to it at the same level of compensation and responsibility they held when they left.

Yet it remains troubling that Church-sponsored institutions or entities lag far behind—even when compared with other charitable institutions (including religious nonprofits)—in offering those options[11] that would make the ideal of service to the Church and service to the family possible:

1. Flexible schedules, allowing for the natural rhythms of family life to take place without placing an undue strain on either mother or father;

2. Paid maternity and paternity leave so that our places of employment acknowledge in both word and ac-

---

10   Janne Matlary, "New Millennium, New Feminism," *Pravda.ru*, April 23, 2001.

11   To be fair, in speaking with my friends who work in secular institutions, I know that what is offered "on paper" is, in fact, sometimes resented by other employees who might be inconvenienced by a women's maternity leave or flexible schedule. When my sister, an officer at a large bank in Chicago, told her team that she had arranged, per the bank's "family friendly" policy, to work each Friday from home, a fellow team member (who happened to be male and unmarried) sarcastically said that he, too, would like to have every Friday off to play golf, but unfortunately the bank "didn't have a policy for that."

tion that each human life is a gift to be celebrated and welcomed;[12]

3. For Church employees with children, assistance with tuition for Catholic education at all levels, so that parents who are called to vocations in the Church are not consequently precluded by tuition costs (and lower salaries) from obtaining a religious education for their children;

4. Time and funding for retreats and/or spiritual direction as well as ongoing formation in the Catholic faith, so that the "assiduous" prayer that the Holy Father mentions can be a more intentional part of the workplace. In my experience, it is not at all common for either ongoing formation in the Church's theology or social teachings or spiritual direction to be made available on a regular basis for Church employees, even when those employees are responsible for ministerial tasks where such guidance and education would be invaluable.

Sandberg and others in leadership roles in for-profit corporations have widely noted that one of the primary reasons for offering such family-friendly policies and incentives is that it helps the bottom line: Employee retention is far greater in an organization that provides flexibility for its employees. And long-term employees save companies time and money that would otherwise be spent recruiting, hiring, and training new employees to replace those who leave.

While prudence and an obligation to use resources wisely can and should motivate Church-sponsored institutions to weigh those considerations, the primary consideration for of-

---

12   This type of benefit, of course, must in prudence be weighed in light of the Church's responsibility to use her financial resources wisely, as numerous studies have shown that the cost of maternity leave, including the maintenance of a woman's health insurance while she is on leave, can have a significant impact on an organizational budget, whether for-profit or nonprofit.

fering family-friendly policies should be, simply, that it is the right thing to do. In order to allow mothers and fathers to do justice to their primary vocations as spouses and educators of their children, Church-sponsored places of employment must never engage in practices that undermine or discourage family life. These family-friendly policies would reinforce not only the Church's teachings on what Pope Saint John Paul II called "responsible parenthood,"[13] but also the Church's teachings on women, who are inextricably linked to their children and who are likewise to be treated with justice and equality.

In July 2004, in its *Letter to the Bishops of the Catholic Church on the Collaboration of Men and Women in the Church and in the World*, the Congregation for the Doctrine of the Faith endorsed "labor policies that do not force women to choose between a career and motherhood...and calls for women to have access to positions of responsibility in politics, economics and social affairs."[14]

The document states:

> It cannot be forgotten that the interrelationship between these two activities—family and work—has, for women, characteristics different from those in the case of men. The harmonization of the organization of work and laws governing work with the demands stemming from the mission of women within the family is a challenge. The question is not only legal, economic, and organizational; it is above all a question of mentality, culture, and respect. Indeed, a just valuing of the work of women within the family is required. In this way, women who freely desire will be able to devote the totality of their time to

---

13   Pope John Paul II, General Audience, "Responsible Parenthood Linked to Moral Maturity," EWTN, September 5, 1984, *http://www.ewtn.com/library/papaldoc/jp2tb120.htm*.

14   John L. Allen Jr., "Vatican Document Rejects Combative Feminism, Seeks 'Active Collaboration' for Men and Women," *National Catholic Reporter*, July 31, 2004.

the work of the household without being stigmatized by society or penalized financially, while those who wish also to engage in other work may be able to do so with an appropriate work-schedule, and not have to choose between relinquishing their family life or enduring continual stress, with negative consequences for one's own equilibrium and the harmony of the family.[15]

If it is true that strong social policies are strong family policies, then the Church's own teaching on women and family should be more fully implemented in her own structures, where arguably she would have the most control. Some arch/dioceses offer paid maternity and paternity leave, but many do not. Some offer assistance with Catholic school tuition for children of employees, but many do not. Some offer flexible work schedules, work-from-home arrangements, or job-sharing opportunities, but most do not. Sadly, countless arch/diocesan agencies and ministries have seen faithful, competent, and committed Catholic women leave their ranks for no other reason than they simply cannot manage to survive economically and continue to work for the Church. As their careers progress, they leave the ranks of the Church workforce—either by choice, to stay home and raise their families, or by necessity, to earn a higher salary elsewhere so they can adequately provide for and educate their children. Ironically—and sadly—this is especially true for those married couples who have made a deliberate and generous decision to raise a large family—see *Humanae Vitae*[16]—and who by their very presence and witness would bring great insight about the needs of families and the

---

15 Congregation for the Doctrine of the Faith, *Letter to the Bishops of the Catholic Church on the Collaboration of Men and Women in the Church and in the World* (2004), *http://www.vatican.va/roman_curia/congregations/cfaith/documents/rc_con_cfaith_doc_20040731_collaboration_en.html.*

16 Pope Paul VI, encyclical *Humanae Vitae* (On the Regulation of Birth) (1968), *http://www.vatican.va/holy_father/paul_vi/encyclicals/documents/hf_p-vi_enc_25071968_humanae-vitae_en.html.*

truth of the Church's sexual teachings to their Catholic school communities, their work, and their parishes.

The Church's voice could contribute so much to eliminating the drama to which Matlary refers and to which Sandberg devotes several chapters of her book. But before that can happen, the Church must more clearly articulate its teachings on women, their dignity, their gifts, and their roles, alongside those of men. There is simply not enough clear and consistent teaching at every level of the Church about the equality of women and men, the value of complementarity, and the responsibility on the part of all to ensure genuine collaboration among women and men so that both voices are equally present. We do a great disservice—some would term it violence—to a woman when we ask her either directly or by circumstance to suppress her maternity in order to follow the professional vocation God has given her. Women should not be forced to make this decision. Nor should family life suffer harm when a person is employed by a Catholic institution.

The Church—as an organization called to be prophetic and to be an example—should set an example for the secular world in its hiring and family policies. Sadly, it is often the secular world that is setting the standard for us in this regard. When *Glassdoor*, the online job community website, published its annual "50 Best Places to Work" list for 2014, not one Catholic institution was among them.[17] Not one. And the "Top 25 Companies for Work-Life Balance"?[18] The Church isn't there, either. Options for paid maternity leave, on-site day care, flextime, and part-time work should be given for any woman working for the Catholic Church. It damages the Church's voice on a whole host of what are often seen as "women's issues" when we ourselves do not provide women

---

17 "Best Places to Work," *Glassdoor*, 2014, *http://www.glassdoor.com/Best-Places-to-Work-LST_KQ0,19.htm*.

18 "Top 25 Companies for Work-Life Balance," *Glassdoor*, 2014, *http://www.glassdoor.com/Top-Companies-for-Work-Life-Balance-LST_KQ0,35.htm*.

with the support they need when they strive to balance family and vocation. Why is it that the secular world has often responded to the needs of working women in ways that the Church has not? And it not only has hurt Catholic women; it also has hurt the Church itself, because the gifts that women could be bringing to a variety of roles, both administrative and ministerial, are absent due to economic forces.

Finally, in his *Letter to Women* at the time of the Beijing Conference, Pope Saint John Paul II called for "an effective and intelligent *campaign for the promotion of women*, concentrating on all areas of women's life and beginning with a *universal recognition of the dignity of women*. Our ability to recognize this dignity, in spite of historical conditioning, comes from the use of reason itself, which is able to understand the law of God written in the heart of every human being."[19] I'm not sure what happened to that call—or if the campaign ever really materialized—but it's high time we revitalize it!

Over the past three decades, the New Evangelization has shaped and empowered Catholic women to influence others, with enthusiasm and good humor. Women can often contribute in ways—or be present in situations—where a priest would not be heard with the same credibility, or simply would not have the life experience to speak authoritatively. Examples that immediately come to mind are those women who work to end legal abortion, human trafficking, or pornography (all of which almost exclusively affect women), teach natural family planning, or speak on domestic-violence issues. This type of collaboration cannot be a mere accident—women with the appropriate academic and professional credentials need to be sought out and engaged to help the Church proclaim her message in a way that is understandable and appealing.

At the same time, Church leadership needs to avoid any appearances of tokenism. When women are called to speak for the Church, it needs to be made clear that they are not simply

19   Pope John Paul II, *Letter to Women*, 6.

window dressing, but rather experts in their respective fields who—of their own volition—seek to affirm and explain the Church's teachings. One way to achieve a public perception that women speak with authority in the Church would be to model hiring practices that seek to utilize women's expertise in areas beyond issues of sexual morality. In this way, everyone benefits: The woman who serves as the Church's messenger fulfills her baptismal call to bring Christ to others, and the Church's teachings are proclaimed in ways that are both accessible and credible.

As noted above, many secular companies go to great lengths to keep employees engaged and happy, because the longer an employee is with an organization, the more valuable he or she becomes. Women cannot be an *incisive presence* if we are not *there*, and so the Church's response to the needs of working mothers and families becomes ever more critical.

The Church needs to develop a more organized, concerted effort at the parish level to engage the many women who can be of service in building up local communities so that they become true spiritual homes. A growing concern among parishes in the United States and throughout South America is the number of baptized Catholics leaving the Church for evangelical, Pentecostal, or mega-church communities. While there are admittedly a myriad of reasons (including a lack of catechesis on the Eucharist) that families abandon the Catholic faith for Protestant communities, one factor consistently cited is the fellowship and social outreach dimensions. Just as women create homes where family members feel included and loved (but at the same time can be corrected or disciplined!), so too can women's gifts be put to use to make parish families more welcoming and inclusive. However, in the same way that arch/diocesan structures need the "incisive presence" of women in a variety of positions, so too should parish communities reflect women's levels of education, experience, and skill.

Having been charged by Vatican II to save the "future of humanity," Catholic women cannot help but *lean in*. Yet in our leaning we need to know that there is a sturdy structure present to support us. With the Church at all levels fully recognizing, accommodating, and using women's gifts, we will speak to and change the world far more profoundly than any *New York Times* bestseller.

Mary Hallan FioRito, JD, is a wife, mother, attorney, and twenty-nine-year employee of the Catholic Archdiocese of Chicago. FioRito served for twelve years as the executive assistant to Cardinal Francis George, OMI, now the archbishop emeritus of Chicago. Prior to her position with the cardinal, she worked as a vice chancellor and associate chancellor for the archdiocese and headed the Archdiocesan Respect Life Office. She is well known to many Chicagoans as a pro-life spokesperson and is frequently interviewed on television and radio. She serves on the board of directors of Aid for Women, a Chicago-based pregnancy resource center and maternity home and the national board of directors of Project Rachel. She has been published or quoted by the Wall Street Journal, The New York Times, *the* Chicago Tribune, *the* Chicago Sun-Times, *and numerous religious publications. Other distinctions include being named one of "40 Under 40" by* Crain's Chicago Business *and one of the "Women of the New Century" by* Newsweek. *She and her husband, Kevin, are the parents of three daughters.*

CHAPTER ELEVEN

Offense, Defense, and the Catholic Woman Thing

Mary Eberstadt

A prominent Catholic columnist told me recently that his biggest fear in life—his biggest fear—is that his own children will come to hate what he stands for. That same fear burdens many Christians, because every Christian in the chilly public square has felt the temperature drop. But that fear is exactly what I want to address, because we need to change fear into hope, and we need women to do that. Let me explain.

Following recent losses in the culture wars, anxiety in some places is running high. Not only in the United States, but also across the Western world, an aggressive secularism, emboldened by recent victories, now presses for more victories, in the courts, in the public square, in private industry, and even in the streets, quite literally. In the United Kingdom, for example, two preachers were lately threatened with arrest for reading passages from the Bible aloud on the street.[1] In light of such troubling cases, many people suspect that religious believers in all these societies are entering darker and more difficult times. Most likely they are right.

The rewriting of laws and customs along radical new lines has surely only begun. How many Christian students, teachers, priests, nuns, ministers, counselors, professors,

---

1   Andrew Alderson, "Preacher Threatened with Arrest for Reading Out Extracts from the Bible in Public," *The Telegraph,* August 15, 2009, *http://www.telegraph.co.uk/news/religion/6034144/Preacher-threatened-with-arrest-for-reading-out-extracts-from-the-Bible-in-public.html.*

and so forth will be ostracized or worse in their schools and workplaces—it's already happening—for being "extremists"? Will the United States go the way of the United Kingdom, where the British Equality and Human Rights Commission barred[2] a Christian couple from serving as foster parents because, under the new dispensation, the couple stands "on the wrong side of history"— that is, on the side of religious traditionalism concerning sexual morality? Or will we follow Canada, where even Catholic schools are required by law[3] to include student groups forthrightly subversive of exactly those same teachings? Father Raymond de Souza of Canada warns: "Many young priests I know expect that the prospect of one of us spending some time in jail for teaching the faith is not a distant or unlikely proposition. It is a plausible reality to be prepared for."[4] How long until American men and women of the cloth say the same? As these and other examples show, there's plenty worth fretting about out there, beginning with the fact that just being a religious believer, from here on out, will require more courage and endurance than before—in some cases, much more.

But what about the rest of the big picture? After all, discrimination and persecution have failed for more than 2,000 years to put Christianity out of business. Are we really and finally and only now facing its terminal decline on account of this one foe, the sexual revolution?

2   Benjamin Mann, "British Court Says Christian Couple Can't Be Foster Parents Due to Beliefs," Catholic News Agency, March 1, 2011, *http://www.catholicnewsagency.com/news/british-court-says-christian-couple-cant-adopt-due-to-beliefs/*.

3   Benjamin Mann, "Catholic Schools Will Follow Ontario's Gay-Straight Club Requirement," Catholic News Agency, June 7, 2012, *http://www.catholicnewsagency.com/news/catholic-schools-will-follow-ontarios-gay-straight-club-requirement/*.

4   Mary Eberstadt, "Faith and Family," *National Review Online*, May 20, 2013, *https://www.nationalreview.com/nrd/articles/347192/faith-and-family*.

When one considers the sweep of history and the many challenges and critical battles the Church has faced before, to say nothing of the Holy Spirit, one can only conclude that the answer to that question is no. But we must reckon with the reality of our times. This reality extends far beyond Saint Peter's Square, to the homes and workplaces of the Church's daughters and sons around the world. This new reality tells public school children that Christianity is backward and hateful. It tells the United Nations[5] that the Holy See must rewrite canon law to conform to whatever its hungry political adversaries desire at this particular moment.

Under this new wanton intolerance, men and women who never gave a thought to speaking their minds as Catholics must now worry about their standing in the public square—the good opinion or lack thereof among their friends and employers. They may even worry about what children, their children, will make of their faith down the road, as pressure mounts in influential places to stigmatize that very thing.

So what's to be done? We can't simply surrender. We couldn't even if we wanted to. The Church isn't a piece of real estate to be traded. It's the embodiment of truth on earth, and it's the patrimony as such of every human being. So if we can't exactly stay where we are, and we can't exactly go away, what should we do? That is the question that I want to take up, as a particular reflection on the opportunity we have, as women, to make a difference. I offer these thoughts not as a theologian, but as a strategist in the public square.

My title—"Offense, Defense, and the Catholic Woman Thing"—is an ironic title, first, because its metaphor draws from gamesmanship, and what we are about isn't re-

---

5   Associated Press, "Vatican Slammed by U.N. Human Rights Committee over Abuses," *CBC News*, February 5, 2014, *http://www.cbc.ca/news/world/vatican-slammed-by-un-human-rights-committee-over-sex-abuse-1.2523737*.

ally a game; it's the most serious business on earth. There are souls at stake.

It's an ironic title, second, because offense and defense are familiar as football terms. Fully two generations of male relatives, brothers, nephews, and now a son have tried to teach me the rules of football, as patiently and for as many years as Penelope waited for Odysseus. All to no avail. (This experience has given all of us an intuitive understanding of invincible ignorance, because in the matter of football, among other matters, I am an invincible ignoramus.)

And the title "Offense, Defense, and the Catholic Woman Thing" is ironic, third and most obviously, because the world of sport, dominated as it is by men, might seem an odd rubric for reflections on the role of women. But I've chosen that title deliberately and even mischievously for that very reason. It illustrates my point exactly: that women can take things made by men and make them new again.

Arguments, rhetorical fillips, and plain words sound different coming from a woman. Nuances and graces, intuitive to women, change the way those words are heard. Logic—formal, symbolic logic, of the kind that some of us have studied—is sexless. Validity and soundness are sexless. But *who* makes the argument is something else.

The duty of the public Catholic woman, one might say, is to take what men have made and to perform social and moral alchemy on it, the better to attract those who have shut their heads to logic and, in some cases, have shut their ears to *any* arguments made by the sons of the Church. Deborah Savage, in her chapter, "The Genius of Man," helpfully expounds the point that there is masculine genius too. The proposition to consider is that the feminine genius the current pope invokes, the one he sees as necessary to holding this very Church on earth together, lies here: in allowing the daughters of the Church to put what men have made into softer and sometimes more dexterous hands.

Consider these examples: one, where it would help to have women play more defense, and the other, where it would help to have women play more offense.

First, to the question of defense, when I hear the pope call for women to step up in the Church, that call is, of course, filtered through my very particular corner of life, —that is, that corner where thinkers and communicators hang out.

This is a very particular, but also potentially very influential, piece of intellectual real estate. And when I look at that real estate as a strategist, both inside and outside the Church, the first two alarming words that come to mind are *turf wars*. Turf wars are what sometimes happen when men control most of the intellectual real estate. Again, to observe that is not to pay disrespect to husband, brothers, son, quasi-adoptive sons, friends, and such. I've spent my professional life in worlds dominated by men. Most of my closest intellectual companions are men. Even the hobbies to which I'm drawn, such as philosophy, Texas Hold 'em, cocktail hours, and chess, are dominated by men.

Because we know and love them, women know also that our male brethren—including writers, bloggers, journalists, great and small—spend more time than their female counterparts on turf wars. They spend lots of time shooting BB's at one another—which is understandable and useful, unless and until it obscures the fact that whole bazookas are trained on all of us from elsewhere. As if we had eternity to figure these things out. Left to their own devices, some of our brothers will spend precious time tearing each other down rather than building up any new coalitions. This is partly, no doubt, because of their more territorial natures. But it's there—just as the feminine stamp on other aspects of life is there too. If you have any experience with the blogosphere, you will know exactly what I mean. Some would rather launch attacks on other writers of generally like mind than engage the other side—or even our side—constructively. (I invented a word, loosed here for the first time: "snarticle," meaning a snarky article, or a piece masquerading as objective that's really just an excuse for sarcasm. There's a lot of that going around.)

The negativity enhanced by the Internet is not only a problem for writers. It's a problem for the Church. Men of the cloth at every level are men of God, but they are also men, and as such, subject to infighting and turf wars too. Nor are they alone, of course. Columnist Ashley McGuire has written about similar turf wars among the laity over issues such as natural family planning and the like.

When Pope Francis, therefore, calls for women to heal the Church, that rings as a mandate—a mandate to do what women do organically in our families and communities. Not always, not nearly often enough, but at our best, we mend fences—rather than burn them down. We blur lines—rather than draw them so starkly as to frighten off other people who, with just a little work, might be inside our tent instead of out of it.

No, not nearly often enough but at our best, we do what Martha did. We provide the warmth, the feminine heart, the organization that makes it possible for men to be together without having to assert themselves nonstop. As Margaret McCarthy observes in her chapter on "The Feminine Genius and Women's Contributions in Society and in the Church," the presence of women is a correction to the temptation to power. So, in short, the message here, part one, is to play defense within our own ranks: We must resist the urge to go after one another and, instead, do what we can to shore up and protect what we have, in the way that women are uniquely and intrinsically gifted to do.

Now let's talk about the related matter of playing offense out there, and how women, *qua* women, might be able to do that in a unique way. Once more, logic is sexless. If you were to translate what follows into symbolic logic, it would look identical no matter who was making the argument. But atmospherics differ—and atmospherics matter. We know this from the domestic realm. Think how different a kind reprimand sounds, depending on whether it comes from a mother or a father, a loving grandparent, or an older sibling. The same words sound different. The same is true in the public square, especially in a politicized time polarized by gender issues. Herewith a couple of specific illustrations of how women *qua* women can play better offense in the public square.

Exhibit A: pornography. An overwhelming abundance of evidence,[6] including accumulating empirical evidence, proves that pornography causes harm. As Catherine Pakaluk points out in her chapter, "With Motherly Care: Addressing the Crisis of Human Flourishing in Our Time," we in the Church need to build better bridges to social science. The issue of pornography is a preeminent instantiation of that point. Empiricism is on our side.[7] The testimony from therapists, doctors, reporters, including secular reporters, and other sources unassailable in the secular world, all testify to this truth: Pornography causes harm.

Now, it's not as if men can't make these arguments. Exceptionally brave ones do. The pastoral letter by Bishop Paul Loverde of Arlington, Virginia, on pornography[8]

---

6   See, for example, two landmark books on pornography published by the Witherspoon Institute: Mary Anne Layden, *The Social Costs of Pornography: A Statement of Findings and Recommendations* (Princeton, NJ: Witherspoon Institute, 2010); James R. Stoner Jr., ed., with Donna M. Hughes, *The Social Costs of Pornography: A Collection of Papers* (Princeton, NJ: Witherspoon Institute, 2010)., *http://www.socialcostsofpornography.com/*.

7   Ibid.

8   Paul S. Loverde, *Bought with a Price: Pornography and the Attack on the Living Temple of God* (Arlington, VA: Diocese of Arlington, 2006), *https://www .arlingtondiocese.org/documents/bp_boughtwithaprice.pdf.* For a similar example on the topic of contraception, see the pastoral letter by Bishop James Conley of Lincoln, Nebraska, entitled *The Language of Love.* Zenit.org News Agency, "Bishop Conley Releases Pastoral Letter on Contraception," Zenit.org, March

does so admirably. Here again, though, women can amplify those arguments uniquely. Why? In part, because many men don't want to talk about pornography.

Many[9] are implicated or feel implicated—and fall silent. Even more so because pornography goes to the heart of the lie spread by the sexual revolution: Sex is for recreation simpliciter, and recreation simpliciter is victimless.

It isn't. So on the subject of pornography: Play offense, not defense.

How? Consider the recent situation of a college student from Duke who made a splash in the blogosphere and elsewhere when it was revealed that she was financing her higher education by becoming a pornography star.[10] I'm no victim, she insisted. The hard core of the libertarian wing of American thought went wild with cheers. To them, she proved the point: Pornography is a victimless crime. Playing offense on this issue means challenging her narrative, perhaps like this:

Dear Ms. Pornography Star,

Let's take you at your word. Let's say you aren't a victim. That's fine. But have you ever counted the ways in which you (and everyone like you) are victimizers?

You are a victimizer, first, of all the young women like you whose boyfriends and husbands will have been romantically poisoned by the images you sear on their minds. Those young women, like you, deserve

25, 2014, *http://www.zenit.org/en/articles/bishop-conley-releases-pastoral-letter-on-contraception* accessed August 22, 2014.

9   Meredith Somers, "More Than Half of Christian Men Admit to Watching Pornography," *The Washington Times*, August 24, 2014, *http://www.washingtontimes.com/news/2014/aug/24/more-than-half-of-christian-men-admit-to-watching-/?utm_source=RSS_Feed&utm_medium=RSS.*

10   Jane Stancill, "Duke Student Says She Pays Tuition with Porn Star Earnings," *The Seattle Times*, February 26, 2014, *http://seattletimes.com/html/nation-world/2023001075_dukepornxml.html.*

men who love them wholeheartedly and without visual reserve. You will help to destroy that option for them. You're a victimizer of the wives struggling to help raise a family—Herculean work under any circumstances—who will someday find the consolations of their bedrooms missing because their husbands have come to think them inadequate compared with a flickering screen. You are a victimizer in the intimate sense that you will teach a generation of young men to be lousy lovers. You are a victimizer of the children of the homes that will break apart because you have helped to render the men in those homes incapable of satisfaction with a three-dimensional woman. Divorce lawyers report that their business is up because pornography is more and more an issue in divorce cases. If that's not clear evidence of harm, what is? You are also a tertiary victimizer of people who will never see you—those who pick up the pieces of these broken families, such as the good brother struggling to help his sister, a newly single mother. Or, the newly fatherless children who now will face a lifetime of heightened risks.

And so on.

That kind of response is one example of how the evil of pornography becomes real when women make the argument and play offense, because women are the most credible witnesses to that particular evil. They can testify to its harms on them and on their children in a way that shoots straight to the heart, including even the hardened secular heart.

This brings us to another example of how women can and should play offense on this particular issue—one that goes out especially to potential activists, even more than to armchair communicators. All must study the example of Mothers Against Drunk Driving and adopt their tactics.

The genius behind that movement, the reason for its astonishing success, is that it is founded on what is still the unique moral standing of mothers, all mothers, single as well as married, secular as well as religious. This is another place where bridges can be built, including to the secular world. What's needed more than anything is an organization similarly patterned, *Mothers Against Pornography*.

Think about that. Mothers who do not want their sons poisoned and rendered less than manly; mothers who want to protect their daughters from men who have already been so poisoned. This is an idea whose time is long overdue. Somewhere in the world, we have to hope some brave women will breathe institutional life into it—and that effort couldn't help but make real inroads into the public square.

So now let's talk about one more way in which it would help to have women playing offense. From time immemorial, women have been particularly identified with the care of the weak, the old, and the most vulnerable. Yes, men in the Church have done this kind of work too, but generally speaking it's women who change the diapers, women who staff the soup kitchens and volunteer in the nursing homes, women who brighten the days of the unwanted elderly and tend to their bedsores and other unglamorous physical needs.

The aggressive secularism that says the sexual revolution comes first makes the work of these people harder in all kinds of ways—and this truth needs to be shouted till it's heard. Wanton and aggressive secularism attempts to strangle Catholic Charities—as if Catholic Charities weren't one of the most important institutions in America actually *serving* the poor and the worse off; as if there weren't destitute immigrants and patients and homeless families who would say, "Thank God they exist to help me." Again, the point needs to be pounded over and over. The HHS mandate isn't only constitutionally questionable (hats off to the people fighting that fight), it is also *morally* questionable, not least because it drains resources from the saintly people who do this kind of work—work that no one else wants to do.

The Little Sisters of the Poor say that refusing to comply with the mandate will cost them a considerable chunk of their budget in fines. Let's make it clear that they are talking about a budget that goes to feed and house and buy Depends for unwanted people the rest of society has written off and thrown out. To repeat, aggressive secularism aimed at protecting the sexual revolution above all else is having blowback of the worst kind imaginable. It is amputating the resources of those who serve the poor and unwanted—and, in that way, hurting the poor and unwanted themselves.

This isn't just a Catholic problem. I was at Baylor University recently, and there was similar talk of the town among the many people worried in the Christian world all over about the federal government impeding good works by just such ideological fiat. Evangelical churches, evangelical campuses, evangelical charitable organizations—all now have similar heightened worry. Secularism is kneecapping the efforts of all kinds of pro-life groups to take care of single mothers and babies, to give just one example. They are under litigious siege by Planned Parenthood.

That's not just a transgression against the polity. That's a transgression against the needy. There's lots of room for an ecumenical movement to make common cause on these issues and other issues. And, once again, to draw on the particular genius of women, making these kinds of cases in the public square.

Women today are being called upon to do nothing less than to change reality itself—to replay it through the higher keys of a feminine heart and mind. Not often enough, but at our best, that is what we do. And in doing it we lend a lightness of tone and also, again at our best, clarity to the larger human symphony.

Mary Eberstadt is a senior fellow at the Ethics and Public Policy Center in Washington, D.C., where she explores issues relating to American society, culture, religion, and philosophy. She is the author of several influential books: How the West Really Lost God: A New Theory of Secularization *(West Conshohocken, PA: Templeton Press, 2013);* Adam and Eve after the Pill: Paradoxes of the Sexual Revolution *(San Francisco: Ignatius Press, 2012);* The Loser Letters: A Comic Tale of Life, Death, and Atheism *(San Francisco: Ignatius Press, 2010); and* Home-Alone America: The Hidden Toll of Day Care, Behavioral Drugs, and Other Parent Substitutes *(New York: Sentinel HC, 2004). Eberstadt previously served as a speechwriter to former Secretary of State George P. Shultz; a special assistant to the U.S. ambassador to the United Nations, Jeane J. Kirkpatrick; and as research fellow at the Hoover Institution. She and her husband are the parents of four children.*

CHAPTER TWELVE

Promise and Challenge

Mary Rice Hasson, JD

I see clearly...that the thing the Church needs most today is the ability to heal wounds and to warm the hearts of the faithful; it needs nearness, proximity.

—Pope Francis, *America* interview, 2013[1]

Pope Francis has opened wide the doors of welcome, encouraging women's greater participation in the mission—and structure—of the Church, and inviting[2] women to help shape the direction of their contributions. We are called to be part of "a new chapter of evangelization" marked by "the joy of the Gospel,"[3] proclaiming an unchanging message of God's "immense love," revealed in the "crucified and risen Christ."[4] In so doing, Pope Francis reminds us, we will find "the source of authentic per-

---

1   Antonio Spadaro, SJ, "A Big Heart Open to God: The Exclusive Interview with Pope Francis," *America,* September 30, 2013, *http://americamagazine.org/pope-interview.*

2   Pope Francis echoes previous popes, particularly Pope Saint John Paul II, who wrote: "If anyone has this task of advancing the dignity of women in the Church and society, it is women themselves." See Pope John Paul II, post-synodal apostolic exhortation *Christifideles Laici* (On the Vocation and Mission of the Lay Faithful in the Church and in the World) (1988), *http://www.vatican.va/holy_father/john_paul_ii/apost_exhortations/documents/hf_jp-ii_exh_30121988_christifideles-laici_en.html.*

3   Pope Francis, apostolic exhortation *Evangelii Gaudium* (On the Proclamation of the Gospel in Today's World) (2013), 1, *http://w2.vatican.va/content/francesco/en/apost_exhortations/documents/papa-francesco_esortazione-ap_20131124_evangelii-gaudium.html.*

4   Ibid., 11.

sonal fulfillment," the realization that "life is attained and ma-
tures in the measure that it is offered up in order to give life to
others."[5]

The contributors to this book, responding to the
Church's call for "women's participation in the prophetic mission of Christ and his Church,"[6] have proposed some specific
thoughts for discussion, covering a range of relevant ideas in
their chapters. In this final chapter, I draw out several themes
for emphasis—and add some new ideas[7] to the mix. For this
book is a conversation starter, a discussion of unfinished business, unfolding priorities, and emerging opportunities. And
how could it be otherwise? Our work for the Lord—to evangelize, to serve, and to love in Christ's name—requires us to
embrace both the promise and the challenge inherent in any
human endeavor, relying on God's power, not our own.

When it comes to expanding the presence of women
in the Church, then, what themes might provide a framework
for action?

First, as the Church travels the path toward greater
complementarity in action—that is, as men and women collaborate in greater numbers and to greater effect, furthering
the Church's evangelistic mission—the way forward will require humble service, loving fidelity, prayerful discernment,
and trust, on the part of both men *and* women. Incorporating
women more fully into the work of the Church is not simply

---

5   Ibid., 10.

6   Pope John Paul II, *Christifideles Laici*, 51.

7   This chapter includes some ideas that arose during the closed-door ses-
sions of the symposium on women in Washington, D.C., on April 10, 2014,
co-sponsored by the Ethics and Public Policy Center and the Catholic Information Center. The symposium, formally titled, "Women and the Church: Present
Considerations and Future Directions," included presentations by the scholars
contributing to this book and closed-door discussions among the panelists and
attending scholars. The closed-door discussions were an opportunity for frank
engagement on the topics, from all angles, with the promise that no quotes
would be attributed to particular individuals. Thus comments from the discussions are referenced in general terms.

an exercise in diversity. As Pope Francis warns, "When we, for our part, aspire to diversity, we become self-enclosed, exclusive, and divisive; similarly, whenever we attempt to create unity on the basis of our human calculations, we end up imposing a monolithic uniformity."[8] Rather, "diversity must always be reconciled by the help of the Holy Spirit; he alone can raise up diversity, plurality and multiplicity while at the same time bringing about unity"[9] in the service of evangelization. In short, greater collaboration will require interior growth, openness to the Holy Spirit, and an enduring orientation to God's will, from all of us. The watchwords are not power, position, or prestige, but humility, service, and evangelism.

Second, more theological work lies ahead in order to illuminate, in greater depth, the meaning and significance of complementarity. In her "commitment to evangelization," Pope Francis notes, the Church encourages theologians to "advance [their] dialogue with the world of cultures and sciences." In this way, insights into "human experiences" will assist the Church's "discernment on how best to bring the Gospel message to different cultural contexts and groups."[10] In a world that is quickly losing sight of the truth about the human person, where adults and adolescents find themselves lost in the fog of confusion surrounding sexuality, gender, and family, this task is crucial. In particular, as Sister Sara Butler notes in Chapter Two, it seems appropriate to pursue deeper explanations of the male genius, the relationship between fatherhood and motherhood, and the significance of integral complementarity, especially in light of opposing cultural messages. In addition, as the Marian, pastoral face of the Church assumes a higher profile in Francis's pontificate, the theology underlying the Church's Marian and Petrine aspects requires more attention; the practical meaning of a more feminine ap-

---

8   Pope Francis, *Evangelii Gaudium*, 131.

9   Ibid.

10   Ibid., 133.

proach to the Church's pastoral work seems ripe for further discussion as well.

Third, because the cultural clamor renders it more difficult to communicate the truth to those who "have ears and do not hear" (Jer 5:21, NAB), the "language" of evangelization, apologetics, and general civic discourse must be sensitive to and refined in light of cultural realities. Pope Francis urges us to see the Church as a mother, reminding us that, "a good mother can recognize everything that God is bringing about in her children, she listens to their concerns and learns from them."[11] For women, this is a high priority; their concerns need to be heard and understood by the Church.

Pope Francis also sees translation as a necessary part of evangelization. In *Evangelii Gaudium*, he observes that "today's vast and rapid cultural changes demand that we constantly seek ways of expressing unchanging truths in a language which brings out their abiding newness."[12] As Erika Bachiochi points out in Chapter Nine, women formed in a secular, feminist mindset need to hear the Church's teachings on sexuality and reproduction translated into language consonant with their experiences and capable of touching the wounded heart. But translation presupposes that the translators are conversant in both languages. Those in the Church charged with such a task must first listen well to women's concerns and experiences—and indeed women should be among the translators. Women will then be poised to become messengers, front and center, of the Church's teachings. For as Mary Eberstadt notes in Chapter Eleven, women are well-suited to "take things made by men—and make them new again."

Fourth, the Church must amplify and implement its teachings on women in particular ways. Confident in the power

---

11 Ibid., 139.

12 Ibid., 41.

of truth, the Church must amplify its message regarding the dignity of women, the meaning of human sexuality, and the importance of marriage and the family so as to reach all people, but especially the poor and vulnerable. The poor, in particular, suffer materially as well as spiritually when these truths are disregarded. To the extent that the laity exhibits widespread disregard[13] for difficult Church teachings, particularly the teachings on contraception, some clergy suggest those teachings do not reflect the *sense of the faithful* and must be wrong,[14] or, if true, those teachings are merely an "ideal"[15] that must bend to the "conscience of the couples."[16] However, the decades-long failure[17] of the clergy to promote these teachings widely, with conviction and moral clarity—and the consequent rejection of those teachings by the laity—proves only that equivocation, silence, and timidity are unpersuasive. Moreover, significant numbers of women fall into the "soft middle," where they currently reject the Church's teachings on contraception, but remain open to rethinking those views.[18] And a solid core of Catholic women,

---

13   Jerry Filteau, "Bishop: Synod Questionnaire Shows Most Reject Teaching on Contraceptives," *National Catholic Reporter*, February 24, 2014, *http://ncronline.org/news/faith-parish/bishop-synod-questionnaire-shows-most-reject-teaching-contraceptives*. The article reports the statement of Bishop Robert Lynch of Saint Petersburg, Florida, that "Catholics have made up their minds and the *sensus fidelium* [the sense of the faithful] suggests the rejection of church teaching on this subject."

14   Ibid.

15   Vatican Radio, "Cardinal Kasper: Synod to Model Pope's 'Listening Magisterium,'" October 1, 2014, *http://en.radiovaticana.va/news/2014/10/01/card_kasper_synod_to_model_popes_listening_magisterium/1107667*.

16   Ibid.

17   Patrick Craine, "New York Cardinal Dolan Says Church Failed to Teach Against Contraception," LifeSiteNews, April 2, 2012, *https://www.lifesitenews.com/news/ny-cardinal-dolan-says-church-failed-to-teach-doctrine-on-contraception*.

18   Mary Rice Hasson and Michele Hill, *What Catholic Women Think About Faith, Conscience, and Contraception*, Preliminary Report, Women, Faith, and Culture Project, Ethics and Public Policy Center, 2012, *http://s3.amazonaws.com/eppc/wp-content/uploads/2013/07/What_Catholic_Women_Think_Contraception-Aug_2012.pdf*. Our research sampled churchgoing Catholic women

particularly younger women,[19] embrace Catholic teachings on family planning and are well positioned to witness to God's mercy and grace—and to the blessings that flow from living in accord with the Church's teachings. Surely these "ambassadors" would welcome consistent leadership on this issue in every diocese and every parish.

It's important also for the Church to implement her teachings about women in a way that manifests the Church's conviction that women's participation *is essential* to the Church's mission. Women's collaboration with men signifies deep truths about the human person, relationality, and the Church; collaboration brings added value to the Church's work and benefits society, which sorely needs "a revolutionary model," as Helen Alvaré describes it in Chapter One, a model that affirms sexual difference, human dignity, and the benefits of male-female collaboration. Even as Church authorities affirm the value of women's inclusion, they also must ensure, as Mary Hallan FioRito points out in Chapter Ten, that their employees, particularly women, receive the practical support and accommodations they need to allow them to care for their

---

ages 18-54 on their views of Church teachings on contraception, sexuality, and reproduction. The results offer a more nuanced picture of the attitudes of Catholic women and suggest that dissenting views are far from unchangeable. ("Churchgoing" covered a spectrum of attendance and included women who attended Mass at least weekly to those who attended at least a few times per year.) We found that although only 13% of women overall fully accept the Church's teachings on family planning, that number doubles (27%) among younger women (18-34) who attend Mass weekly. Moreover, women who do not fully accept the Church's teaching still reflect some openness toward the Church's position. A strongly plurality (44%) of women expressed agreement with parts, but not all, of the Church's teachings on family planning, and more than half (53%) of this "soft middle" said they would be open to learning more about those teachings. Disagreement with Church teachings is correlated with sacramental frequency (or infrequency): Although one-third (37%) of churchgoing women overall completely reject the Church's teachings on contraception, the number of dissenters drops to 24% among weekly Massgoers and to 12% among women who both attend Mass weekly and have received the Sacrament of Reconciliation within the past year.

19   Ibid.

families as they participate in the work of the Church. Women's needs in this area differ from men's.[20]

Fifth, while the female perspective needs to be incorporated and valued "wherever decisions are made" at parish, diocesan, and Vatican levels, the "presence" of women needs to be recognized, valued, and fostered in the "capillaries" of the body of Christ—*wherever* women nurture, teach, and care for others. As Professor Alvaré writes, "What women are doing already— their loving, merciful, person-centered ways of working and living—are what the Church wants to be." Progress regarding women's presence in the Church should be measured less by the

---

20 Raising children is not the task of androgynous parents, but of mothers and fathers. Just as men and women are different, mothers and fathers are different in their approaches to work, child-rearing, and family responsibilities—differences not overcome by egalitarian sharing of chores and errands (a matter of family preference). Over the years, women with children at home consistently say they prefer part-time work to full-time work, but men do not. Perhaps it's time to listen to what women are saying, instead of assuming they don't really mean what they say. When asked, "If money were no object, and you were free to do whatever you wanted, would you stay at home, work full-time, or would you work part-time," 52% of men would work full-time, while just 27% of women would choose full-time work; 30% of men would select part-time work, while 49% of women would choose part-time. And 22% of women would choose to be at home full-time, compared with just 16% of men. See W. Bradford Wilcox, "Moms Who Cut Back at Work Are Happier," *The Atlantic*, December 18, 2013, *http://www.theatlantic.com/business/archive/2013/12/ moms-who-cut-back-at-work-are-happier/282460/*. Men also are more likely to work longer hours—50 or more hours per week—while women look for more balance between work and family. See Youngjoo Cha, PhD, "Brief: Overwork May Explain 10 Percent of Men's Wage Advantage over Women," *Council on Contemporary Families*, July 30, 2014, *https://contemporaryfamilies.org/gender-revolution-rebound-brief-overwork-explains-wage-differences/*. In a similar vein, women who take time off from work to care for family members rarely regret the career sacrifice. According to a 2013 Pew survey, 53% of working mothers with children under 18 "have taken a significant amount of time off from work," and 51% "have reduced their work hours to care for a child or other family member." The vast majority (94%) of women report that they have no regrets about those sacrifices and were "glad they did it." Thirty-three percent of all women, but only 21% of men, say they have taken some time off of work to care for a family member. See Pew Report, "On Pay Gap, Millennial Women Near Parity—For Now," Pew Research Center, December 11, 2013, *http://www .pewsocialtrends.org/files/2013/12/gender-and-work_final.pdf*.

numbers of women appointed to significant positions within the Church's structure (although that is surely important) and more by the transformative impact of an integral complementarity put into practice more broadly, in parish ministries, education, social work, business, and health care.

Sixth, it's important to underscore that the public Catholic woman has a vitally important role to play in creating what Pope Francis calls "an evangelized culture," a culture "marked by faith" and "authentic Christian values."[21] The degree to which women, and motherhood itself, are becoming ever more degraded, and the pace at which society is embracing increasingly deformed views of the person, the family, and even love itself make this an urgent task. At the heart of the problem, Pope Francis writes, is "[t]he process of secularization [which] tends to reduce the faith and the Church to the sphere of the private and personal. Furthermore, by completely rejecting the transcendent, it has produced a growing deterioration of ethics, a weakening of the sense of personal and collective sin, and a steady increase in relativism. These have led to a general sense of disorientation, especially in the periods of adolescence and young adulthood which are so vulnerable to change."[22] Catholic women cannot be bystanders as families and the culture around them disintegrate. This is the world we need to evangelize. Our task begins in the family and springs from the family to the Church and the larger community, through witness, personal relationships, and our daily interactions.

Additional Insights on Women, Motherhood, and the Meaning of "Presence"

In addition to the insights presented in the preceding chapters, the symposium that served as a springboard to this book gener-

---

21 Pope Francis, *Evangelii Gaudium*, 68.

22 Ibid., 64.

ated further observations[23] that deserve mention. I share them here, in summary fashion, to round out the conversation and to encourage, in another forum perhaps, further analysis and development.

The Theology of Woman and "Motherhood"

While traditional Catholic theology, as expressed in Pope Saint John Paul II's *Mulieris Dignitatem*,[24] describes "virginity and motherhood as two particular dimensions of the fulfillment of the female personality"—reflecting different ways of living the "self-gift" at the heart of human fulfillment—some scholars have observed the difficulty, in today's culture, of linking women and their vocation so strongly to motherhood.

Consider the cultural backdrop of a young woman's life today. Marriage and motherhood are no longer considered integral to a well-lived life, or to a thriving society. According to the Pew Research Center, shrinking numbers of Americans— just 46 percent—believe that marriage and children should be a priority for society. Worse, two-thirds of younger Americans (ages 18-29) say that "society is just as well off if people have

---

23 These additional points, which emerged in the symposium closed-door discussions and post-symposium follow-up, should not be interpreted as consensus ideas or priorities; they are offered here to provide a fuller sense of the range of insights that arose in discussion and from feedback. As mentioned in note 7 of this chapter, the comments are reported generally, without attribution to particular individuals, in keeping with the aims of the closed-door session.

24 Pope John Paul II, apostolic letter *Mulieris Dignitatem* (On the Dignity and Vocation of Women) (1988), 17. In Mary, "*virginity and motherhood co-exist,*" allowing all women to see, in her person, "how these two dimensions, these two paths in the vocation of women as persons, explain and complete each other." Pope John Paul II, echoing the Second Vatican Council, also reminds us that human fulfillment lies in "a sincere gift of self," and that the "*mutual gift of the person in marriage*" opens the possibility of "the gift of a new life." Concretely, "motherhood implies from the beginning a special openness to the new person.... In this openness, in conceiving and giving birth to a child, the woman 'discovers herself through a sincere gift of self.'" Thus "motherhood *is linked to the personal structure of the woman and to the personal dimension of the gift.*" See *Mulieris Dignitatem,* 17-21, http://www.vatican.va/holy_father/john_paul_ii/apost_letters/documents/hf_jp-ii_apl_15081988_mulieris-dignitatem_en.html.

priorities *other than* marriage and children"[25] (emphasis added). These attitudes play out in practice.

Almost 20 percent of American women today remain single as adults,[26] and that number is projected to climb. According to Pew Research, 30 percent of Millennial women "will remain unmarried by age 40" if present trends continue.[27] The drop in marriage rates has hit women of color the hardest,[28] as the number of single black women who remain unmarried has quadrupled, while the number of never-married Latino and white women has doubled. And in spite of the low marriage rates, out-of-wedlock births to women of color have risen sharply.[29]

While nearly half of all single adults would like to be married, another third express ambivalence, and a smaller percentage of singles (13 percent) choose that life deliberately.[30] The plunging marriage rates have created a marriage divide: high-income, well-educated Americans are still marrying, although at older ages and often after cohabiting, and they generally wait to have babies until they are married; low-income, poorly educated people have seen their marriage rates

---

25 Wendy Wang and Kim Parker, "Record Share of Americans Have Never Married," *Pew Research, Social and Demographic Trends*, September 24, 2014, *http://www.pewsocialtrends.org/2014/09/24/record-share-of-americans-have-never-married/.*

26 Ibid. The number of never-married women, however, varies somewhat by race and ethnicity: 36% of black women 25 and older have never been married, while 26% of Hispanic women and 16% of white women 25 and older have never been married. Asian women remain single at rates slightly higher than white women.

27 Tami Luhby, "Millennials Say No to Marriage," *CNN Money*, July 20, 2014, *http://money.cnn.com/2014/07/20/news/economy/millennials-marriage/.*

28 Gene Demby, "Marriage Rates Are Falling, and for Some, Faster than Others," *NPR Codeswitch*, September 26, 2014, *http://www.npr.org/blogs/codeswitch/2014/09/26/351736134/marriage-rates-are-falling-and-for-some-faster-than-others.*

29 "The Fraying Knot," *The Economist*, January 12, 2013, *http://www.economist.com/news/united-states/21569433-americas-marriage-rate-falling-and-its-out-wedlock-birth-rate-soaring-fraying.*

30 Wendy Wang and Kim Parker, "Never Married," *supra* note 25.

plummet as their out-of-wedlock birth rates have skyrocketed.[31]

The statistics on motherhood tell a similarly disheartening story. A steadily rising number of women, almost one in five,[32] will end their childbearing years without ever having children. Roughly half of these women purposely choose the "child-free"[33] life; others find themselves childless for lack of a partner or because of infertility. Radical feminists and social liberals have normalized casual sex, universal contraception, and easy abortion, fostering a mindset within which a child becomes a burden rather than a gift, and motherhood is a "punishment"[34] unless carefully planned or desperately desired.

Perhaps most troubling, fewer and fewer of America's most educated young women even *aspire* to motherhood. Twenty-three years ago, 79 percent of female college students said they intended to have children. Today, at least one study suggest that number has dropped dramatically among highly educated women: just 43 percent say they intend to have children.[35] For the majority of these young women, "mother" is an identity that they no longer expect, or even desire, to assume.

31 "The Fraying Knot," *The Economist, supra* note 29.

32 Lauren Sandler, "Having It All Without Having Children," *Time*, August 12, 2013, *http://content.time.com/time/magazine/article/0,9171,2148636-2,00.html.*

33 Melanie Notkin, "The Truth about the Childless Life," *The Huffington Post*, March 4, 2014, *http://www.huffingtonpost.com/melanie-notkin/the-truth-about-the-childless-life_b_3691069.html.*

34 President Obama infamously remarked that if one of his daughters ever became pregnant, he would not want her "punished" with a child. David Brody, "Obama Says He Doesn't Want His Teen Daughters Punished with a Baby," CBN News, March 31, 2008, *http://blogs.cbn.com/thebrodyfile/archive/2008/03/31/obama-says-he-doesnt-want-his-daughters-punished-with-a.aspx.*

35 Stewart D. Friedman interview by Jeffrey Klein, "'Baby Bust': Why Fewer Young People Expect to Become Parents," Wharton School, University of Pennsylvania, October 31, 2013, *http://knowledge.wharton.upenn.edu/article/stew-friedman-new-work-family-choices-men-women/.* Friedman, the founding director of the Wharton Work/Life Integration Project, tracked the attitudes of two generations of Wharton students toward work and family. His research is published in his book *Baby Bust: New Choices for Men and Women in Work and Family* (Philadelphia: Wharton Digital Press, 2013).

Is that a good thing? Surely not. But it is the reality of the culture shaping today's young women. This warped cultural lens projects a distorted image of *woman* very poorly aligned with the Church's beautiful teachings. Even Catholic women well-disposed toward femininity and motherhood will not be immune from the influence of those cultural distortions.

Given this context, the Church's teaching on women—in which motherhood is a central aspect of woman's dignity and vocation—may seem puzzling, counterintuitive, or even oppressive to some women. And for other women, those who carry the painful cross of infertility with hearts raw with yearning and loss, the Church's celebration of motherhood evokes hope and despair, impossibly intertwined. Their suffering is too often invisible in parishes filled with young children and pregnant moms and rarely mentioned even in prayer intentions. For another group of women, raised in broken, inchoate, or seriously dysfunctional families, the idea of maternal self-giving may seem an alien concept; it does not resonate with them, because they rarely experienced it. These women, too, may find it difficult to connect their womanhood with motherhood, even "spiritual motherhood."[36]

To identify these challenges is not to imply that the Church's teachings on women, motherhood, and virginity are somehow wrong or inadequate. They are not. Indeed, the truths in these teachings are essential to women's well-being, particularly the well-being of poor women. But identifying these challenges does highlight the importance of understanding the cultural challenges that may make it difficult for some women to intuitively grasp and intellectually accept the Church's teachings on womanhood. It also makes clear

---

36   Pope John Paul II, *Mulieris Dignitatem*, 21. He notes that a woman who chooses virginity experiences "a different kind of motherhood: motherhood 'according to the Spirit' (cf. *Rom 8:4*)." In "spiritual motherhood," an openness and self-giving to others "takes on many different forms," and, because the human person is a unity of body and soul, even physical motherhood needs to include spiritual motherhood.

why it's important to find the language and analogies that will reach women in the context of their experiences, pain, and aspirations, helping them to "respond to the God of love who saves us."[37]

Single Women…Neither Married nor Consecrated

Some Catholic single women—neither rejecting marriage nor discerning a call to the religious life—hope for a fuller discussion of their vocation and role in the Church. For these women, the virginity-motherhood descriptions in *Mulieris Dignitatem* seem not quite apt, at least as applied to their concrete circumstances. Some women question[38] whether the single life is a separate state in life, distinct from the call to be married or to the consecrated life. The Church often emphasizes the more relevant distinctions between the ordained ministry and laypersons, and the general call to holiness.[39] Still, it's clear that some single women would welcome a deeper theological reflection on their lives and their place in the Church. On the practical side of things, the single state in life seems to create some awkwardness within the Church, as contented singles perceive that some priests and laity regard them, by default, as

---

37   Pope Francis, *Evangelii Gaudium*, 39.

38   See, for example, Mary Beth Bonacci, "Is Single Life a Vocation?" Catholic Match Institute, January 5, 2014, *http://institute.catholicmatch.com/2014/01/is-single-life-a-vocation/*, and Emily Stimpson, "Is the Unconsecrated Single Life a Vocation?" *Our Sunday Visitor Newsweekly*, July 13, 2011, *https://www.osv.com/TabId/735/ArtMID/13636/ArticleID/4580/*.

39   For example, the Diocese of Sacramento lists the "Single Life" under the heading of "Vocations," but describes the shared lay vocation: "All are called to live their life joined to Christ in Baptism. For many, single life becomes the best way to fulfill their vocation whether being 'single' is a choice or a circumstance. Accepting the vocation of the single life means choosing to serve God as a member of the laity. Single persons serve the Christian family through acts of love and service, in a variety of lay ministries." See *http://www.diocese-sacramento.org/vocations/single_life.html*. Germain Grisez and Russell Shaw describe the desirability of every person discerning a personal vocation: Germain Grisez and Russell Shaw, *Personal Vocation: God Calls Everyone By Name* (Huntington, IN: Our Sunday Visitor, 2003).

unfulfilled vocations to marriage or unrecognized vocations to the religious life. Neither placement fits.

The "Presence of Women": in the World and in the Pew

Much of the excitement generated by Pope Francis's comments about expanding the presence of women, especially into decision-making arenas, centers on the possibility of more women appointees to influential positions—for example, as Vatican advisers. In these high places, women's sensitivity to persons and to the *whole* seems likely to inform teachings and influence pastoral practice for the better. Indeed, the Church seems receptive[40] to the idea that Catholic women—and Catholic laymen—should be placed in roles that allow them to bring their insights, particularly as they relate to the married vocation, sexuality, and family life, into Church discussions at the highest levels. However, efforts focusing primarily on presence in official Church institutions, particularly female appointments to high-level curial, national, or diocesan positions, risk missing other dimensions of presence important to the Church. Pope Francis, of course, warns against clericalizing the laity, in light of the Second Vatican Council's emphasis on the laity's mission in the world. Women play a role in the Church's evangelizing mission wherever they encounter others—in neighborhoods, parish activities, universities, medical centers, and in far-flung missionary outposts. Similarly, women's natural inclinations and chosen professions often afford them prime opportunities to humanize the culture. Catherine Pakaluk argues in Chapter Eight, for example, that women's gifts are particularly needed in the social sciences, the Church's social work, and in revitalizing and perhaps reshaping Catholic education. These areas are ground zero in the battle for the

---

40   See, for example, the increased participation of married couples and lay experts at the Synod of Bishops on the Family in 2014. Gerard O'Connell, "Fourteen Married Couples Among 253 Participants at Synod on the Family," *America*, September 9, 2014.

family, places where women are uniquely suited to proclaim the dignity of the person and to bring the healing power of Christ's love. Similarly, Margaret McCarthy, in Chapter Five, emphasizes the crucial nature of women's "hidden" work at home and raising a family, and why the Church needs to value and support this work as indispensable to the task of humanizing the culture and transmitting the faith. The family is the first school of love and the first field of evangelization.

In a related vein, the symposium discussions surfaced concern for the ordinary Catholic woman. In too many places, as one participant observed, "the Church is not caring for the woman in the pew." This applies on several levels. There's a sense that many women in the average Catholic parish do not find themselves growing spiritually or deepening their intellectual understanding of the faith; they feel disconnected and rarely avail themselves of parish spirituality programs.[41] For some women, the teachings of the Church seem theoretical and inapplicable[42] to the real struggles of their family and personal lives—and few parishes seem to have practical approaches that bridge that gap for women. Women searching for spiritual growth, fellowship, and practical guidance—on prayer, child-rearing, financial stewardship, and marriage, among other issues—too often come up empty in Catholic parishes.

Women themselves can be part of the solution. The Church needs to foster the presence, at the parish level, of small-group ministries where women on fire for the Lord can manifest Christ's saving love—and the truth of his teachings—to other women. In the process, women with evange-

---

41   Our research found that 16% of churchgoing Catholic women participated in Catholic spiritual activities (apart from Mass and reception of the sacraments) within the past twelve months. See this report for insight on women's involvement in the parish and receptivity to Catholic teachings on conscience and contraception: Hasson and Hill, *What Catholic Women Think About Faith, Conscience, and Contraception*, note 18.

42   Ibid.

lists' hearts make the parish more of a home, a welcoming community. Two programs in particular, Endow[43] and Walking with Purpose,[44] both operate on the parish level with the local bishop's support. Although different in focus, each succeeds in connecting women more deeply to the Church— they change lives and revitalize parishes. No doubt other strong programs have a similar impact. But programs like these seem to be too few or remain unknown to many pastors, parishes, and bishops.

In addition to encouraging woman-to-woman ministries, the Church might encourage formation programs to train female spiritual directors and establish mentoring programs[45] between older and younger women. As one woman active on the parish level noted: "The truth is, fewer and fewer women are being mothered well. So many women are hungry for mentoring, to be loved, and to be coached in terms of how to live life well." Women, formed well by the Church, have much to give, particularly to other women. And when women help other women grow spiritually, and encourage them to

---

43 Endow, a women's faith program supported by bishops in many dioceses, has active groups in every state. Where no program exists, women are encouraged to approach their diocese about forming a group. Endow appeals to "women from all walks of life who are at various places on their faith journey," as well as to "pre-teen and teenage girls who are discovering their individual and spiritual identity." Endow groups build friendships, faith, and understanding through "a comprehensive program that is understandable and embraced by women and girls in the pew—because that is who we are too: faithful wives, mothers, daughters, and career women." See *endowgroups.org.*

44 Walking with Purpose enjoys ecclesiastical support and is active in an increasing number of dioceses across the country. Its mission is "to bring women to a deeper personal relationship with Jesus Christ by offering personal study and small group discussion that link our everyday challenges and struggles with the solutions given to us through the teachings of Christ and the Roman Catholic Church." It offers a parish-based program of small-group meetings ("Connect Coffees") to discuss the weekly lessons (Bible studies) or watch an inspirational video. See *walkingwithpurpose.com.*

45 Mentoring programs would encourage older women to share their wisdom with younger women, not only in spiritual areas but also in practical areas such as work-family balance, child-rearing, and marital growth.

integrate their Catholicism with their daily life decisions, it bears great fruit beyond the women themselves, extending to their families and the larger society.

Indeed, rather than clamoring for influential positions in strategic "territories" of the Church, the vast majority of Catholic women ought to focus, as one leader phrased it, "on being more effective influencers in the territory we already have." She pointed out that the United States has roughly 76 million U.S. Catholics (66 million of whom are parish-connected),[46] and women represent about half that number— an enormous untapped potential for the work of evangelizing and humanizing the culture. Women have a natural inclination to accompany others in their suffering and in their joys. Open to others, women tend toward (in Pope Francis's words) "a fraternal love capable of seeing the sacred grandeur of our neighbor, of finding God in every human being, of tolerating the nuisances of life in common by clinging to the love of God, of opening the heart to divine love and seeking the happiness of others."[47] As a result, this leader notes:

> [W]omen are uniquely gifted by God to minister to one another. Our relational abilities equip us to enter into places of brokenness and need with sensitivity and compassion. When we love one another well, there is nothing more effective than women ministering to other women.… A stronger woman can strengthen a marriage. A stronger marriage results in a stronger family.… Stronger families mean better communities. Strong and healthy individuals in our communities are able to reach out to our broken world.

---

46   CARA, "Frequently Requested Church Statistics," Center for Applied Research in the Apostolate, Georgetown University, 2014, *http://cara.georgetown .edu/caraservices/requestedchurchstats.html.*

47   Pope Francis, *Evangelii Gaudium*, 92.

In *Evangelii Gaudium*, Pope Francis invites the Church to be open to change—not doctrinal change, but other changes that will contribute to the success of the Church's evangelizing mission: "I dream of...a missionary impulse capable of transforming everything, so that the Church's customs, ways of doing things, times and schedules, language and structures can be suitably channeled for the evangelization of today's world rather than for [the Church's] self-preservation" (27). The Church is on a mission to evangelize the world with the truth of the Gospel message, and women are an indispensable part of that mission. Without a doubt, this is a promising—and challenging—time to be a Catholic woman.

Mary Rice Hasson, JD, is a fellow in the Catholic Studies Program at the Ethics and Public Policy Center in Washington D.C., where she writes on Catholicism, sexuality, and family life. She co-authored, with Michele Hill, the groundbreaking report What Catholic Women Think about Faith, Conscience, and Contraception *(2012) and is completing a book that explores Catholic women's views on faith, sexual morality, and reproduction. An attorney, She writes commentary for a variety of websites and publications and has been interviewed by media outlets such as CNN, MSNBC, EWTN, the BBC, and the AP, as well as numerous Catholic radio programs and print publications. The mother of seven children, she also has served the Catholic Church in a variety of apostolates focused on women, marriage, family, and education.*